Growing Your
Business Globally
First Edition

Robert A. Taft

THOMSON
™

Australia · Canada · Mexico · Singapore · Spain · United Kingdom · United States

To Guy Tozzoli
Who Gave the World Its Trade Centers
And the Twin Towers
Which We Sorely Miss
And Will Never Forget

THOMSON

Growing Your Business Globally,
First Edition

Robert A. Taft

COPYRIGHT © 2005 by Texere, an imprint of
Thomson/South-Western, a part of
The Thomson Corporation.
Thomson and the Star logo are
trademarks used herein under license.

Composed by: Central Park Studios

Printed in the United States of America by Phoenix
Color

1 2 3 4 5 08 07 06 05

This book is printed on acid-free paper.

ISBN: 0-324-20303-9

This publication is designed to provide accurate and
authoritative information in regard to the subject
matter covered. It is sold with the understanding
that the publisher is not engaged in rendering legal,
accounting or other professional services. If expert
assistance is required, the services of a competent
professional person should be sought.

For more information about our projects,
contact us at:

Thomson Higher Education
5191 Natorp Boulevard
Mason, Ohio, 45040
USA

Asia (including India)
Thomson Learning
5 Shenton Way
#01-01 UIC Building
Singapore 068808

Canada
Thomson Nelson
1120 Birchmount Road
Toronto, Ontario
M1K 5G4
Canada

UK/Europe/Middle East/Africa
Thomson Learning
High Holborn House
50/51 Bedford Row
London WC1R 4LR
United Kingdom

Australia/New Zealand
Thomson Learning Australia
102 Dodds Street
Southbank, Victoria 3006
Australia

Latin America
Thomson Learning
Seneca, 53
Colonia Polanco
11560 Mexico
D.F. Mexico

Spain (including Portugal)
Thomson Paraninfo
Calle Magallanes, 25
28015 Madrid, Spain

TABLE OF CONTENTS

INTRODUCTION

In the mid-1960s, two countries in Africa gained independence. Zambia, the second most prosperous country on the continent at the time, had a popularly elected government to go with large lucrative copper mines and a seemingly bottomless pot of foreign aid. Botswana, on the other hand, was described by a British diplomat as being "a useless piece of property". One of the world's poorest nations, however, it suddenly found diamonds under its desert sands.

Given the relative conditions of these two countries, what could they do to better their economic situations? They wanted their own turf – their national sovereignty – but would they prove responsible enough to earn it?

In Zambia, Kenneth Kaunda established a one-party socialist government and nationalized – or put under government control – everything from dry cleaners to car-part retailers. He assumed that the copper mines would generate revenue for the country for as far into the future as the eye could see. But that future lasted for only about ten years when worldwide copper prices dove. To bail out the nation, the International Monetary Fund, the World Bank Group, and individual countries gave Zambia so much money that international aid ballooned to eleven percent of the nation's gross domestic product. Years later when a new president, Frederick Chiluba, tried to privatize industry, angry ministers, who benefited from corrupt patronage, prevented him from doing so. When the IMF demanded that Zambia correct its problems and enact free-market reforms, leaders would at first agree and then reverse such policies.

In Botswana, the government plowed the profits from the newfound diamond mines into infrastructure, health and education. Private business flourished and foreign investment was welcomed with open arms. Aid projects were approved only if they were sustainable, had value-added to the local economy, and did not duplicate the work of others.

So what happened from the mid-sixties to the mid-nineties in both countries? Did they succeed as viable, responsible nations in the world order?

The World Bank said that if Zambia had used the aid they received appropriately, its per capita income would have been more than $20,000 in 1995. Instead it was $400. Conversely, Botswana pulled itself out of the economic dregs and achieved $3,000 income per head. While the government leaders of Zambia lived in mansions, drew exorbitant pensions and cruised *around in Mercedes limousines, those in Botswana opted for locally assembled Hyundai sedans.*[1]

Why start a book about international business here? Because the global marketplace is made up of 232 countries, each as different as Zambia and Botswana, presenting different challenges to the companies that approach them. While the speed of communications and transportation seem to be shrinking the globe, companies should not accept this conclusion unwittingly. Whether venturing into foreign markets through exporting or investing, they should gain an appreciation for the multifaceted world they want to deal with and read the lay of the land before they tread too far.

Before we delve into the mechanics and strategy of exporting and investing abroad, let's see how the global marketplace has evolved and what it means to companies that operate in this environment.

When people ask me what was the most significant set of events in the twentieth century, I tell them the creation of the Bretton Woods Agreement, the Generalized Agreement on Tariffs and Trade (GATT, now known as the World Trade Organization – WTO), and the United Nations. Created in the mid 1940s, all three still exist and espouse national alliances, openness, and peace. They resulted in the aftermath of two global wars and an ugly depression: three happenings that shared two common culprits – "protectionism" and "isolationism". To eliminate wars and depressions, the representatives of Bretton Woods claimed that the world needed greater distribution of wealth among nations and the only way for countries to generate new wealth was to trade and invest with other countries. This seemed like a simple enough formula for success, but to achieve it, the Bretton Woods representatives believed they needed to do four things:

- Establish an international monetary system that truly worked, where all countries could participate and different currencies could flow freely across borders.

- Ensure that trade and investment among countries was, in fact, free by eliminating protectionist barriers through the international organization now known as the WTO.

---

[1] Staff, "Helping the Third World: How to Make Aid Work," *The Economist*, June 26, 1999, p. 24 – 25.

- Set up the International Monetary Fund to bail out second-level countries that were experiencing temporary economic woes.

- Create the World Bank Group, which by providing funds for infrastructure, health, and education would help third-level countries survive and begin prospering.

To spread the wealth more equitably, the IMF and the World Bank would be based on the "Robin Hood Principle": rich nations would provide the bulk of funding and the poorer ones would receive it. The chief proponents of these initiatives were Europe, North America, Australasia, and Japan, subsequently known as "the West".[2]

Has the Bretton Woods formula worked? Critics say "no", advocates, "yes". The first view contends that big corporations have used these institutions to gain world power. The IMF has insisted that countries that ail economically must tear down barriers to trade and investment and let capital flow freely across their borders, similar to what Botswana did. But, unfortunately, this approach has not worked well for all nations. For example, Argentina at the insistence of the IMF tied its peso to the U.S. dollar, lifted all barriers to trade and investment, liberalized its financial markets, and cut public services. Trying to become competitive in the global marketplace, it forced local firms to trim down and passed a labor law that weakened Argentine unions. This prompted civil unrest and when the dollar began to rise in the mid-1990s, the strengthening peso made Argentine exports uncompetitive price-wise.[3] Foreign companies in that and similar situations, where they had little host government restrictions, can come and go as they please, reaping resources like cheap labor or raw materials, and leaving the economic risk to the countries themselves. Also, while the World Bank Group funds projects for poor countries, the ultimate recipients of these project funds are actually large foreign firms that win the contracts.

On the other hand, advocates for free trade and investment hold that the world is better off. From 1990 to 2001, countries that opened their borders and globalized grew at an average annual

[2] Staff, "Radical Birthday Thoughts," *The Economist*, July 2003.
[3] Anderson, Sarah, "Argentina and the IMF," *Institute for Policy Studies*, from Kavanaugh, John, et al., *Alternatives to Economic Globalization*, Berrett-Koehler (San Francisco) 2002, p. 43.

GDP rate of over four percent while those that did not averaged less than one percent.[4] Although there is still a large gap between rich and poor countries as we shall see below, when measured as the distribution of individual incomes within nations, the gap has narrowed considerably and has resulted in creating burgeoning middle classes across the globe, especially in Asia.[5]

Critics of globalization also point to the fact that countries like the United States devote less than one percent of their budgets to foreign aid. But the World Bank admits that aid money is not spent properly. So why should rich nations give more? According to the Bank, which doles out $20 billion a year, an extra $10 billion dollars should lift 25 million people out of poverty; however, as used in the late 1990s, aid could only accommodate at most seven million.[6] Since the days of Bretton Woods, rich nations have given poor countries over $1 trillion in aid, but it has done little to spur economic development in these countries. Much of it has gone for nonproductive purposes, like buying and distributing copies of the Koran in Saudi Arabia, or, as in the case of Zambia, to corrupt politicians who have fleeced most of the funds. In a study of 56 aid-receiving countries, those with good economic policies, low inflation, and lean government institutions with little corruption and strong law enforcement benefited from aid. Those with poor policies and institutions did not.[7] The same can be said of second-level countries where initiatives to revamp economies – called "structural adjustment" programs – have succeeded or failed largely based on the effectiveness of the institutions in those countries.[8]

Whether individual governments or worldwide institutions are to blame, there is a widening economic gap among nations. The richest fifth of the world's population produces nearly 75 percent of all goods and services while the bottom fifth generates only two percent. Of the 6.5 billion people on earth, nearly half make less than $2 a day. Of the two hundred plus countries, 35 percent have a per capita annual income of about $785 a year or less; 39 percent between $786 and a bit over $3,000; ten percent between $3,100 and $9,700; and sixteen percent over $9,700. If almost nine out of ten people live on less than $10,000 annually,[9] how many will likely

---

[4] Staff, "Radical," p. 5.
[5] *Ibid.*, p. 5.
[6] Staff, "Helping," p. 25
[7] *Ibid.*, p. 25.
[8] Dollar, David, "Eyes Wide Open," *Harvard International Review*, Spring 2003, p. 51.

buy flat-screen TV's?

Ironically this economic inequality was exactly what Bretton Woods saw as the villain in the first half of the twentieth century and resolved to conquer through free and open trade and investment. Also ironic, during the Cold War, IMF and World Bank loans went to anti-communist dictatorships, which were generally regarded as more reliable than democracies.[10] In the 1970s and 1980s, however, these institutions took a more laissez-faire approach to countries, pushing hard on a formula of free trade and investment with democracy as the political means necessary to achieve economic prosperity. Since 1980 eighty-one countries have taken significant steps toward democracy, including civilian governments replacing 33 military regimes.[11] To sell this formula, rich countries tried to make a deal with poor ones during the Uruguay Round of the GATT, when the World Trade Organization was established. Looking logically at comparative advantage, the rich advocated that if poorer countries would open their consumer markets and liberalize their financial markets, essentially allowing multinational corporations to operate among countries unhampered, the developed countries would reduce or eliminate tariffs and quotas on the agricultural and textile products of these poorer countries. Since the developed countries controlled the purse strings, many developing countries were forced to adopt liberalizing policies, but the removal of domestic farm subsidies and textile trade barriers against poorer countries has never really happened.[12]

Meanwhile, in the late 1990s, Europe announced its intent to form an economic union to look more like the United States with a single currency and free flow of the factors of production across

---

[9] The World Bank, *World Development Report 2003.*

[10] Finnegan, William, "The Economics of Empire," *Harper's Magazine*, May 2003, p. 44.

[11] Staff, "Radical," p. 5.

[12] Developed countries impose tariffs on many agricultural items that range from 200 to 300 percent. Regarding textiles and apparel, a report to the WTO in 2000 showed that few quota restrictions by developed countries had been lifted (13 of 750 by the United States, 14 of 219 by the European Union, and 29 of 295 by Canada: Source - Khor, Martin, "The Hypocrisy of the North in the WTO," *Third World Network*). Further, since 1986 when the Uruguay Round commenced, domestic farm subsidies in developed countries have actually risen by over fifteen percent. These subsidies, which developing farmers can ill afford to pay to their farmers, effectively close rich markets to many poor-country food producers, while letting big agricultural corporations flood foreign markets with inexpensive food (Finnegan, p. 49). Since subsidies favor the rich over the poor and over fifty percent of today's employed work the land, this situation serves to widen, not lessen, the wealth gap. The new Doha Round of trade talks, geared to resolving this problem, has so far failed to do so.

national borders. Other members of The West – the United States and Canada – countered with a regional alliance of their own. In the early 1990s, they added Mexico to make a larger integrated market than a combined Europe. Such commercial integration has increased dividing the world into larger chunks than nations. Imagine if the world was split up that way. Consider the ramifications if the world could accomplish what Europe has: each country sacrificing its autonomous right to make monetary and fiscal policy to achieve a bigger, stronger economy. There would certainly be far fewer and stronger currencies and a more comprehensible array of trade and investment barriers to contend with. Markets would be more homogenous and company supply chains operating within them more manageable and cost effective.

When the Europeans and North Americans began their new alliances they both included rules of origin and anti-dumping/countervailing duties in their guiding principles. Essentially rules of origin state that if a company selling in the integrated market imports parts or materials, these items will be tariffed. And antidumping/countervailing duties warned foreign companies (and countries that were home to them) that if they attempted to sell goods and services below fair market value in the integrated market, those companies would face significant duties as well. Both of these measures told corporations that if they wanted to be successful in the integrated market, they not only had to have an assembly plant there, but they had to develop new technology and, in effect, run a domestic firm there as well.

This development occurred in the early 1990s when the global economy was coming out of a small recession and fair winds lay ahead. Companies with limited resources and faced with positioning themselves differently in these larger markets, saw mergers and acquisitions with foreign companies as the fastest, surest way to secure much needed market access. The timing could not have been better. Softer government policies on foreign direct investment and a collectively kinder host government view towards mergers and acquisitions paved the way for this approach. Moreover healthy, reinvigorated stock markets worldwide welcomed such business arrangements, allowing companies to finance these with equity rather than debt. Typically these company combinations increased the market value of the stock. Investors and companies enjoyed windfall profits, which allowed for more mergers and acquisitions, causing what I refer to as the "M&A Spiral". The spiral enabled just five companies in six key industries – consumer goods, automotive manufacturing, aircraft manufacturing, electronic components and steel – to control over fifty percent of the world market in those industries.[13] In one year in the mid 1990s, the value of cross-border M&As soared by nearly forty percent to $544 billion.[14] By 1998 there were over a half million foreign affiliates operating worldwide, established by nearly 60,000 parent companies.[15] Global foreign direct investment inflows flourished from a mere $160 billion in 1990 to $1.5 trillion in 2000.[16] By the end of the 1990s foreign-affiliates' sales had outpaced exports by nearly 65 percent, and affiliate employment was rising significantly faster than domestic employment.[17] Unfortunately for better distribution of wealth, two-thirds of FDI inflows move between the richer countries and this trend is likely to continue for the next five years.[18] Why? Mainly because a number of paranoid poorer countries, rightfully or wrongfully, still maintain trade and investment barriers.

While critics claim that global corporations are running amuck in foreign markets and becoming rich at the expense of helpless countries, the facts show that FDI does improve a country's economy. And while parent companies control the majority of research and development expenditures, technology has been flowing across borders at about the same rate as FDI. Further, in 2002, 111 countries boasted inflows of direct investment of at least $100 million dollars, compared to just 45 countries in 1985.[19] Unfortunately, those countries that put up protectionist barriers are indeed falling further behind economically and technologically.

Ten years ago developing countries participated in international production largely through foreign affiliates in their countries, which greatly boosted their economies. Today these same countries produce their own multinational firms that now account for over fifteen percent of all FDI outflows in any given year.[20] Moreover, eighty percent of all investment in developing countries is not done by

---

[13] *Alternatives*, p. 123.
[14] *World Investment Report 1999*, p. 11.
[15] *Ibid.*, p. 2.
[16] *The Economist*, p. 98.
[17] *World Investment*, p. 14 – 15.
[18] *The Economist*, p. 98.
[19] *World Investment*, p. 18.
[20] *Ibid.*, p. 21.

rich country corporations, but by multinationals from other developing nations. While the magnitude of this investment is still relatively small, it shows that FDI and international production are playing a role in integrating countries in the developing world.[21] This regionalism is likely to strengthen and grow over time, creating much larger, more homogenous markets similar to what it has taken Europe over fifty years to achieve.

The free and open trade and investment formula, coupled with democracy and all promulgated by the rich West, has caused friction with the rest of the world. The Central Intelligence Agency declared in its *Global Trends 2015* report that globalization will increase the economic divide among countries.[22] Given this imbalance and global corporations' ability to overproduce, there is a "product excess" today. Many would-be consumers who actually work the factories to make these products cannot afford to buy them. Consequently, to absorb this surplus, the United States has set itself up as the "buyer of last resort".[23] For the past twenty years, this country has imported far more than it has exported, witnessing an almost threefold increase in its trade deficit from 1995 to 2001. To pay for this needless excess, the United States borrows heavily from the Japanese, and even poor countries. Perhaps the greatest irony to the Robin Hood Principle – and maybe the crowning sore point between rich and poor countries – lies in The West's formula for the global financial system. Essentially the system has let the United States become the world's biggest borrower, absorbing $40 billion monthly to finance trade and budget deficits. Since poor borrowing countries must finance their debt in U.S. dollars for the most part, they have amassed over $2.4 trillion to pay off their debt, a figure that realistically swells $160 billion a year. These idle funds are largely U.S. dollar instruments, like Treasury bills, that poor countries buy from the United States, revenue that the country then uses to pay off its own debt.[24] In effect, developing countries lend to the United States to help finance its spending binge, enabling the most powerful nation to be the largest debtor as well. Did John Maynard Keyes have in mind the "buyer of last resort" concept as the ultimate

[21] *Ibid.*, p. 24.
[22] Cavanaugh, John et al, *Alternatives to Economic Globalization*, Berrett-Koehler (San Francisco), 2002, p. 30.
[23] *Ibid.*, p. 52 – 53.
[24] Stiglitz, Joseph, "Dealing with Debt," *Harvard International Review*, Spring 2003 (Vol. 25, No. 1), p. 56 – 7.

savior of the world economy? Hardly. But now that is does exist, how long can it last?

In civilization terms, the West is very much a minority, but since it has the most power and money, it has dictated to the rest of the world how economic development should be. For many nations and cultures the formula has worked; democracy has replaced authoritarian rule and economies are prospering. But even the IMF has learned quite painfully that their structural adjustment formula does not apply equally to all countries and situations. Plus, different cultures often resent the imposition of Western values, such as violent movies, fast food, and poorly respected sex. Further, critics view the globalization process simply as powerful corporations lobbying their governments to force the free trade agenda on the entire world. The result, they contend, has been an environmental disaster where rich companies get richer without having to account for or compensate for their waste and abuse. Numerically, there is some truth to this allegation. Between tax breaks, paying sweatshop wages in several markets, and dumping untreated wastes in the environment, one study suggests that global public costs of corporate welfare may exceed $10 trillion annually.[25] By the same token, over the past twenty years or so, the top two hundred firms grew faster than national economic activity. If one listed the top one hundred economic units in the world, more than half would be corporations and the rest countries.[26]

For many around the world, globalization translates into Western capitalistic imperialism, and on September 11, 2001, we saw the resolve of opposition to it. Terrorism has changed the way the world and international businesses operate. Clement Henry characterizes the radical Islamic resistance to the free trade formula as a "clash of globalizations".[27] Ironically, many of the tools terrorist groups employ resemble the modern corporation: the Internet, decentralized empowerment of the work force, the supply chain, and free capital flows. Also, oil that has been the key to prosperity in the West has empowered Middle East dictators. Revenue from the precious liquid allows them to resist democracy that authoritarian regimes in other parts of the world have lacked. And, of course, it has been shown that oil revenue has fed terrorist efforts

---

[25] *Alternatives*, p. 142.
[26] *Ibid.*, p. 122.
[27] Henry, Clement, "A Clash of Globalizations," *Harvard International Review*, p. 60.

too.

Beyond terrorism, though, there is a fundamental disconnect between global companies and their host countries. Many countries feel threatened by foreign corporations. True, they employ more where they expand, although jobs are not necessarily leaving the developed world and resettling in new markets. Consider the fact that total assets of the top 100 companies ballooned by almost seven hundred percent from 1980 to 1995, but employment decreased by eight percent.[28] The reason for this is firms going global have found a new way to function, which allows them to be lean and cost efficient while producing quality goods. This converts into healthier earnings and better market value with which to attract investors and customers alike. Because of a smaller world with faster information and capital flows, more companies have access to technology. Over the past twenty years, the key question for expanding companies has not been where to produce goods and services, or which ones to produce, but rather *how* to produce them. By focusing on their core competencies – what they do best – the answer increasingly for firms is not to erect new facilities with gobs of workers, but to order parts and materials from suppliers in poor countries. At the same time, especially with the sensitivity to Westerners since 9–11 and the overall backlash to globalization, foreign companies have put more emphasis on becoming better corporate citizens in host countries. Among other things, this involves customizing products more for different customers, instead of selling "one-size-fits-all" to everyone.

As a result, the core of the new international business model has shifted from "do it alone" to "collaborate". The need for reliable suppliers on the one end and strong distribution and retail partners on the other has allowed companies to concentrate on what they do well and search for ways within their "supply chains" to find their competitive advantages. The supply chain has always been there; it has simply become significantly more important with the shrinking role of the focal company in the middle that used to control it all.

This, then, is a brief description of the lay of the land and how we arrived at this point. Over the past twenty controversial years, companies have indeed prospered, but real per capita income has also soared by nearly thirty percent and many more people enjoy freedoms, can buy property, and participate in representative gov-

---

[28] Finnegan, 48.

ernment. These developments auger well for continued healthy expansion of the global marketplace. Over the next fifty years, global income is projected to rise by 3 percent a year, which would translate into a fourfold pitch in world GDP. But how will that increase materialize in terms of better income distribution and a healthier marketplace? Population growth will surge to nine billion and, for the first time in history, most people in developing countries will live in towns and cities, not farmland. Unfortunately, over a billion people will continue to live on fragile lands - semi-arid, mountainous, or forest land – while the vast majority will congregate in cities and megacities, too many close to the sea.[29] This predicament will put considerable stress on the environment, and while technology does or will exist to manage this situation, will governments and corporations apply it responsibly?

Now that we have created this global environment, how can companies deal with it? This book does not have all the answers, but it does try to help firms approach international expansion in a logical, well-prepared fashion. In going global, companies normally do not just plunge into it, but move through a progression from exporting, where the company essentially stays at home and sells abroad through agents and distributors, to investing, where it owns property and conducts business in one or more host countries. In the first part of the book, we will look in depth at some common mistakes firms tend to make when exporting, how to determine their export-readiness, various international business arrangements, and the exporting process itself: how to prepare for it and how to execute it properly. In the second part we will explore investment abroad and the mechanism by which companies increasingly do it: the global supply chain. We will explore ways to strategize, organize, and prepare financially for investing in such chains abroad.

This book is a practical guide, mainly geared to help relatively inexperienced companies, small and medium in size, or even large ones that need a nudge or two, become active global players. While we tend to discuss products more than services, it is only because products are more tangible and somewhat easier to describe. In reality, services and products follow the same logic and steps, whether we are discussing exporting or investing. The book can also

---

[29] World Bank, *World Development Report 2003*, p. 2.

benefit advanced international business students, especially those who seek a practical approach for designing and setting up an international company.

Whether exporting or investing abroad, the keys are a) good analysis, b) attention to detail, and c) building a solid achievable strategy on a strong financial base. This book deals with all three of these. It contains several examples and tools for working through the concepts. Chapter 10 provides a comprehensive framework for doing this and includes all the key points covered. This framework will aid a company to strategize and organize for international expansion, as well as determine the right target markets and develop strong financial underpinnings.

Large corporations have traditionally dominated international business. But although they achieved over 70 percent of the total value of U.S. exports in the year 2000, small and medium-sized companies accounted for over a 300 percent increase in the total number of U.S. exporters during the nineties. Companies with fewer than 500 employees now make up over 97 percent of all U.S. exporters. In fact, firms with fewer than 20 workers constitute nearly three-fourths of all American exporters.[30]

What does this prove? Simply that any company with a competitive product and good common sense can go international. Looking at the increase in these numbers from 1990, you can see that total exporters, not only in the United States but around the world, can easily more than quadruple if those companies are inclined to export and commit to doing so. And while the opportunities are vast in venturing overseas, so are the challenges, which is why so many firms still resist the pull of distant markets. Some companies have slipped into the global marketplace through the Internet and have found electronic sailing to their liking. Still others, though, have had to make major adjustments that take longer to reap the rewards they seek. In either case, the elements are the same: different cultures and supply chains.

Regardless of a company's approach, the prevailing attitude is that in today's world of rapid communications, the rush to go global waits for no one. Yet if companies are not careful, they will fail.

So where should a company begin?

---

[30] U.S. Department of Commerce, "Highlights from: A Profile of U.S. Exporting Companies," *Commerce News*, July 2000.

To look outward and meet the challenges, a company must first explore itself inwardly by assessing its capabilities not as an international company, but as a company. The assessment process described in Chapter 1 is geared for small to medium-sized companies, although it can work well for larger firms inexperienced in international business.

For *any* company looking to expand abroad, they should be prepared to do the following three things:

- *Evaluate:* A company has to evaluate its ability to export. What a company does regionally, or even nationally, does not necessarily translate across borders. Underestimating that transnational plunge as many companies do can lead to a firm's downfall.

- *Plan and Commit:* Even though a company has evaluated its ability to do business internationally, the proof is in the execution. Will the company be there for the long haul? If a company does not have the executive time, resources, and funds to plan well and go abroad, it should not take the plunge.

- *Prepare at Home and Go Abroad:* A company should do as much homework at home before venturing abroad. Once it has decided on a plan of action and target markets where the product or service should sell well, company representatives should go overseas to do more homework and find well-rooted, lasting business.

Let this book assist you and your company through these steps and the ones that follow them to achieve long-term global success. Enjoy the ride.

CHAPTER 1
THE SEVEN SINS OF EXPORTING AND THE 4C CURE

Even before 9/11 the U.S. economy was headed south. Paul Edison, CEO of Waterford Laser Projects, saw a huge increase in competition from foreign producers. With the domestic market becoming saturated and a recession looming, Paul brought his senior team together.

"It's time to expand abroad," he said to an audience reluctant to do so. His team had been working for the better part of twenty years without ever having to venture overseas. They knew nothing about foreign markets and, frankly, some of them were too old to start learning now.

Paul studied their skeptical faces. "I don't care how we do it," he said at length, "but I want to generate leads from abroad." He had few people to choose from. "Okay, Al, get on it."

"How?" asked the dubious lieutenant. "I'm a domestic marketer."

"I understand our embassies overseas can help," the boss said. "Contact them. They actually have an office, believe it or not, called an Export Assistance Center."

"What if they charge for their services?" Al asked.

"We don't want to spend much money," Paul replied. "See if they can give you some phone numbers."

"Hey," Doug Porter cut in. "The university library has international phone books." A pack of confused faces looked his way. "Don't you see? If we can get our hands on the Yellow Pages of, say, five or six cities in Europe or South America, we can just contact potential distributors directly."

"What if they don't speak English?" Joe Morrison said.

This was not what Paul wanted to hear. "Everyone in business speaks English," he said. "Besides, who wouldn't want what we manufacture? Everyone knows that American products are the best by far."

Which of the Seven Sins described below is Waterford Laser guilty of? Let's have a look at the sins.

Company A has never done international business before. It decides to advertise in an international magazine. From just the one ad, it receives four orders for samples from overseas. Enthused by the orders, it sends 12 samples to interested parties in four countries. What is wrong here?

This is a case of *ecstasy from interest.* The company is reacting to positive feedback and believes unconditionally that the inquiries are from viable potential business partners. In its new enthusiasm to venture abroad, the company does not take the time to investigate either the market or those interested. The firm exacerbates the problem by sending samples. By responding to the advertisements, potential agents fish for samples; if they are lucky enough to receive them, they may very well sell them without ever intending to do business with the exporter. Once a company sends out samples, it loses any leverage in the relationship. The opportunistic agents now have the product and can copy it or produce a cheap imitation, leaving the exporter with nothing.

Overseas orders for Company B are increasing. The president of the company wants to be involved but does not have the time to devote to it, so he hires a recent college graduate at $25,000 a year to handle the international business leads, telling the graduate to report directly to him. The graduate develops business opportunities in seven Latin American countries based on leads and follow-up calls with international agents. The president tells the graduate, "That's great, but right now I'm much too busy to get involved." What's wrong with this picture?

This is a classic case of *appendage exporting.* The company receives a stream of international inquires that it doesn't want to ignore but it has no plan for how to handle them. The president wants to do something international, even makes a minimum investment in it. But is the company ready to expand? Not if it can't devote the time, energy, and resources necessary to do it well. The resourceful graduate proves there is business to be had, but when it comes time to pursue it, he gets no support. He is left hanging like an unwanted appendage, rather than an integral part of the business. Soon he will become disenchanted and leave. The export potential of the firm will go unrealized.

Company C is having difficulty in its domestic market. With the economy slumping, it decides to explore business opportunities abroad to boost operations. After getting the names and addresses of chambers of commerce and trade associations in several countries, the firm faxes these organizations in search of trade leads. What's wrong here?

The company is taking a *shotgun, not a rifle*, approach. When domestic sales slide, whether for cyclical reasons or a slump in the domestic economy, companies tend to look overseas for quick new sales. Legitimate overseas organizations that receive obviously mass-mailed solicitations call these desperate messages "e-mails heard around the world." They usually find their way into the recycle bin. Alternatively, companies search the Web and other sources for international Yellow Pages. Once a company gets access to them, it identifies potential agents and distributors and writes to them in the working language of the company, not the prospective partners. This is usually a colossal waste of everyone's time.

Company D has a product it believes is the best in the world: "The product will sell itself." It decides to write in English to a few agents in Latin America, France, and South Korea. When the firm gets no response, it visits two or three countries and makes cold calls on these and other potential business partners. What's wrong with this picture?

This is a lethal combination: *the monolingual monkey who is impressed with his own "unimportance."* In many parts of the world, companies need third-party introductions to reach good prospective business partners. Quite often unsolicited letters or e-mails, especially those in a foreign language, even English, are total turn-offs. They are discarded instead of read. Using another's language is all about respect; not using that language is arrogant and presumptuous, particularly if you are asking for something like an appointment. Because not securing the proper introductions in advance may also violate the customs of a potential partner, such rudeness could jeopardize a future relationship.

Even worse, some pathetically argue, "Well, everyone speaks English." This generalization is exactly why a serious businessperson overseas does not entertain "cold" letters. It is the same myopic view some companies use to view their own products and services. Those who think in this highly competitive global marketplace that their products are so unique that they will sell themselves should definitely do more homework before venturing abroad.

Company E has market opportunities in several regions of the world, but its cash flow is bad and production capacity is running at about 85 percent. Does it have the ability to produce and deliver on time to unfamiliar foreign markets? The president wants to expand abroad, yet insists on manufacturing at home to protect the firm's technology. He deals with distributors using only confirmed letters of credit payable in U.S. dollars. What's wrong here?

The company suffers from *control syndrome.* True, new exporters are well advised to trade on a confirmed letter of credit, payable in U.S. dollars. Nevertheless, companies often limit themselves when they do not entertain other possibilities. Many companies prefer safety to real expansion; others will take calculated risks to achieve greater returns. By being too inflexible, the firm may overlook its vulnerabilities and miss opportunities for which it is better suited. If the firm evaluates itself properly, it may determine that its domestic cash flow is too weak to support international expansion, or that its production capacity and unfamiliarity with shipping options will cause serious delivery problems down the road.

Company F sends a shipment to Madrid, Spain. Time passes, three months, four, and the company hears nothing from the overseas agent. When someone from Company F calls, the agent reports that he never received the goods. What's wrong with this picture?

The company has experienced a *Murphy's Shipwreck.* Murphy's Law states: "Anything that can go wrong will go wrong." In this case, which involved a Miami-based firm, the exporter fired the importer, only to find out later that the goods were still dock-bound in Miami. The devil is in the details, as they say. Unfortunately, this company did not pay enough attention to the details.

Company G with 30 percent excess capacity pays several thousand dollars to develop trade opportunities overseas. It receives major orders from importers in Brazil, Canada, and Peru. This new business could fill capacity to nearly 95 percent but, panicked by the sudden flood of new orders, the president takes the easy way out and declines to move on any of the orders. What is wrong here?

The company has fallen into the *dark hole.* In this case, the company actually paid $4,000 to find potential business partners in five countries. When the results of the search were better than anticipated, rather than prioritizing the new opportunities, the company president decided not to pursue any of them. Why? His commitment to exporting from the start must be questioned. He has the excess production capacity and, thankfully, now the avenues to fill it. Yet because the firm has not prepared for next steps, it abandons legitimate opportunities instead of figuring out how to deal with them.

What do all these cases have in common? A lack of evaluation, planning, and preparation, the three steps mentioned in the introduction. For starters, all of these firms failed to grasp their domestic business well. Normally a company must understand its current capabilities to set a solid base for strategizing and executing any cross-border expansion.

How should a company evaluate, plan, and prepare? Those within the firm must begin by being honest with themselves. This surely is one of the hardest things for a company to do: compare itself to the competition and talk openly about what it does well and not so well. For example, an American company that specializes in a few hi-tech products was convinced that it had the only technology of its kind not only in the United States but across the globe. When it went to Hong Kong and Singapore, though, it found that not only did it have competition, but similar and even superior products had filled the marketplace there for some five years.

Why is it so difficult for a company to be truthful to itself? Good companies, after all, must tell the truth if their business plans are to be airtight. They state their costs, possible markets, proposed management structure, projected sales . . . but unless they are truthful and conservative in their estimates, the sharp eye of an investor will not see a real rate of return. If initial business plans must be crafted with such well-honed blades, why would international expansion not deserve the same scrutiny?

Honesty cannot only rest with top management. The best way for a company to assess its ability to go global is to do so with input from as many company members representing as many functions as possible. Only then will there be a solid foundation that will ensure that international expansion is well integrated into future operations.

The vehicle for honest inclusiveness should be a series of meetings—one is never enough!—where parties from all levels participate. The discussions should focus on four C's:

- *Commitment*
- *Competitiveness*
- *Cash flow*
- *Capacity (or capability)*

These critical areas span the range of company operations. We will use them throughout this book to evaluate, plan, analyze, and strategize for global expansion.

1. The First C: Commitment

A company will most likely spend more of its money, time, and resources on its international business than on its domestic business. But like honesty, commitment cannot rest solely with top management. Too often the vision at the top blurs as it works its way down the organization. Involving employees as well as management in the international expansion process will greatly enhance the likelihood of success. If just top management alone believes in what the company should do, achieving success will be difficult and frustrating.

How does a company determine its commitment? A simple way is to measure the company in the following areas:

- *Reason for Expanding:* Some companies expand overseas because they are pushed by the competition or elect to get a jump on the competition and lead the way abroad. Others find that their product or service is more salable overseas than it is domestically (although that does not happen often). Some venture overseas to reap cost efficiencies, such as gaining access to cheaper labor or materials, or they license a product abroad to improve domestic cash flow. Still others expand because their own market is becoming saturated. Whatever the reasons, they must be justifiable in terms of overall company operations and doable in terms of what the company can afford.

- *Company Status:* Before a company expands, it should have a solid domestic base. Going abroad will normally cost more, at least initially. Companies tend to finance their first attempts overseas either by incurring debt for working capital or using internal funds to finance the expansion. Perhaps they subsidize products for export to make them more price-competitive in a new market. Regardless, most approaches require an infusion of funds. That means that companies that expand abroad to boost cash flow are likely to fail.

- *IB Benchmarking:* A company should define the amount of international business it seeks to do over time in percentage terms relative to its domestic business. I call this "IB benchmarking". For example, a firm may currently be doing 5 percent of its business internationally and it wants to raise this to 25 percent within five years. That is an admirable goal, but it cannot be achieved if the firm is not ready to commit the funds, management, employee time, and other needed resources in at least the same percentage terms. By doing IB benchmarking, a company can stay the course and measure its progress in terms of benefits achieved and costs incurred.

- *Organizational Changes:* Many companies grow internationally on an ad hoc basis, but the international process should be inclusive, with input and growth opportunities available to everyone in the company. Similarly, as the company expands abroad, the company culture and organization must assume a different face. The more adaptable the company's culture and organization, the more it can accommodate global changes. A company that wants to be truly international and integrate its overseas operations into the business as a whole should commit to flexibility from the start of its expansion.

- *Company Risk Profile:* In venturing overseas, companies often expect too much. If a product sells domestically, why would it not do well abroad? Unfortunately, this does not necessarily follow. Companies should set realistic goals and objectives for what they hope to accomplish overseas, and set realistic payback periods. Failure to do so has made many companies that start exporting abandon the effort within three years.

2. The Second C: Competitiveness

Generally, a product should do well in the domestic market before it can do well overseas, though, of course, generalities always have their exceptions. Selling through the Internet, for instance, allows companies without the resources to expand across borders physically to do so virtually, accessing a universal marketplace without being confined geographically. Others, imaginatively, have ventured abroad and raised working capital from international advance sales to finance domestic operations. Nevertheless, if a product or service cannot do well in its home market, the chances of its doing so in countries with different cultures, languages, customs, and preferences are normally slim.

How, then, should a company evaluate its competitiveness for overseas markets? There are many competitive factors that we will discuss later, for now, at a minimum, a company should consider the following:

- *Reasons Why the Product or Service Sells:* This addresses both need and want: Why does the customer buy the product? More important, what features about it attract the customer? Motivational marketing 101? Not exactly. Too many companies observe the buying patterns in their home markets and transfer them exactly into other markets, with devastating results. Yet it remains important to understand the domestic buyer and use that buyer as a benchmark from which to appreciate the needs and preferences of foreign buyers.

  Appreciating what motivates domestic customers helps a firm appreciate differences in consumer tastes in new markets. For example, while a product may have a mass market at home, customer sophistication and buying power coupled with significant price increases may demand a customized or niche marketing approach elsewhere. Sensitivity to domestic customers lets a company recognize the need for changes in other markets.

- *Product Modification:* Companies not only have to adjust their thinking and expectations when approaching new markets, often they also have to adapt the product or service itself to meet customer needs. Companies from the United States or other large lucrative markets must realize that their target market may be much smaller not only in numbers but also in sheer buying power. Prices must cover higher margins and additional costs, making the product more expensive in these markets that have less purchasing power.

  On the other side, certain features, such as colors or electrical current, that work well at home may not be attractive in other countries. Further, a firm may have to change its packaging and advertising. Management has to address decisions to modify products up front, expending money in the hope of recouping the costs through future sales. As with the payback period, a company must also determine its "modification expense tolerance." Usually done on a percentage basis, this refers to the amount a company is willing to spend adapting the product or service to achieve sales targets.

- *Knowing the Competition:* It is amazing how many companies profess to understand their competition but really do not. It is not enough to know the major competitors or even just their products or services. As is discussed in detail later, a key to global growth is to find a firm's niche, doing something the rest of the competition does not. These niches increasingly emerge from improvements in a company's supply chain. Thus a firm must know not only the products and services of the competition but also their methods for creating and delivering them. Many companies fail because they base their plans on hearsay of what the competition is likely to do.

If a company cannot get a handle on the competition in its own backyard, it will be much harder to do it in a foreign market. There, competition will consist not only of the familiar faces a company sees in its own backyard but also local entities that may produce at lower quality but certainly also at much lower prices. This reality, together with a different customer base, makes understanding the competition all the more critical.

- *International Business Arrangements:* In evaluating its competitive edge, a company should weigh the types of business arrangements it can afford and feel comfortable with. Traditionally, most new exporters want to be paid in U.S. dollars, using a confirmed letter of credit. This is a safe way to do business: the company gets paid when the goods are shipped, it does not have to worry about foreign exchange risk, and it can better protect its proprietary technology. But this approach may price the product out of the foreign market.

Alternatively, companies that have short-term cash flow problems and want to work on the next iteration of their technology may want to consider licensing to reap cash upfront through license fees or reaching out for local contract manufacturing to stay price-competitive in the local market. Regardless of the motivation, the overseas business arrangement will have cost implications and should be evaluated in this competitive stage.

3. The Third C: Cash Flow

Normally, international business requires an upfront commitment of funds. If domestic operations are not doing well, trying to sell abroad will only worsen the situation, because of the added expense, unless the product or service is better suited to an overseas market. Nevertheless, many companies expand abroad because domestic business is slipping and they expect to hit the mother lode overseas over an unrealistically short period of time. Unfortunately, they discover all too soon that expansion abroad usually requires positive cash flow from the domestic business first.

How should a company evaluate its cash flow? It should consider the following at a minimum:

- *Its Financial Position:* A company should evaluate the fundamentals of the company by applying a variety of financial ratios. It should look first to its profit margin because international sales will incur more and generally higher costs. It should also consider its debt situation and its ability to access capital or incur more debt.

- *Two International Budgets:* A firm venturing abroad needs two budgets: one to explore possible target markets and the other to actually penetrate those markets. The first consists of the funds needed to cover the steps, discussed in chapter 2, that a company needs to follow to determine which markets to pursue and the best way to pursue them. The second applies to the costs of actually entering the markets long-term. While the implementation budget will vary with each new market, a firm should first draft both budgets to assess its ability to finance its plans. Once the ultimate goals and strategies are set, the company can refine its earlier estimates, but at this stage it needs to decide whether it can proceed or not.

- *The Payback Period:* Again, companies should not be overly optimistic in determining the likelihood of positive cash flow from overseas sales. Instead they should set conservative timelines and not expect the international side to bail out the domestic.

4. The Fourth C: Capacity (Capability)

A company must have the capacity to produce and deliver on time. While this is of course true domestically, it is particularly important for dealing overseas with multiple markets and often intriguing shipping problems. In most countries other than the United States, European Union members, and Japan, there are far fewer agents and distributors because developing markets are smaller and have less spending power. These agents deal with lower inventories and higher markups than the typical U.S. distributor. What they are looking for are smaller quantities but prompt deliveries. The exporting company cannot over–commit; it has to adapt its production and logistics systems accordingly.

How should a company evaluate its capacity? To start the exporting process, it should look first at the following:

- *Its Resources:* An expanding company should consider its company structure, its organization, to see how well it is handling domestic operations and whether it has the critical mass to accommodate expansion. Too many companies think they can just add international business to their existing portfolios. These firms grow awkwardly, without adjusting their corporate culture to reflect their markets and without figuring overseas activity as a logical extension of total operations. In short, they append international activities to domestic activities rather than integrate the two. This generally leads to budget shortfalls, among other financial problems, that will have to be corrected somewhere down the line. Why not organize properly from the start?

- *The Domestic Supply Chain:* A company's supply chain, as will be discussed later, consists of its suppliers, manufacturing, and distribution. The firm may procure parts and supplies from one or more vendors in the same city where it manufactures a product or it may have sources in many countries. It may buy supplies at home and contract production overseas. It may sell directly to retailers or work through a web of distributors. However it operates, the company needs to understand the range and flexibility of its supply chain to analyze whether it can adapt to expanded markets. Can new markets be accommodated within the current chain? If not, what changes need to be made and what additional partners and alliances will be needed? Are the changes acceptable from a risk point of view and affordable from a cost point of view?

For example, if a U.S. company wants to export products to Latin America, how will the products move from, say, the company in New York to the customer in Buenos Aires? How much will each stage cost, starting with international shipping, spanning long or short distribution channels in the host country, and arriving safely at a retail store where it can reach a happy customer? Would it be cheaper to source materials from Latin America, outsource the manufacturing there, and reap the benefits of selling as a domestic firm? A host of variables affect business arrangements and methods of delivering goods and services. A company should try to anticipate possible changes early on for budget and preparation reasons.

- *Production Capacity:* As a potential exporter, a company should evaluate four things in its production area:
  1. Whether it has excess production capacity, including what it manufactures internally and what it outsources,
  2. The age and condition of its equipment,
  3. The reliability and timeliness of sourcing supplies and fitting them into the production system, and
  4. The current delivery record.

Problems in any of these four areas will make expanded production for overseas markets a nightmare. For example, if the equipment is old and prone to breakdowns, additional orders will be extremely difficult to fill. If a company is having a hard time making deliveries domestically, think of the headaches it will have if it adds customers in perhaps five different countries.

- *Expansion Capabilities:* At this point a company should decide whether it can expand its capacity, either internally or through outsourcing. It does not want to venture too far, accept orders, and only then figure out how best to fill them.

This assessment process helps a firm determine its export readiness. Appendix 1 contains a questionnaire covering the areas that will help a company through it. To be inclusive, firms should invite representatives from all levels and functions to fill out the questionnaire. What management may think can differ greatly from how others view the world, or the company. Having everyone's input from the beginning can help management understand where future problems may lie and how best to navigate the transition to international operations. The appendix also includes a scoring chart so that a company can evaluate its results.

Once the assessment is done, a company is ready to explore target markets.

CHAPTER 2
THE BACKWARD EXPORT PROCESS

John Smith bought rights to micro-encapsulation from the 3M Corporation. This technology compresses the smell of many different things for application to objects. Once the compressed scent is scratched, it emits the smell. The company contracts with a T-shirt manufacturer and decorates the shirts with fruits and their encapsulated smells; if the shirt had an apple on it, for example, you could scratch the apple to smell like apples.

Smith needs working capital to begin a small factory to apply the fruits to the T-shirts and other scents to other products. He has spent most of his savings on buying the rights to the technology and cannot get working capital from his bank, but he still has $7,000 in the bank. He thinks he can be more successful overseas than in the domestic market because he can generate orders on a letter-of-credit basis and apply for working capital loans based on the advance orders. Should he venture overseas? If so, how?

Before seeing what Mr. Smith did, let us review how he might want to proceed.

After assessing its ability to do international business, a company needs to determine how and where it wants to go abroad and whether it wants to trade or invest. The rest of this book delves into what is involved in both areas. This chapter discusses a basic 15-step method for trading or exporting:

1. Learn how best to utilize the available trade infrastructure.
2. Identify target markets and craft plans and budgets for determining how and when to explore each one.
3. Identify potential business partners.
4. See how shipping and trade financing work between the exporter's and importer's countries.
5. Identify an attorney in the target markets to deal with local laws and to register the company's products and name.
6. Visit the target countries.

7. Investigate the 5Ps and 2Cs to determine the company's comparative advantages and potential market niche.
8. Interview potential business partners.
9. Determine the best time to enter the target markets.
10. Commit to modifying the product as needed to fit the market.
11. Determine the best business arrangement for each target market (e.g., agency or distributorship, licensing arrangement, etc.).
12. Price the product or service.
13. Negotiate a contract with a business partner.
14. Position the product so that the customer will remember it in a certain way.
15. Set out the company's business objectives and market penetration strategy in a business plan and draft an implementation budget for each target market.

The order of these steps appear somewhat backwards; most people have been taught to start with goals, objectives, and strategies and fill in the blanks along the way, but many companies that use that approach to penetrate new markets overseas usually get frustrated and fail. Why? Because companies tend to base their international goals on their domestic experience. This is unrealistic and leads to overly optimistic projections. By preparing well and following these 15 steps, a company can "back into" its goals, objectives, and strategies, arriving at ones that are achievable.

Let's look at the steps in detail.

1. Learn how best to utilize the available trade infrastructure.

Because international trade has become a high priority for a growing number of countries, government and private resources worldwide are available to companies looking to trade and invest in other markets. The range of services they offer stretches from market research reports to hands-on services to help companies identify and connect with potential business partners. In addition to services a government provides its companies, each country has a trade infrastructure consisting of industry associations, chambers of commerce, banks, law firms, and universities, among other groups.

Contacts within these organizations can provide potential exporters and investors with more or less neutral insights into the target market. In identifying countries to enter, a company should investigate their trade infrastructures.

Figure 2.1 shows the trade infrastructure of the United States, what it offers companies both domestically and internationally.

Figure 2.1
The U.S. Trade Infrastructure

Domestic Side	Target Country (International) Side
• Universities	• Universities
• Banks	• Banks
• Export Assistance Center	• Embassies/U.S. Commercial Service
• World Trade Center	• World Trade Centers
• U.S. Chambers of Commerce	• American Chambers of Commerce
• Trade Associations	• Trade Associations
• Trade Show Organizers	• Trade Show Organizers

The *domestic side* of the U.S. trade infrastructure consists of the following:

- *Universities, Banks, and Consultants:* These organizations can provide valuable trade and investment information. The global marketplace has put a premium on international business as a college discipline and many of the better schools now offer degree programs in this field; most are looking for practical ways to educate their students in this area. A company can contact universities in its area to obtain interns who, usually for credit and not big bucks can conduct much-needed market research. International banks, and those that have corresponding relationships with banks in other countries can help exporters with financing options. Consultants, usually for healthy fees, offer expert advice as well.

- *World Trade Centers (WTO):* There are membership organizations; there are over 340 World Trade Centers worldwide. Many are connected electronically to one another and all belong to the World Trade Center Association. They offer their members brokering services, such as market research and contacts. Some centers provide reciprocal privileges to members free, though some charge for services. Some centers offer a full line of services, others do not. Interested companies should check with the nearest center to see what services they can access locally and globally by visiting WTCAOnline (*www.wtca.org*).

- *Export Development Commissions (EDC):* These are local government organizations that provide trade and investment services. They typically put on country or trade seminars, organize trade missions or other trade events, host foreign business visitors, and try to attract foreign investment.

- *Trade Associations and Chambers of Commerce:* These local and national groups provide trade services to members. They may focus on a particular country or industry.

- *U.S. Export Assistance Centers (EAC):* These are the domestic arm of the U.S. Commercial Service (USCS). There are some 70 offices throughout the United States that provide a host of services for companies looking to export. They are directly tied to U.S. embassies (see below) around the globe. In addition to giving trade-related counseling, they link exporters to counterparts abroad and to the services embassies offer, many of which are described below. Also in these centers are the regional offices of the U.S. Small Business Administration and the Export-Import Bank, which offer companies loans for international working capital and often work in partnership with state financial institutions that do the same.

The *international side* of the trade infrastructure provides the following:

- *World Trade Centers:* Centers similar to those described for the domestic side also operate abroad.

- *U.S. Embassies:* The overseas offices of the USCS are typically located in the embassy, though several are located outside for easier access for businesspeople. While each country program has a set of core export services, the individual offices are encouraged by Washington to undertake initiatives to tap opportunities in the local marketplace and business community. Headed by American managers, these facilities feature foreign service nationals (FSNs), trade specialists who each concentrate on one or more industries. Their job is to conduct market research and stay in contact with potential business partners and business leaders in their industries. They are the on-the-ground support for U.S. companies; the Export Assistance Centers are the conduits for companies to reach these valuable overseas resources.

The USCS has over 130 offices spread across more than 70 countries. Where the Service does not have a presence, State Department economic officers assist American companies.

- *The American Chamber of Commerce (AmCham):* Many countries have American chambers that are tied into the U.S. Chamber of Commerce in Washington, D.C. While they lobby in their host countries, they help build stronger business ties between the United States and those countries. Their members include U.S. companies resident in the host country or local firms that are doing or want to do business in the United States. Thus they are an excellent source of market information and contacts.

Before actually going overseas or at least while exploring a target country, a company should make appointments to meet as many people in the trade infrastructure as possible. It is a good way to learn about the market, its strengths and weaknesses, and to broaden the contact base. Insights from representatives of these organizations also prepare company executives for detailed interviews and negotiations with potential business partners.

2. Identify target markets and craft plans and budgets for determining how and when to explore each one.

A firm wants to answer two questions at this stage: (a) where will its products or services sell, and (b) will it be safe to sell. The second questions covers whether the company can collect what is owed to it and whether it can protect its proprietary technology.

Chapter 4 discusses factors companies should consider here, especially those looking to invest abroad. Suffice it to say here that there are a number of sources available on the Internet to learn about possible markets. A good place to start the search is the National Trade Data Bank (NTDB), a resource created under the 1988 U.S. Trade Act. With data supplied by over 20 government organizations, the NTDB contains information on more than 130 countries. For each, the database has two key sets of documents: (a) a Country Commercial Guide that explains how to do business in that country, and (b) Industry Sector Analyses, market research reports that tell which types of products are likely to sell best in the country. New information becomes available monthly. Available on-line at STATUSA.com, the NTDB can be bought on a subscription basis but it is free through many libraries. It can be very helpful to a company in narrowing its search for target markets.

A company should identify as many as 10 potential markets and then concentrate on the best two or three based on its own priority criteria (see chapter 4). Ultimately, the company will want to send representatives to these markets; keeping the number of prospect markets small will keep the exploration affordable in both time and money.

Once the markets have been identified, a company can draft an initial budget and plan for each. Both should cover the 15 steps already described. To explore properly, sooner or later a company will need to send representatives overseas to the examine markets firsthand. Appendix 2 contains a format for an initial plan and budget.

3. Identify potential business partners.

Typically, most embassies provide services to companies from their country. The USCS offers a range of services, though they may vary from one embassy to another. It is wise to check the USCS country websites for a thorough list of the services. Local export assistance centers can also help by providing details about the following four core tools:

- *Catalog Shows:* Companies send their literature and international business objectives to an embassy. The staff procures space either in the embassy or a hotel or other outside venue, sets out the catalogs, and invites prospective agents and distributors to view them. Each show features products or services in a certain industry. Agents register their interest in products they may want to represent. These leads are given the companies that entered the show for follow-up.

- *Commercial News USA:* This magazine is published in New York ten times a year. Each issue deals with products from a certain industry. A company can place an ad with a picture and description of its product and its overseas business objectives. This service is useful to throw a net over the world, because the magazine is shipped to about 130 embassies worldwide, where the FSNs distribute copies to contacts like agents, distributors, and other potential business partners in the industry featured in that issue. Thus each issue is targeted to a very specific audience. Some companies have done years of business from placing just one ad, but using this approach can also attract agents who are just fishing for samples.

- *Agent/Distributor Service (ADS):* Once it has determined its two or three target markets, the exporter can send either its product literature or a few samples, along with its business objectives, to the embassies in those countries. The FSN responsible for the exporter's industry then contacts potential business partners and sends them the material to review for interest in doing business with the exporter. After about six weeks, the FSN sends the exporter four to six names of interested parties, together with some market research about the salability of the product in that market. This service is especially effective if the FSN can vouch personally for the potential business partners.

- *Gold Key Service:* This service functions like the ADS except that the exporter commits to going to the target countries to meet with interested parties. While there company representatives have access to FSNs or contract hires who are normally available to escort the representatives to their meetings and provide translation. This service has about an 80 percent success rate at finding reliable business partners. Geared to help small and medium-sized companies, the Gold Key, like all embassy services, help companies save time and money. In this case the money is very little: the company stays at home while others do the initial screening. It is leveraging at its best. By the time the firm's representatives arrive in a country, meetings with the right people have already been set up. To do a Gold Key right, representatives should also enlist the help of their embassy to arrange appointments for them with host country trade infrastructure officials. While a company would be hard-pressed to accomplish all the steps in an exploratory trip in a short time, it can make significant progress on this first trip.

4. See how shipping and trade financing work between the exporter's and importer's countries.

Before going abroad, company representatives should learn about trade financing and shipping possibilities for the target countries. In the finance area, the key is to find a domestic bank that either operates a subsidiary or affiliate bank in the target country or has a corresponding bank relationship with a bank in that country. In the latter relationship, neither bank has ownership in the other. They simply work together to help mutual clients with trade transactions. In the shipping area, the exporter should meet with two or more freight forwarders to learn shipping terms and options, including transportation costs and length of delivery time to the target markets.

When interviewing agents and distributors, an exporter should be able to discuss shipping and finance knowledgeably. Most exporters dealing with agents or distributors want to be paid in dollars or other hard floating currency under a confirmed letter of credit. Prospective business partners, on the other hand, want to know that the exporter can produce and deliver on time. For the two sides to have this discussion, the exporter needs first to find out what is possible.

Appendix 3 deals with trade financing and shipping. There are volumes written on these subjects, but the material in the appendix can help familiarize you with them. Exporters should view shipping and trade finance as inseparable. To be paid under a letter of credit, the shipping, packaging, and export documentation must conform to the terms set in the letter of credit. As the appendix shows, if there are problems with the documents or if deadlines for shipping are not met, the exporter may not get paid.

5. Identify an attorney in the target markets to deal with local laws and register the company's products and name.

Next, an exporter should find a good trade lawyer in the target countries, for several reasons:

1. Any contract with a business partner must follow the laws of that country and be written in the country's working language.
2. A lawyer can discuss the obstacles involved in doing business in that country, such as the need for import licenses, payment of duties, intellectual property protection for copyrights and trademarks, and government restrictions.
3. A lawyer will explain labor law and the contractual or employment relationship the exporting company would have with a local business partner.
4. The lawyer will advise on how to register the product and company names.

Some attorneys disagree and downplay the importance of having international patents and registering names. It is true that universally recognized names like IBM and Burger King are better protected from piracy than they used to be. Smaller companies with less recognized names often do not think their names would attract international pirates. Nevertheless, thievery of names and technologies occurs daily. The registration process is usually not that costly, sometimes less than $500. Yet pirates have been known to register product and company names and then offer to sell them back to the firm for outrageous amounts. Name registration and patent protection is a case of "better be safe than sorry." A small upfront investment can save embarrassment and headaches down the road.

Try to get the names of good lawyers overseas from a domestic international law office that has contact with firms in other countries. Alternatively, embassies maintain lists of lawyers and law firms in the host country, although many embassies are prohibited from making recommendations in case companies have bad experiences with a law firm.

6. Visit the target countries.

A company should try to touch base with as many business groups in the trade infrastructure as possible when going abroad. It should approach overseas markets in an organized way so as not to waste time or be taken in by opportunistic business people. Use the Gold Key Service or another avenue, such as:

- *Trade Missions:* These are groups of companies, organized by trade organizations like economic development commissions or state foreign affairs departments, that help firms explore potential overseas markets and make international contacts. Many of these missions, though, are more political than commercial because they are headed by public figures, or they are simply too large and socially programmed to get much company-to-company business accomplished. They can help open certain doors to key business and government contacts, but the same can normally be done through an effective Gold Key.

- *Trade Shows:* These are exhibitions where products, usually from all over the world, are displayed and sold. Hundreds of shows are held annually in many countries. A well-targeted show can be an excellent way to find agents and distributors and possibly other types of business partners, especially if the event restricts its audience to people in the trade, not the public. Companies planning to participate should find out what is the target audience before entering. Because of the cost of transporting products and equipment, trade shows are relatively expensive, but they bring potential partners and buyers to the exporters where they can demonstrate and explain their products and services face-to-face.

- *Post-Initiated Promotions:* The commercial sections of embassies often hold mini trade shows or catalog shows where one or more companies demonstrate their wares and services. The embassy recruits attendees for the event. This, too, is an excellent way for a firm to leverage. Moreover, unlike a big trade show, because these promotions feature no more than a few companies, they can be tailor-made to fit the exhibitor's specific objectives.

- *Invitation of a Potential Business Partner:* Some companies make that first trip overseas at the invitation of an agent or distributor after the agent has contacted the exporter, maybe even placed an order. A company in this situation should try to learn as much about the host as possible, usually through the commercial section of the embassy. The host obviously has some interest in the product, but if he thinks that the exporter will not be circumspect, he may try to take advantage of the situation.

Whichever approach the exporter takes, it should contact the commercial offices of the embassy. Services through these offices are usually well targeted and inexpensive; much of the legwork is done for the exporter in advance by experts in the know. Since it is in the best interest of an embassy to see its companies succeed abroad, the staff will help follow up with potential business partners as well.

7. Investigate the 5Ps and the 2Cs to determine the company's comparative advantages and potential market niche.

Once its product and company names are properly registered in a target market, the exporter should explore the marketability of its product or service. A good way to do this is by investigating the 2Cs and 5Ps. The 2Cs are the *customer* and the *competition*. The 5Ps are *product, promotion, price, place, and partner.*

In exploring the 2Cs the exporter wants to know: Who can and will buy the product? Under what conditions? Who else is selling something similar there?

In other words, is the customer base, with available discretionary income, sizable enough to support a profit? How do customers buy? Where do they buy? How do they learn about goods and services? Moreover, what does the potential customer not know they are missing? For example, when Baskin and Robbins first went to Australia, it learned that Australians were very familiar with vanilla, strawberry, and chocolate ice cream but had never in their wildest imagination dreamed of flavors like rocky road, crème de leche, or mocha almond chip.

On the other side, the exporter will want to assess competitors active in the market, both domestic and international. Local firms will probably offer cheaper but inferior alternatives, but not necessarily. The number of international competitors that are present indicates the demand for the product or service, the tolerable price differential between similar domestic and imported products, and the relative size of the upper end of the market.

The exporter should then explore the 5Ps. Notice there are five, not four as in classic domestic marketing. Here the exporter wants to discover what products and services are provided, what features they have and lack, how products get to market, how competitors advertise, and how they sell. In particular, the company should assess the availability of and restrictions to marketing (e.g., advertising) in the country and the length and breadth of the distribution channel (see chapter 6). Since the key to evaluating both requires local input and ultimately someone on the ground to do the work, it is important to involve potential business partners like agents in this evaluation. During this stage, the exporter has an excellent opportunity to weigh exactly what each prospective partner can bring to these critical areas.

The 2C and 5P evaluation process should start with comparison shopping—touring the marketplace where products similar to those of the exporters are sold to observe customers, check out prices and point-of-purchase advertising, and interview customers and retailers. Appendix 4 lists questions to ask to gather information from these sources.

Once the information is gathered, the company will want to analyze the results to determine the *competitiveness* of its product or service. A good way to do this is by using a gap analysis. Many companies find "gaps" or "holes" in the marketplace by investigating two areas. First, customers in another country may be accustomed to doing things a certain way or believing that a particular product is the best of its kind since it is the only one available or they have not been exposed to alternatives. A better product or different way of doing something may exceed the customer's grasp. In other words, he may not know what he is missing. Second, what the competition is providing may be lacking as well. In either case the company should consider both of these possibilities to find what it can provide that would be unique to fill existing gaps. Gaps may occur in one or more of the 5Ps.

Figure 2.2 presents a simplified version of a gap analysis.

Figure 2.2
A Gap Analysis

"P" Area	Customer (Doesn't know he is missing)	Competition (Provides)	Company (Can provide) to fill gap)

Product
  - Features
  - Accessories
  - Quality
  - User friendly
  - Packaging
  - Instructions
  - Warranties
  - Color			

Price
  - Discount/sale
  - Loss Leader			

Promotion
  - Brand recogntion
  - TV
  - Newspapers
  - Point of sale			

Place
  - Suppliers
  - Distribution
  - Retail			

Partner - Leverage*			
* Degree of local support or endorsement for product, company or brand.			

Using this matrix approach, a firm can identify market gaps. If it can fill in these gaps, the company can find its comparative advantages or niches. These advantages are not necessarily product- or service-based but can also emerge from the supply chain. By the same token, finding an advantage is not that simple. To fit the market or create a niche, a company may have to modify or adapt a product or service, which will cost time and money. Worse, the company may discover that it simply cannot fill the gaps or its advantage is not strong enough to dislodge existing competition or gain appreciable market share. In that case, it may be best to just move on.

8. Interview potential business partners.

Ideally, now it is time to narrow the search for the right business partner. Hopefully a company has used the resources of potential partners to navigate the 5Ps and 2Cs, which means the company is ready to settle on the best partner. But cramped schedules often make this due diligence process difficult, and the exporter finds that marketplace conversations have to be held in agent's offices rather than in the market itself.

In any case, the exporter and the importer want to find out as much as possible about each other. The more knowledgeable the exporter is about the market, the more impressed the partner will be and the less likely to exaggerate the situation in his country or his own company's capabilities. This obviously argues for the exporter to do as much homework on the ground as possible before entering serious negotiations. Yet typically the time-restricted exporter wants to sign an agent, agree on terms, and leave before the weekend. On the other side, the potential partner, even one who has expressed interest in a product or service of the exporter, wants time to get to know the company and its people.

Exporters around the world tend to be impatient and quick-paced, looking to make relationships and ultimately sales as fast as possible. Truly viable potential partners, from agents to licensees, tend to move much more slowly, looking to build a reliable relationship on trust. This takes getting to know the other side quite well. It is not unusual that the partner will want to invite the exporter to dinner, even at home to meet the family or talk about family and other topics outside of business. On a Gold Key, for example, an efficient exporter may try to cover two countries in a week, only to find that the agents or distributors interviewed are not eager to sign on the dotted line. Despite the time and travel involved, exporters should not be in a rush. Signing contracts may take more than one trip abroad. Ideally, too, the exporter would invite the potential business partner to visit the company's facilities first.

Before business negotiations actually start, however, companies may find the questionnaires in appendix 5 useful. Essentially what the exporter wants to know about the importer or agent is wrapped in the S A I D formula:

- *S – Sales and Service:* How many people work in the partner's company? How many will be devoted to promoting and selling the company's products or services and providing after-sales service? Further, does the partner handle products that *complement* or *compete* with those of the company?

- *A – Advertising:* Can the partner advertise the company's products and how will that be done (radio, TV, newspaper ads, point of sale, etc.)? If not, what marketing and advertising alternatives are there and how much do they cost?

- *I – Inventory:* Does the partner have the space to keep a sufficient supply of the company's product on hand, in good condition?

- *D – Distribution:* Can the partner get the products through customs and into the market?

With regard to distribution, the exporter needs to know:

- Whether the importer knows the right tariff nomenclature to be able to get shipments through customs. The importer needs to provide the right tariff numbers for duty purposes or the shipment may not be released by customs in the importer's country.

- The credit rating of the importer. This is important to determine whether a partner can afford to purchase products and move them to the marketplace.

- The reputation of the importer, not just in the local community but especially in the exporter's industry. The importer should have the contacts to move product from customs to the retail level.

9. Determine the best time to enter the target market.

Timing is critical in entering an overseas market. For example, a country with political instability today may make a good market six months to a year from now. The company's home country may be unpopular in the target market at a given time and thus business for the exporter may be risky and less than profitable.

Place is probably the most important P with regard to timing. Part of a market may yield success when other parts may not. Before entering negotiations with a potential partner, an exporter must explore the timing issue. Once again, the embassy may be helpful here.

10. Commit to modifying the product as necessary to fit the market.

In filling in the market gaps, a company may learn that its product could be quite successful if it were modified to fit the market better. A classic example of a product not fitting the market was when General Motors advertised a new Chevrolet in the Latin America market with its U.S. name, the Nova. "No va" in Spanish means "does not go"—not an appropriate message for motivating customers to buy a car.

Perhaps companies have seen their products, including advertising and packaging, do very well in the domestic market, only to find that the same does not hold true overseas. In such cases a firm must swallow some pride and concede to cultural differences if it wants long-term success. If analysis shows the product must change, the exporter must make the changes or accept less than optimal market share.

How should an exporter determine if the changes needed are worth the effort? Many companies start by measuring the size of the projected market. If the product modifications will cost a relatively small percentage of projected sales, they are probably worth it. What is a "relatively small percentage"? Each company has to answer that question for itself. Some will sacrifice sales by doing nothing. Others put a limit of 5 to 10 percent. Others will venture as much as 30 percent or more.

Key questions include:

- How much risk is the company willing to accept?
- What is the payback period for the company to turn a profit in the overseas market?
- How much investment in change can the company justify? This is usually tied to its cash flow situation.
- How reliable are the sales estimates?

Once these questions are answered, the company should commit to making affordable modifications at this point in the process.

11. Determine the best business arrangement for each target market (e.g., agency, distributor, etc.).

At this point the exporter needs to decide which business arrangement to enter into. (These possibilities will be discussed more fully in the next chapter.) The arrangement will affect not only price and market entry strategy but also the efficiency of the firm's supply chain (discussed in detail in chapters 5 and 6).

12. Price the product or service.

Before entering into contract negotiations, the exporter must have a handle on price limits for each product or service. A service will more likely than not involve a presence in the target markets from which the service will be delivered. A typical service might be a restaurant or hotel, a law office, or a bank. It might take the form of a franchise, management contract, joint venture, or Greenfield investment (when a company owns and controls 100 percent of an offshore investment). In other words, a service would start with an investment, not a trade. Thus, services require local pricing, based on costs plus the value added of the service company.

The price of a product, on the other hand, depends greatly on the business arrangement used. Selling directly through an agent or distributor would involve the extra costs that international sales entail, such as shipping, duties, and higher than domestic wholesale markups. Licensing or contract manufacturing implies that the product would be produced and delivered locally, so some of those international costs would not be incurred. The same is true for products produced under an in-country joint venture or Greenfield investment.

Assume a company would work through an agent or distributor. The exporter should estimate the price of the product in the target country's retail market before finalizing an agreement with the partner. Some partners downplay the importance of pricing, saying the price can be changed later if necessary. That is not practical. Now is the time to compute a competitive price. To do so, the following information is needed:

- Factory price of the goods
- Domestic freight
- Insurance
- International freight
- Import duties
- Merchant marine tax (percent of freight)
- Warehousing
- Terminal handling charges
- Custom brokerage fees
- Financing charges (for letter of credit)
- Value-added tax
- Importer's commission and markup
- Retail markup
- Consumer price

Wow! Why bother? At first glance the exporter may have a heart attack, thinking it would be impossible to sell in the target market at a price high enough to cover all these costs, especially if the target market is much smaller than the company's domestic market. Smart exporters, though, while acknowledging that the overseas markets they pursue will generally be much smaller than their own and that the number of people in it that are capable of buying their product are far fewer, also know that this small proportion of the people will buy imported products because they have ample discretionary income and like to boast of that fact by buying expensive imports. Consequently, it is not unusual to see American products selling for two and three times as much in a much smaller and poorer market than they do in the United States.

Ideally, the exporter and importer should agree on the price together. To be both profitable and long lasting, the relationship between the two partners has to be based on honest and open communication. This honesty is nowhere better demonstrated than in working out the price. All hidden costs have to be disclosed; if the importer is insisting on too high a margin, now is the time to resolve that. The ultimate price can then be compared to local and other imported prices of similar products to see how competitive it is, or even whether the product's competitive advantage can justify a significantly higher price. Appendix 2 compares domestic and export pricing.

13. Negotiate a contract with a business partner.

The company is now ready to hook up with a business partner. The firm has explored the market and understands its competitive niche and the type of business arrangement that makes sense to be competitive. Company representatives should also be sufficiently knowledgeable about the market and how it works to enter into negotiations with a citizen or resident of that country.

Until now, discussions with potential partners have been exploratory only, with the parties getting to know each other, learning as much as possible about each other, and gaining valuable market data. A good partner will appreciate the exporter's due diligence and respect the company for its sincerity and its desire to do things right.

14. Position the product so that the customer will remember it in a certain way.

Product positioning is simply the message the company conveys to get the customer to remember the product in a certain way. For example, when Japanese companies entering the U.S. automobile market ran into resistance from Detroit producers, Honda and Toyota stressed the superior quality of Japanese cars, to justify to the American people the higher prices of vehicles imported from Japan.

Positioning ties directly to product niche or competitive advantage. Once it has been determined that the product is competitive, for whatever reason—price, distinguishing features, quality, more efficient supply chain—the exporter should work with host country groups like advertising firms and the importer to position the product. Since the exporter is dealing with a different culture, it is important to get the positioning right by working with people who know the culture. What works well in one country does not necessarily do so in another.

This is also the time to seek out local endorsements by celebrities, sports figures, and even political leaders. Having the weight of a local name backing a new product gives needed market leverage. Of course, such endorsements do incur additional cost, which must be figured into pricing.

15. Set out the company's business objectives and market penetration strategy in a business plan and draft an implementation budget for each target market.

With the due diligence done and the information needed in hand, the exporter can "back into" its final plan and budget, both usually projected for one year and five years. Many contracts have a trail period, sometimes less than one year, with performance incentives for sales targets. If this is the case, the plan should cover that period only so that both sides know exactly what is expected. The exporter, though, should have a longer-term plan to prepare for a contract extension or other business arrangement.

Finally, the business plan is first tested in the budget. Both sides must show a financial or resource commitment if market penetration is to be successful. If the budget is inadequate or does not allow for exigencies or down-the-road adjustments, there could be significant problems later. Now is the time to anticipate and prepare for them.

These, then, are the steps in a well-designed export process. Most successful exporters have used this or a similar method. The order of the steps may change slightly, although as presented they represent a logical approach. As a result of using this entry method, a company typically will think smaller, adjust its expectations lower, and set its sights more realistically over a longer period, giving it a much better chance of success.

Postscript: Other points to consider before exploring overseas markets.

While walking down this 15-step path a company needs to be streetwise on the international highway as well. Here are a few additional points to consider along the way.

Who is a citizen's best friend overseas?

Its embassy. Embassies are unjustly maligned. Since they are part of the government, people naturally think that they are political, bureaucratic, and generally a waste of time. Yes, they are political and bureaucratic because any organization, including a good company, is that way, as are individuals: Everyone is concerned about protecting turf. Human politics is as inherent as hair color and the sense of smell.

Beyond normal bureaucracy, embassies are a veritable contact machine. Their function is to know the people and lay of the land in the host country. Unless company representatives have pre-arranged contacts (or even if they do), touching base with their embassy or consulate, especially the commercial section, is smart business. Generally, embassy staff are insightful and objective. They can give an independent view, which is most helpful, before company representatives meet with potential business partners. Also, having an informed FSN accompany the representatives on their appointments signals to prospective partners that the representatives have been well briefed.

Further, if a company has a complaint with a firm or partner in another country, the embassy can help resolve it. The embassy can raise the issue, say, a nonpayment problem, directly with the local partner, or even with the government. If it is serious enough, the complaint can become a trade issue between the two countries, or an issue for international arbitration if the local courts fail to act properly. At some point in the trade complaint process, the embassy may advise the grieving company to pursue the matter in local court, but often the fact that the embassy is inquiring about the matter or is likely to move it to the government level suffices to spur the local firm to resolve the problem.

If company representatives lose their passports or money, the embassy can help them. And many company representatives have tried to walk the streets of a country to conduct market research and business on their own, only to turn for assistance at the end to their embassies. Though some, regrettably, have had unfortunate experiences with their embassies and swear never to return to one, smart companies that understand the power of leveraging let those more familiar with a situation help them.

Which of the following markets would you approach if you had to pick just one on the information given?

- *Brazil: 165 million people, $5,000 per capita GNP*
- *Argentina: 29 million people, $10,000 per capita GNP*
- *Ecuador: 13 million, $2,000 per capita GNP*
- *Mexico: 105 million, $4,600 per capita GNP*

Most companies would chose Brazil or Mexico and very few Ecuador, because the population and per capita income are so much greater in the two former countries. Since most companies tend to pursue the largest markets, these markets tend to have more competition as well. As competition mounts, agents and distributors become less interested in taking on new products. Companies that pursue smaller, less popular markets often find a much warmer reception and much less competition, ensuring better overall success.

How do agents and distributors in large markets differ from those in small markets?

Agents and distributors in large markets normally deal on high volume and low commissions; the opposite holds true for those in small markets. Agents and distributors in small markets do not maintain large inventories and want products that will move quickly to produce profits. Because they deal on lower volume, they are more inclined to represent several competitors in the same industry, putting extra effort behind the products that sell best.

Exporters from larger markets should be wary of this situation or a scenario like the following may occur: The exporter and agent agree to terms, although the agent makes it clear that he believes that working on a confirmed letter of credit basis adds unnecessary expense. The exporter, properly insists on being paid on a L/C basis. After further discussion they agree that they will begin their relationship with small shipments of 100 units only, for which the importer will pay with a letter of credit. This works well the first time: the exporter is paid in advance at time of shipment and the importer sells the product swiftly. A win-win situation.

The partners repeat the cycle with the same result. At this point the agent argues that the relationship has run so well that it is time to increase the size of the orders. The exporter agrees. But the importer says that the cost of an L/C for larger shipments will be excessive. Consequently, the exporter agrees to ship 1,000 units on open account. The risk has suddenly been transferred from the importer to the exporter. Instead of being paid at time of shipment, the exporter gets paid as the units are sold. If the importer cannot move the large number of units, which are consuming an inordinate amount of his limited inventory space, the excess product may mysteriously disappear and the importer may claim that they arrived damaged, although he never reported it.

Frustrated, the exporter decides to fire the agent, only to find that under host country law the agent is considered not a contractor but an employee of the exporting company and is entitled to severance pay. The exporter's only recourse is to pursue the matter as a trade complaint with its embassy or through the local court system. Do you think the chances of winning are good? All of this points to the need for safe, reliable financing and an understanding the company-agent relationship under local law before actual negotiations even begin.

Why would a company that is successful in a large domestic market venture overseas to a smaller market with less purchasing power?

Companies have been wrestling with this question for years. This is why most U.S. firms have been slow to export. They have been spoiled by a relatively easy and lucrative domestic market.

While smart companies acknowledge the limits of smaller markets, they set their expectations lower. Take a market like Uruguay. It has a population of less than four million people and per capita income of about $6,500. Why would a company in the United States, whose population is 270 million with per capita income of $35,000, try to enter Uruguay? One reason might be that competition in the United States is ever increasing, so that the market is becoming saturated. Maybe sales there are slow due to cyclical problems. Or maybe the company understands that international business may be its best source of growth and that penetrating a few small markets may reap good rewards down the road.

Whatever the reason, the company knows that Uruguay will not bring it huge success. Given import costs, the firm estimates that only 5 to 10 percent of that small market may have the wealth or disposition to buy its goods initially. But it also knows that if it breaks into the market now, its customer base is likely to expand over time. A number of smaller markets, each with some growth potential, can be a solid backup if domestic sales slacken occasionally.

A small company has new technology and the backing of some venture capitalists. It manufactures a device for testing the freshness of food from point to point in the distribution chain. It promotes the product to several large companies like Coca Cola and Wendy's. While all of them say the product is terrific, the small company makes no sales. What should the company do?

Many companies tend to evaluate their products in terms of the domestic market only: If the firm cannot sell there, it will not sell anywhere. That simply is not true. Facing rejection in the domestic market, the company mentioned ventured abroad where refrigeration was not as good as in the United States. Over time most of the firm's business was overseas in markets where food freshness is at a premium, but there are lapses in good refrigeration within the distribution system. In a global marketplace, companies should view the salability of their products and services in terms of that entire marketplace, not just their home market. Like the company above, several others have found that their goods are actually better suited to sales abroad.

Finally, remember John Smith. Here he was with $7,000 in his pocket and contemplating expansion abroad before his first domestic sale. This is risky but sometimes it can pay off beautifully. Once again, an overseas market may be kinder to a company than its home base. In this case, John Smith went to Europe and visited four trade shows in five weeks, all related to clothing, housewares, or related industries. With help from his embassies in these countries, he hired children of embassy employees to wear the T-shirts and walk up and down the rows of the shows. The exhibitions were filled with agents and distributors who were so impressed by the novel concept that they placed orders for the shirts.

When John returned home with the advance orders, he was able raised the capital necessary to start up his factory and fill the orders. He retired from that business as a millionaire at the tender age of 32.

CHAPTER 3

THE INTERNATIONAL BUSINESS LADDER: BUSINESS ARRANGEMENTS

GopX Corporation is a new company producing a sophisticated database management system that has useful applications to several industries. It has focused its limited resources on health care, but there is potentially an even larger market in the chemical and automotive industries. The firm's system is far better than other systems on the U.S. market but the company has heard about an upstart venture in Europe that is pursuing similar technology. GopX has limited resources. While it has commercialized its product, which is selling well in the United States and Canada, it needs an infusion of new capital.

Two venture capitalists are anxious to contribute. One is encouraging the firm to expand abroad before the competition does. The president of the company wants to use new funds to develop a new iteration of the system to keep it ahead of its European competitor. Some in the company believe it would be better to ignore international competition and expand horizontally across other industries at home.

What should the company do? Assuming it gains new funding, should it jump overseas into unfamiliar territory? Should it attack the domestic market, build a solid reputation and brand image, and then venture abroad? If it goes overseas, how should it do so? Manufacture product at home and sell through agents or distributors in selected countries? Does the company have the critical mass—the resources—not only to produce its product for domestic and overseas markets but to devote time and effort to nurturing new foreign markets?

Step back a moment. How can GopX even address these strategic questions until it understands the range of options open to it overseas? Because it needs an infusion of funds, maybe it should simply expand horizontally in the home market, which would certainly cost less. The firm has several possible ways to go here. Each of the arrangements available to it has different financial and operational implications. Before a company can make decisions like the ones before GopX, it should understand the methods and consequences of expanding.

The International Business Ladder

A good way to view the possibilities for growth abroad is to imagine a ladder, a progression of options. For example, most companies venturing overseas want to start with an easy, safe transaction. They want to be paid in U.S. dollars, using a letter of credit as the financing tool so they can be paid when they ship the goods, and send the goods to an agent or distributor overseas, who will have the worry of selling the goods. This is a classic export situation.

If business overseas grows to where the company can no longer keep up with demand in this fashion, it may consider licensing the goods to an overseas partner. Under a licensing or franchise arrangement, the company can get an upfront license fee based on the potential sales volume of the product, plus royalties on each unit sold. The company does not have to expand production or worry about shipping and trade financing, though it does have to transfer its technology to the licensee.

As business grows overseas, the company may enter into strategic alliances, management contracts, and joint ventures in which it would have to invest people and money.

Finally, if a company believes the overseas market is worthwhile long-term, it may do a Greenfield investment, where it acquires an existing company or starts one from scratch and owns 100 percent of it to maximize its control.

Companies move from exporter to investor for many reasons. Smaller firms do so because they learn the market and realize that local production can lower costs and increase sales. Larger companies tend to invest as part of a global strategy; investment positions the company strategically not only for that particular market but for the entire region. As we will discuss in later chapters, many factors go into the investment decision. For now, I would simply point out that the motivation of the company is what typically drives the investment decision. For example, in expanding does the firm want to own property and resources to control them? Or to leverage the situation by transferring technology to another company and gaining profit from the effort of that company? In the first case the firm may try to acquire a company in the host country to gain immediate market presence there and benefit from local knowledge. In the second case, a company may license its technology to a local company and reap a license fee and royalties without incurring the risk and expense of manufacturing and marketing product in that market.

Whatever the motivation, a company should set the stage for the transition from exporting to investing early on. By looking at the growth ladder, a company can see the transitions it might ultimately make (see figure 3.1).

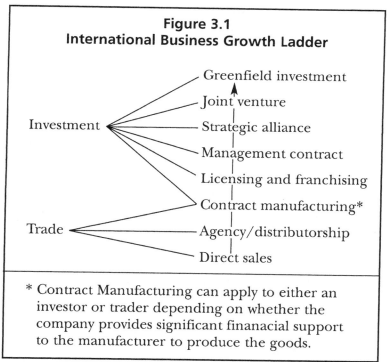

Figure 3.1
International Business Growth Ladder

Investment
- Greenfield investment
- Joint venture
- Strategic alliance
- Management contract
- Licensing and franchising
- Contract manufacturing*

Trade
- Agency/distributorship
- Direct sales

* Contract Manufacturing can apply to either an investor or trader depending on whether the company provides significant finanacial support to the manufacturer to produce the goods.

The decision to move from exporting to investing is strategic. It requires much thought and analysis, as we will discuss in depth later in the book.

Business Arrangements and Their Pros and Cons

Let's look at the pluses and minuses of the various international business arrangements:

Agency/Distributorship

Here a representative in a foreign market agrees to sell, market, or distribute the exporter's product. Distributors buy goods from a manufacturer, they may break them down from bulk into smaller portions, and they resell them at a profit to other wholesalers or retailers. An agent will represent the producer in securing arrangements with wholesalers or retailers, working on a commission or markup basis. Usually both can provide warehouse space for inventory, a sales force, marketing support, and any after sales service that may be required.

The product is generally shipped whole from the country of origin and the distributor or agent has to clear the goods through customs in its country. Either may agree to do assembly of the product and thus get credit for being a local manufacturer. Since most foreign markets have relatively few customers, agents and distributors tend to work on high margins and low inventory, pushing products that sell well and abandoning those that do not. A company needs to ensure that the margins do not price their products out of the local or regional markets. This is especially important if the distribution channel is long and wide, using many wholesalers and retailers to bring the product or service to market (see chapter 6). Figure 3.2 shows the pros and cons of an agency-distributorship relationship.

Figure 3.2
Agency – Distributorship

<u>Pros</u>	<u>Cons</u>
Less chance of technology transfer unless product can be disassembled	An agent or distributor can represent competitive products
Can ship to importer and be paid at time of shipment under a L/C	Importer prefers to deal on an "open account" basis; less expensive but risk falls to exporter
Similar to domestic business	Difficult for exporter to manage and monitor agent's performance

Figure 3.2
Agency – Distributorship (cont.)

Pros	Cons
Someone else works the overseas market; an extension of the company	Added product costs: shipping/tariff and finance charges
	Importer may be considered an employee, not contractor, in some countries with the possibility of a severance pay requirement
	Commission and/or markups can make product non price-competitive

Licensing

Under a licensing agreement, the exporting company contracts with an overseas partner to manufacture and distribute the product in that market or region. This arrangement normally involves a transfer of the company's technology: patents, trademarks, designs, or trade secrets. For protection, the exporter should ask for up to 50 percent of the product's value up-front for disclosing the technology secrets, though this is difficult for potential licensees to accept. *Franchising* is a form of licensing popular with service and chain operations where the parent company sells the franchise formula either individually or to a master franchiser, who then peddles sublicenses. Figure 3.3 lays out the pros and cons of licensing.

Figure 3.3
Licensing

Pros	Cons
Least expensive and less for exporter to do	Little control of overseas operations
Licensor does not incur shipping problems and expenses	Licensee owns rights to the technology

Figure 3.3
Licensing (cont.)

Pros	Cons
Royalty income, usually 3%	Host government regulations can restrict expatriation of profits, or impose a royalty tax
Licensor can learn from partner	Licensee can become a competitor
Up-front license fee can help company cash flow	

Management Contract

A company can also sell its experience and know-how to another company by managing a process or running the business of the overseas buyer or investor. Since many countries still insist that domestic companies be held by domestic, not foreign, interests, this approach allows the foreign company (our exporter) to build and, to a large extent, control the business, even lend its name to it, without the normal risks of ownership. This is particularly appealing for hotels or restaurants in countries with relatively high political and commercial risk. A company can gain exposure and name recognition while managing the process and waiting to do more until investment in that market is safer and more desirable. Figure 3.4 shows the advantages and disadvantages of a management contract.

Figure 3.4
Management Contract

Pros	Cons
Minimum investment abroad	Lacks the rewards of ownership
May have some or much control over operations	May be short-term, no lasting market presence
Provides opportunity to explore market before investing	May be the only way to enter market

Figure 3.4
Management Contract (cont.)

Pros	Cons
Good company exposure and opportunity to sell services abroad with limited risk	

Joint Venture

A joint venture usually takes the form of a new business with each partner contributing a percentage of the costs and reaping benefit by the same percentage. Like strategic alliances (see below), companies that can each bring value to an enterprise are likely to form joint ventures. For its share a partner may provide technology, equipment, facilities, capital, labor, management, and other forms of equity. The parties share the risk. In some countries the government restricts foreign ownership, insisting that the local partner be the majority owner. Figure 3.5 lays out the advantages and disadvantages of this form of partnership.

Figure 3.5
Joint Venture

Pros	Cons
Partners benefit from each other	Subject to local tax, labor, and business laws
Shows long-term company commitment to the host country	Subject to political risk, e.g., nationalization of assets and expropriation of funds
Synergy in combining resources	Seven of ten fall short of expectations
Partial control of operations	Share risk
Easier to integrate into local market	Hard to blend different corporate cultures and business objectives

Figure 3.5
Joint Venture (cont.)

Pros	Cons
Bypasses shipping, tariff and trade financing costs	May require local content in products but prices lower than imports

Strategic Alliances

A strategic alliance is a looser form of partnership than a joint venture. In strategic alliances, both parties agree to share risks and contribute to a project, but at a minimum investment or for as long as the project lasts. These alliances have been popular in biotechnology; companies working on related developments combine efforts to reduce their costs and avoid reinventing the proverbial wheel. Figure 3.6 shows the pros and cons of these alliances.

Figure 3.6
A Strategic Alliance

Pros	Cons
Less expensive collaboration	Less of an in-country presence
Less investment and risk	Control can be restricted by foreign company owner
Project-driven, not usually a long-term commitment	
Benefit of local partner's knowledge/contacts	
Synergy of combined operations	

Greenfield Investment

This type of venture is 100 percent owned by a foreign company that has either acquired a local firm or made a totally new investment. This approach may be well received by a host government because of the economic value of the enterprise. At the same time it is subject to local laws and country risk and may can be treated differently from local companies in which there is no foreign interest. (In international trade jargon, that would be a violation of national treatment.) Figure 3.7 presents the pros and cons of this type of investment.

Figure 3.7
Greenfield Investment

Pros	Cons
Strong commitment to the country/market	Company may not benefit from knowledge of local partner
Host government is pleased	Subject to political/economic risk, e.g. nationalization, blocked funds, etc.
Maximum control of operations and can better protect intellectual property	Most expensive form of investment, plus demands from local investors
Local competition is high and market entry may be difficult	Prices are kept lower than imports

Risk of International Business Arrangements

The risk of any overseas business arrangement will ultimately depend on the host country and the company's partners there. Generally speaking, though, agency and distributorships arrangements are considered low to medium risk because they are trade or exporting relationships. The likelihood of theft of intellectual property (IP) is reduced because the product is normally sent already assembled—but if the product does well, the company can expect to see cheaper imitations materialize in the market.

Management contracts are also rated low to medium risk because the company (the exporter) is paid for its services and the local owner (the buyer) of the services bears the major investment risk. However, the exporter does have to provide management and human resources, and these arrangements are typically made in countries with relatively high political and commercial risk.

Licensing is rated medium risk because it requires the transfer of technology and the licensor has less control over production, delivery, and service. The licensor not only needs a partner who is reliable, it also needs to license in a country where IP is protected.

Because international strategic alliances, joint ventures, and Greenfield investments require that the company invest in another country, subject to host-country rules and business environment, these arrangements are considered medium to high risk. A policy of the World Trade Organization (WTO) is "national treatment," that all companies, both domestic and foreign, that are operating in a country should enjoy the same rights. While most WTO member states endorse this policy, violations are not unknown. Figure 3.8 shows the goals of the exporting company in pursuing various types of arrangements and the risk the arrangements normally entail.

Figure 3.8
Goals and Risks of Investing by Business Arrangement

Type	Exporting Company Goal	Risk
Agent/ distributorship	Sell product directly; be paid upfront in U.S. dollars or home currency	Low, if letter of credit is used
Licensing	Good way to expand when firm has insufficient production capacity or company needs capital	Medium, depending on host-country IP laws
Management Contract	Company exposure with little investment; can have control of operations and benefit of local partner and can view country to invest later when conditions improve; may also be only means to enter market	Low-medium, depending on the market/ partner

Figure 3.8
Goals and Risks of Investing by Business Arrangement (cont.)

Type	Exporting Company Goal	Risk
Strategic Alliance	Project-basis so that investment is limited	Medium to high, depending on the market/ partner
Joint Venture	Long-term market presence with good local knowledge	Medium to high depending on market/ partner
Greenfield Investment	Long-term market presence with greatest control	Medium to high, depending on the market/ partner

Suiting the Business Arrangement to the Situation?

Confused? Good. Solid company strategy rarely springs from situations that are perfectly clear from the beginning. It comes from weighing options and considering different possible outcomes. The following examples of companies seeking international business arrangements are based on actual situations. While their choices or possible recommendations are discussed, they are not intended to be the only possibilities. Other companies in similar situations might take different courses of action.

- *Company X wants to protect its technology. It has a healthy domestic market share but its production is running at only 71 percent capacity. A potential international business partner wants to at least partially assemble X's product in its country so that it can gain manufacturing status there. What kind of business arrangement would be good for both parties?*

Since Company X has excess capacity, it can produce cost-effectively for overseas delivery, though it has to determine the demand in the target market to ensure that it has sufficient capacity to meet it. On the other side, the importer can gain a status boost by assembling imported products. By allowing the importer to do the assembly, the exporter gains leverage in the contract negotiations, as long as X's proprietary technology remains safe. Both sides can benefit well by undertaking an agency or distributorship.

- *Company Z has a liquid fuel product that is desirable in several Latin America markets, where it projects sales of $8 million over the first three years. The company wants to ship the product in drums, but the potential agents in Latin America think that shipping and other costs will price the product out of the market. They would rather produce the product there, paying Z license fees and royalties. The exporter has been in business for thirty years and has never had to share its formula with anyone. In fact, it has never obtained patents on its products. What should Company Z do?*

The company should explore the market to determine if pricing is really an issue. If so, it should either look to other markets that may be able to accommodate the added costs, or it should obtain the necessary patents, both domestically and internationally. This firm decided it did not want to make this investment and thus forewent the business. It is still a domestic-only company and may never venture overseas. This is a good example of a company that does not want to spend a relatively small amount to make potentially a large amount.

- *Company Y wants to go global with a package handling service. It wants to open simultaneously in 24 markets. In each it needs a local transport carrier and someone who can handle customs in-country*

The key here is understanding the nature of the business. The package handling industry runs on timeliness and reliability. Though many clients are repeat customers, the business is highly competitive, so a company in this industry must maintain a high degree of control. To open in 24 markets at the same time requires secrecy so that the competition is caught unawares. There are several possibilities open to Y, including joint venturing with sizeable competitors or similar companies in these markets.

Company Y, however, decided to enter into partnerships with small transport companies in each market. It used joint ventures in each case to ensure as much control as possible. The company provided its name and business practices, including managing the operations as it would under a management contract, and all necessary signage and facility redesign. The joint venture partners provided transport vehicles and their own facilities. This kept Company Y's costs to a minimum so that they could open in all 24 markets at once and yet retain the control they needed to succeed.

> • *Company Q has a solar air conditioning system that has a potential market in India of $10 million, but selling the product there would require the expenditure of up to $500,000 for product modifications. The company does not want to spend that much. A potential partner is willing to share half that expense if Company Q will let the partner license the product. Company Q is reluctant because of the political risk in India and the lack of IP protection. What should it do?*

Because India does not have strong IP laws, licensing is risky there. Nevertheless, the potential partner appears willing to make a sizeable investment to achieve success. Still, in addition to sharing the product modification expense, the partner should pay a hefty upfront license fee, considering the projected market is $10 million. Company Q can learn much from the partner's willingness to make the financial commitment. If the partner pays up, it has a vested interest in seeing the business succeed. It will want to protect the technology and product as much as the parent company.

The partner balked at paying more than half the product modification cost. Company Q countered by insisting on forming a joint venture with the partner that would be a separate firm. Company Q provided the technology under a license agreement for its part; the partner provided manufacturing and distribution facilities. As an equity partner in the joint venture, the company had a tighter arrangement and gained significant controls to better ensure production quality and protection of its technology.

> • *Company B manufactures a laser capacitor, a high-tech product, at a rate of 45 per month, which is 90 percent of its production capacity. It has cash flow problems, having had to borrow $50,000 for working capital for export start-up. It decides to deal first with The Netherlands and Great Britain, where the firm believes IP protection is strong and people speak English. A potential business partner in the Netherlands proposes to sell the product throughout Europe. The European Union (EU) represents a market of 30 units a month and the Netherlands is*

a good distribution point. The agent agrees to deal on a confirmed let-
ter of credit basis for at least the first year and negotiate a possible open
account after that. What type of business arrangement should
Company B pursue?

Given its poor cash flow situation and lack of excess capacity, Company B is not in a position to do an agency or distributorship arrangement. Instead it might investigate the possibility of licensing, where the licensee agrees to pay an upfront license fee and royalties. Before doing this, though, Company B should conduct its own market research to determine the true demand in the EU so it can set a realistic license fee. Also, since the proposed arrangement calls for sales Europe-wide, the firm should check the Netherlands' record on IP rights and see how the EU would protect its technology outside the Netherlands, where the license agreement would be established. For example, if the Dutch agent slips the technology to a German manufacturer to produce under a private label, would Company B have access to legal redress from the German firm?

• *Company N, a hotel chain, wants to enter Country M, which it under-*
  stands that one competitor is renovating two hotels it has acquired
  there and another competitor is negotiating for two more hotels to go
  with the five they already have in that country. A new government,
  believed to be less than friendly to Company N's country, has just
  taken power. What should Company N do?

Because Country M poses possible commercial and political risk to Company N, the firm should not engage in a risky venture or invest too much in that country. Further, the fact that competitors are already established there may give them more leverage and credibility with the new government.

Hotels lend themselves to management contracts. By negotiating a management contract, Company N can gain name exposure and good control of operations while the owners of the hotel pay for the facility and any renovations that have to be made. This gives Company N a presence in the market while it buys time to see if the risk subsides, making conditions more suitable for longer-term investment.

- *Company L is a small cash-strapped company that makes unique clothing from rare silk found in its native country. The United States has recently allowed this country to export the silk and clothing made from it duty-free to the U.S. However, the company does not have the capacity or resources necessary to accommodate such a large market. What should Company L do?*

Company L's competitive advantage is its ability to export a unique product to a country duty-free. It should capitalize on that advantage while trying to expand its capacity. The way to do this would be to seek a large clothing producer that would manufacture and distribute the clothing under contract or license. Company L would then provide its patterns and silk for royalties or a percentage of sales. This would allow the company to improve its cash flow while gaining access to a large lucrative market. Alternatively the American producer may simply want to source the duty-free silk from Company L.

Preparing for International Business Negotiations

The aim of an exporter and agent or distributor is to arrive at a win-win situation for both sides that can be articulated in a contract. The contract should include, at a minimum, the following points:

1. The territory that the agent or distributor will cover
2. The duration of the contract
3. The agent's expenses and commission or markup (to determine the ultimate price)
4. The agent's level of effort to sell the exporter's product
5. Method of purchase (e.g. purchase order) and payment terms and timing of payment (e.g. confirmed L/C)
6. Method of shipping
7. Inspection of accounts, audits and performance monitoring
8. Warranties and post sales service
9. The use of exporter's intellectual property (logos, trademarks, trade secrets, etc.)
10. Indemnification against claims, demands, suits or actions against the other party
11. Dispute resolution
12. Other restrictions

To prepare for the negotiation of a contract, both sides need to take care in learning as much about their potential partner as possible. Appendices 4 and 5 are questionnaires geared to help both the exporter and agent or distributor. Appendix 4 deals with information the exporter should want to know about the agent, and appendix 5 does the same for the agent about the exporter. Study both to gain an appreciation for what the other side values most. This empathy will help in the negotiations.

CHAPTER 4

INTERNATIONAL MARKET ASSESSMENT

Tapar International, a multimillion-dollar company, was looking into investing in Indonesia because the country had a huge abundance of barbalay, a conductive material critical to the manufacture of two of Tapar's leading products—a lightweight engine made of ubithium and a smart card that used an alloy.

Chief Executive Officer Robert Hadley, Vice President for Market Development Aaron Watson, and Jason Barlow, the regional director for Southeast Asia traveled to Jakarta to view the investment possibilities firsthand.

"The terrorism situation makes this country a risky investment," Hadley moaned. "And the external debt numbers—just like before the Asian debt crisis in the nineties—are bad. Why, the debt they owe other countries is almost two-thirds of their entire gross domestic product."

"Worse, because of the terrorism situation and the need for more cash reserves, the government is considering new measures to restrict the earnings a transnational firm can take out of the country," Watson added. "The last thing we need is to invest and find out that we can't withdraw our money when we want to."

"But we need the new material and the cheapest source of it is right here, or about a hundred miles from here," Barlow reminded them.

"Yes, but if we open a plant here, can we get reliable labor?" Watson countered. "The material is wonderful, I agree. But the biggest cost savings to us would be if we can manufacture both the engine and the smart card in Indonesia for distribution throughout most of Asia."

"Production will require skilled labor and, with tensions running high, Indonesian management as well," Hadley remarked. "What is the level of skilled labor here? Have we identified any competent managerial talent? If we have, maybe we can strategically position ourselves here. We'll be cost-effective in both sourcing materials and production. which would surely give our supply chain an edge. The competition won't be able to lay a hand on us."

As Hadley smiled broadly, Barlow warned, "That all assumes the infra-structure and supply sources are all reliable."

"We'll develop strategic partnerships or even acquire a few suppliers if need be."

"What concessions will the Indonesian Government give us?" Watson asked. "We'll create jobs, true, but another American company here becomes another target for terrorists. Yes, I want to know what tax incentives there are for investing here and any reciprocal tax arrangements Indonesia has with the U.S. But I also want to know what the government is doing to protect foreign investments."

They both looked quizzically at their regional director. Barlow advised them that he had set up a briefing with the embassy to review the commercial and political risk in Indonesia. When they arrived at the U.S. embassy, the commercial counselor met them and escorted them deep into the cavernous building. Finally they arrived at a small cramped room that appeared to have a plastic sheathing around it.

"What's this?" the CEO asked.

"We'll wait for the ambassador and the others here," the officer said. "Mr. Hadley, we may have to talk about a number of sensitive issues you should consider before you make your investment decision. Welcome to the Bubble."

This scenario is not uncommon. The points Tapar's representatives discussed are all very pertinent to an international investment decision, and the regional director was smart to request what is known as an "embassy country briefing." If embassy officers do not know the answer to something, most likely they can find someone who does. In a country briefing the ambassador and the country team, consisting of the political, economic and commercial officers, advise a company on the risk of operating in the country.

A novice exporter might think that while all this information is fine for investors, why should an exporter have to go to all this trouble? Regardless of whether it wants to export or invest, a company should want to know the same things about foreign markets: demand for its products and services, local and regional efficiencies, the stability of the government, and how difficult it will be to function there.

The difference between an exporter and an investor on these points is just a matter of degree. True, the investor is making a longer-term and more expensive commitment to the target market, but both types of companies should make their decisions based on the country risk and business risk they find there. Country risk covers the full range of political and commercial risk factors, including consumer and country infrastructure sophistication. Business risk relates to the working environment of the host country.

Three Ways to View the World Commercially

In this time of terrorism and corporate regrouping, what market can a company enter that will be both profitable and safe?

Good question. The answer should begin with how a company elects to view the world. If the view is negative, I do not advise pursuing the subject further.

Here is one perspective. Although there are nearly seven billion people on the planet, almost 90 percent of them earn less than $10,000 a year. In 2000, average annual per capita income for the world as a whole was less than $1,400 per year. In terms of productivity, 15 percent of the world's population produces nearly 80 percent of the world's total product. And the rich are getting richer. Recent figures show that per capita income in more advanced countries is growing faster in absolute terms than in developing countries. Unfortunately, the largest increase in population growth over the next hundred years is supposed to be in low-income countries,[1] which are ill prepared to handle such growth.

From this view, a company expanding overseas might say: "Why bother? The situation looks bleak." On the other hand, the global economy is expected to grow at 3 percent a year over the next fifty years. This implies a four-fold increase in gross domestic product (GDP) during that time. Further, over the past twenty years, the world's per capita income has risen 37 percent and illiteracy has been halved.[2] Additionally, democracy is replacing dictatorships across the planet. With increased education, property ownership, government inclusion, and private businesses, income for the general populace of many countries will swell dramatically, and every 1 percent increase in a country's GDP translates into a 0.7 - 0.8 percent increase in that country's international trade.[3]

Or view the world this way: The Group of Seven (the United

---

[1] World Bank, *World Development Report – 2003* (Washington, D.C.: World Bank), pp 2 - 3.
[2] *Ibid.*, p. 2.
[3] Pankaj Ghemawat, "Distance Still Matters: The Hard Reality of Global Expansion," *Harvard Business Review*, Volume: 79 (8) (September 2001): 137 – 47.

States, France, Germany, Italy, the United Kingdom, Canada, and Japan) have combined GDP of nearly $20 trillion. The Big Five emerging markets (China, Brazil, India, Mexico, and Indonesia) have a combined purchasing power of nearly half that. There are over ten emerging economies that companies everywhere cannot ignore because they have shown the greatest rate of growth over the past thirty years.

Why are these markets so important from a business perspective? First, people in these countries are younger and much more numerous than in developed countries. Their productive capacity is potentially greater and less expensive than it is in more advanced nations, and they represent an emerging middle class. Second, it is estimated that three out of every eight middle class consumers will live in the developing world within the next ten years.[4] These consumers will make from $3,000 to $10,000 per annum, an income level at which they will greatly accelerate their consumption.[5] As productivity gains and infrastructure improvements are achieved in these and other markets, the number of middle-class consumers with disposable income should rise significantly. Viewed this way, companies see real promise in expanding beyond their borders.

Thus far we have looked at how a company can proceed to go abroad. Now the question is where to go. Quite properly, most companies start close by, particularly in markets that have a common language or culture. The amount of trade between countries 5,000 miles apart is only about one-fifth of what it would likely be if those countries were only 1,000 miles apart.[6] Nonetheless, as business grows outward, identifying niches and situating strategically as Tapar was trying to do can often drive companies to more distant markets.

An Approach to Market Assessment

For exploring overseas markets, the Internet, the National Trade Data Bank, export and import statistics, embassies, and even chambers of commerce and trade associations in target markets all offer invaluable information. The problem is not a paucity of information, but an overload. What should a company be looking for in its

---

[4] Jeffrey Rosenweig, *Winning the Global Game*, (New York: Free Press, 1998).
[5] James A. Gingrich, "Five Rules for Winning Emerging Market Consumers," in Michael Czinkota, ed., *Best Practices in International Business* (Harcourt College Publishers, 2001).
[6] Ghemawat, *op. cit.*, note 3, p. 138.

initial market research and what questions should it ask? The following three-step approach may be useful:

- *Explore the National Trade Data Bank (NDTB):* Industry Sector Analyses (ISAs), which are a key component of the NTDB, help a company pinpoint where its products or services will sell best in the world. Once it has targeted five or so markets, it can explore the Country Commercial Guides for those markets to determine how to operate in them, and where land mines might be buried.

- *Draw up a Country Profile:* This approach, detailed below, essentially lets a company view a market from six aspects with specific categories in each. For example, the economy would be one aspect and balance of payments a category within it. The information for all 20 categories presented in the profile is available from the World Bank World Development Indicators, which is updated annually to ensure as much fresh data as possible (although many countries do not provide new information that regularly). A company can evaluate several aspects (or categories) of the market through this source, but the profile presented later in the book is limited to some of the more important ones. Once it evaluates a category, a firm can weight it to determine its importance to the company. This way the firm assesses the market based on its own priorities.

- *Compare Country Profiles with Other Sources:* Once a company has its profiles, it should check its judgment against other sources of country evaluations, among them the Heritage Foundation's Index of Economic Freedom (IEF),[7] Freedom House's Survey of Freedom in the World,[8] Euromoney's

[7] Heritage Foundation, *Index of Economic Freedom – 2002* (Washington, D.C.: Heritage Foundation, 2003). This index includes for each country evaluated a weighted average to show a typical tariff on imported goods, the policy on how much earnings a firm can take out of the country, foreign ownership of land and assets, non-tariff barriers, and controls on investment.

[8] Freedom House, *Survey of Freedom in the World*, Washington D.C., 2000-2001. This source shows the relative rights of citizens in countries around the world. For each country evaluated, the survey measures freedom and protection of ownership, both of land and companies; the condition of courts to uphold contracts and other agreements; and the amount of corruption in various institutions.

Country Risk Rankings,[9] and Cavusgil's "Measuring the Potential of Emerging Markets."[10] This comparison lets the firm test its independent country evaluation against expert sources.

The Country Profile

The six aspects of a target country a company should explore are:

- Population and market size
- Effectiveness of the host government
- Infrastructure
- The economy
- The financial environment
- Market receptivity.

The last aspect measures how willing the country is to buy goods from the home country of the exporter or investor. These aspects are discussed in detail below, highlighting key features and categories of each.

Population/Market Size

Here a company can examine several categories to help define the market; for instance:

- The population index gives birth and death rates and whether there is sufficient food reaching the populace.
- Age composition helps measure the relative size of the target customer base.
- Income distribution tests how concentrated discretionary income is.

A key to a sustained healthy economy is a thriving middle class. If the distribution of wealth is unreasonably skewed, with most of the wealth in the hands of a few who control government and business, the middle class will likely be small. Thus, depending on the total size of the population, the market may also be small. Worse,

---

[9] Euromoney Magazine, "*Country Risk Rankings*," London, 2001. These rankings are based on several factors, including political risk, economic performance, debt indicators, debt in default or rescheduled, credit ratings, access to bank finance, short-term financing, and capital markets and discount on forfeiting. This last factor is particularly useful in viewing a country's financial and credit condition and the ability of the government to handle or improve it.

[10] S. Tamer Cavusgil, "Measuring the Potential of Emerging Markets: An Indexing Approach," *Business Horizons*, 40 (1): 87-91.

the possibility of social unrest may be high. Social unrest undermines political stability. A government that feels threatened will adopt restrictive policies, including those that constrain foreign companies. The more unstable a government, the greater the risk to a company of having its assets nationalized or frozen, repatriation of its profits restricted, or value-added taxes imposed on its operations in that country.

Closely related to income distribution are educational and employment demographics. In this analysis a firm can look at the primary, secondary, and college-level education breakdown, as well as the percentage of workers who are skilled as scientists, engineers, or technicians. Further, the company can see the percentage of workers in manufacturing and services and the value these jobs add to the economy. In many countries the government employs people in order to keep unemployment numbers low, but such jobs do not necessarily add much to productivity. To get deeper insight, a firm can look at minimum wages, average hours worked per week, and related items.

The Political Environment

A firm contemplating business abroad needs to know how stable the host country government is and its ability to make and enforce laws. Without a safe environment where there is respect for rules, a company will face significant problems that will negatively affect its ability to conduct business (see "The Economy" below). The company should first determine if the government is democratic, where the people have a voice, or dictatorial, where they have no voice.

A good indication of this is whether the government is entrenched, long in office and protected against popular vote. Entrenchment can lead to paranoia, where the government constantly feels threatened. If this is the case, there is a greater likelihood that the government will impose stringent regulations, especially on foreign companies, and possibly nationalize private firms. Social unrest and bureaucratic red tape are also evaluated in this part of the analysis.

If a country fails to enforce the law or has a weak or corrupt judiciary, a company will probably not fare well in adverse situations. For example, if a country does not do a good job at collecting taxes generally, it may levy substantial taxes on companies, both foreign and domestic, or block funds from leaving the country. In this section of the assessment, a company can also explore the record of the country on protecting IP (patents, trademarks, copyrights, and trade secrets) and whether the country agrees to international arbitration. These further gauge the legal backbone of the country. Refusal to allow international arbitration, for instance, reflects poorly on the judiciary. If there is a risk that its proprietary technology will be stolen, the firm should reconsider that market.

Infrastructure

A company weighs the extent of infrastructure in a country to measure the sophistication of the market and how well a supply chain will work there. Infrastructure includes not just roads and ports but also vehicles to convey information, such as newspapers, TV and radio, personal computers, and the Internet. Information flow not only indicates how well informed customers are likely to be but also how a company can reach the customer base. Data are available on the number of phones and the amount of energy available per 100 people.

How many retail outlets does a country have per 1,000 inhabitants? What about paved roads, railroads, ports, and airports? Measuring the length and breadth of the distribution and retail channels (how many players?) helps a firm gauge its ability to get the product to market. Overlaying the infrastructure aspect is whether the government or the private sector operates this complex system. The private sector tends to perform more efficiently. Information is available on who owns and controls telecommunications, water sanitation, energy, and transportation companies.

The Economy

Here a company should consider both the health of the country's economy and how the country fares economically compared with other nations. Though the external and internal sides of an economy are inexorably linked, they should be examined separately.

Internally, a healthy economy normally has fewer hang-ups than one that is controlled or less invigorated. A firm can assess the vibrancy of the country by looking at key industries and the percentage of GDP each produces. The profile should also survey the business environment in terms of market entry requirements, contract enforcement, tax policies, average import duties, and insolvency resolution. A firm can see how the manufacturing and service industries break down in terms of productivity and GDP distribution, as well as how imports and exports have changed over time. It can judge whether interest rates are generating real returns on investment and how heated inflation is by looking at the country's consumer price index, the real exchange rate of the local currency to the U.S. dollar, and the change in that rate over time.

Externally, a company should read the country's balance of payments: is money entering or leaving the market and at what rate? This helps it determine whether the nation is attracting capital or watching it flee to safer ground. Similarly, how much external debt does the target country have? Is it borrowing money faster than it can pay the money back? Since new funds come from an increase in exports or investment, is this revenue increasing or decreasing at the same rate as debt?

Looking at these external factors in the light of a country's fiscal and monetary policies, such as how it fights inflation or whether it is running trade and budget deficits or surpluses, a company can determine if the government is taking responsible actions to nurture a strong economy. The Heritage Foundation's IEF views the monetary and fiscal policies of a country in terms of government spending and the ability to control inflation and collect taxes.

To be productive, a country's economy needs to be RIPE. It should have:

- *R*easonable interest rates to attract investment and encourage domestic spending,
- *I*nflation that is controlled,
- *P*roductive employment that adds value to the economy, and
- *E*xports that generate income and foreign cash reserves.

Many countries lack ripe economies. If they cannot export because they have little of value to offer the rest of the world or they cannot attract investment, they have to borrow money or rely on aid from other nations or world institutions, like the World Bank Group. Usually the debt of developing companies is denominated in U.S. dollars, so the borrower has to repay in dollars, but if countries cannot export much or otherwise generate foreign reserves, how can they repay debt?

If they simply buy dollars with their own currency, those currencies will cheapen, igniting inflation. Worse for investing companies, the host government will likely block the movement of funds between the parent and subsidiaries in that country or put a hold on dollar or other foreign-denominated transfers. To stop the inflation surge, the government may raise interest rates, which may in turn trigger higher unemployment. People will lose their ability to buy goods, and with inflation and lower productivity, how will a country ever cover its debts?

The prospects of such a downward spin can be gleaned by examining a country's external debt numbers. Unfortunately, many companies—and even governments—tend to overlook them. For example, in the early 1990s, the U.S. Department of Commerce promoted 10 "big emerging markets" that it believed offered the most substantial growth opportunities for U.S. business. One of them was Indonesia, which sat in the middle of the booming economy of South East Asia. Foreign investors poured into the country, ignoring its sizable external debt. When the Asian debt crisis hit in the mid-nineties, investors in Indonesia were caught flatfooted. They lost considerably.

There are three ways to measure external debt against GDP and exports:

- External debt as a percentage of GDP

- External debt as a percentage of exports

- Debt service ratio:

$$\frac{\text{Interest payments} \quad + \quad \text{Annual principal payments}}{\text{Exports}}$$

How can a company tell if these percentages and ratios are within acceptable ranges? This is difficult to judge. It depends on several other factors, such as the nature of the product and the company's business arrangement, but the EU, for example, has set debt at 60 percent or less of GDP as a ceiling for a country to qualify for entry into the EU. Debt service ratios average about 18 percent, with a range from 10 to 30 percent. Debt as a percentage of exports averages 198 percent, with a range of 90 to 275 percent.[11] Credit ratings of government debt by such companies as Standard and Poor's also assess a government's ability and willingness to service its debt

---

[11] World Bank, *World Development Report - 1996* (Washington, D.C.: World Bank, 1996).

in full and on time.[12]

An additional note about a nation's balance of payments: This measure shows how much a country is exporting and importing and the direction in which investment is flowing. Is money entering or leaving the country? How much? How fast? If a country has chronic trade deficits (importing more than it is exporting), what steps are being taken to balance the current account and what effect does this spending have on the country's debt posture?

Mexico ran high trade deficits when its short-term debt came due just after it joined NAFTA. It could not generate enough revenue through oil exports and thus lacked the cash reserves to pay its debt.[13] When the country declared bankruptcy, it had to issue a new currency and borrow an additional $50 billion. After this, many investors not only took their money out of Mexico but also out of much of the rest of Latin America. This became known as the "Tequila Effect".

In this section of its profile analysis, a firm should not only explore a country's balance of payments and external debt, but view it alongside the nation's track record on attracting foreign investment. The World Bank's World Development Indicators give the amount of foreign investment in a country, its credit ratings by services like Standard & Poor's, government restrictions on investment, and how much the country depends on foreign economic aid.

The Financial Environment

A company needs to know how effective the securities markets and financial services industries operate. Is there a stock market? If so, what is its market capitalization and how many firms are listed on the exchange? Can the market serve as a source for debt or equity financing? How healthy are the banks and other financial institutions? To judge this, a firm might explore the percentage of domestic credit that local banks provide. How liquid and profitable are they? Does the government interfere with their decision-making when it results in nonperforming loans? Which do the banks assign a higher credit rating: the government or certain companies in the country?

A company thinking about export should see if subsidiaries or

---

[12] Standard and Poor's, *Sovereigns* (reprinted from RatingDirect April 3, 2002; David T. Beers, analyst). Published by S&P, a McGraw Hill Company, New York (ratingdirect.com and standardandpoors.com).

[13] U.S. Department of Commerce, working papers of the Office of Mexico.

affiliates of its domestic banks operate there and which local banks have corresponding relationships with banks from the exporter's country. It is important to have these ties to home in order to obtain reliable trade financing, such as letters of credit. The National Trade Data Bank is a good source for banking information.

Market Receptivity

After all is said and done, if a market is not receptive to the goods and services of its home country, a foreign company will have a hard time entering the market. For firms in the United States, the National Trade Data Bank and the Port Import Export Reporting Service (PIERS) Global Intelligence Solutions (Newark, N.J.) are good sources of export-import activity. Both provide product information by country destination. To determine how receptive a country is to importing goods and trading in general, World Development Indicators is again a good tool.

Once a company moves through these various analyses to understand the market conditions, it can address buyer behavior. To do this well a firm must visit the target countries to explore buying habits and cultural nuances, using the 5P and 2C approach introduced in chapter 2 and discussed more extensively in chapter 6.

The six factors for analysis cover, to a large extent, the range of country and business risk. The Country Profile shown in chapter 10 is designed to allow a company to gain the vast bulk of the information it needs from one source, *World Development Indicators*. This is a good start to market research. Some companies will want to do a deeper analysis; for that, other sources are listed in appendix 7.

Since an *investment* arrangement normally involves a sizable capital expenditure, though, smart companies follow a set process for making such decisions that combine both quantitative and qualitative features. These firms may also use sensitivity analysis: after receiving input from experts in the target market and throughout the company, they develop "what if" scenarios.

These computerized scenarios apply several sets of risk factors to formulate possible subsidiary situations. They are typically used with the type of capital budgeting described in chapter 9. Say a company predicts that it can gain positive cash flows over a five-year period that will generate a 15 percent return on the investment. What if the country experiences internal strife and the currency devalues by 20 percent over three weeks? How would that affect predicted cash flows? What is the likelihood of that happening?

Companies will select variables randomly to show a range of different results. For instance, if the host country currency devalues by 5 or 10 percent or appreciates by 10 percent, how would these different values affect projected subsidiary cash flows? What if the country amasses too much debt and, needing to hold foreign currency to pay it off, prevents the subsidiary from remitting dividends to the parent? Say the government restricts 15 percent of the income the subsidiary generates. Or 25 percent. Or 45 percent.

Further, firms investing in today's global marketplace must be concerned with proper market positioning. It is not enough to gauge market size and customer demand within one target country; it is necessary to view the investment in terms of how it will contribute to the company's regional or even global strategy. How will the new venture fit into and affect the operation of the company's supply chain? Will the sourcing of materials be simplified and cost-effective? Will finance factors, such as a high host country tax rate or blocked funds, hinder global operations? If yes, to what extent?

Firms should weigh country and business risk against local, regional, and global opportunities to measure the real market value of a target country. These are opposite sides of the same coin.

On the risk side a firm places those factors that it judges to be most critical for a target country, including competition in the market, host government policies affecting business operations, cultural differences between the home and host countries, and the availability of local skilled labor and management expertise.

On the opportunity side the company ranks the potential advantages of making the investment, looking at local and regional demand, how the supply chain and financial operations of the company may benefit, and what corporate values can be brought to bear on the investment to help it succeed. This "opportunity/risk assessment" becomes the basis of the firm's investment decision-making process: Can the company overcome risk and capitalize on possible opportunities? Once it has its country profiles, the firm should view them in terms of all their pluses and minuses, pros and cons.

How to Use the Country Profile

The profile in chapter 10 covers all the market aspects and categories just discussed. Each category is laid out in matrix form for evaluation. Once these are evaluated, a company uses two factors to determine the relative value or importance of each category to the firm. The first factor (Degree) has three possible numbers: 1 for "poor," 3 for "acceptable" or "good," and 5 for "excellent." The second factor (Weight) also has three numbers: 1 – "little importance"; 3 – "important"; 5 – "very important." By multiplying the two factors together, a company can determine the relative value (VAL) of that category in selecting or rejecting the target market. The higher the value, the better the condition and importance of the category. As an example, look at the factor "income distribution" for Indonesia and Mexico in Figure 4.1.

If a company simply focuses on per capita income, it may not see much market opportunity, especially for Indonesia, but a closer look at Mexico reveals that the top one-fifth of the population has purchasing power of over $13,000 annually per capita while the top 20 percent of Indonesians make on average just over $2,000. Viewed this way, Mexico boasts a market of 21 million persons with sizable per capita income. That is larger than most markets of the world! And Indonesia offers a customer base of 47 million with growing spending power. In this case the company sees Mexico as the better market (thus a Degree of 5 versus only 3 for Indonesia). It also considers this category to be very important to its long-term success in any market, thus a Weight of 5 for both countries. Figure 4.2 presents an abbreviated version of the Country Profile in chapter 10. In that chapter a company can also summarize the values or findings in a chart.

Figure 4.1

	Population (M)	GDP/capita	% of Income per 20 Percentile					Degree x Weight =VAL	
			1st 20%	2nd 20%	3rd 20%	4th 20%	5th 20%	(1,3,5)	(1,3,5)
Income distribution									
Mexico	104	$5,500	9	7	13	20	58	5	25
Indonesia	234	$690	8	12	15	19	46	3	15

Figure 4.2 – Abbreviated Country Profile

1. *Population/ Market Size*

	GDP/capita					Degree x Weight = VAL	
Income distribution	10%	25%	50%	75%	100%	(1,3,5)	(1,3,5)
Employment	Unemploy-ment rate	Skilled labor Sci/Eng/Tech	% in Ind. Ser.	Value Added		Degree x Weight = VAL (1,2,3)	(1,2,3)

2. *Political Environment*

	Law enforced	Judiciary strength	Int'l arbitration	IP protection	Degree x Weight = VAL	
Law/order					(1,3,5)	(1,3,5)

3. *Infrastructure Development*

	Newspapers	TV/Radio	PC's	Internet	Tech Exp.	Degree x Weight = VAL	
Information technology						(1,3,5)	(1,3,5)

Figure 4.2 – Abbreviated Country Profile (cont.)

3. _Infrastructure Development (cont.)_

Transportation	Roads	Rail	Seaports	Airports	Degree x Weight = VAL (1,3,5) (1,3,5)

4. _Economy_

External Debt	Debt Classification (Lo/Mod/Hi)	% of GNI (*)	% of Exports	% of Total Debt Short-term	Degree x Weight = VAL (1,3,5) (1,3,5)
Foreign Direct Investment	Amount	Risk Ratings	Gov't Restricts	Aid to GDP	Degree x Weight =VAL (1,3,5) (1,3,5)
Business Environment	Entry Regulations	Contract Enforcement	Insolvency Time/Cost to Resolve		Degree x Weight =VAL (1,3,5) (1,3,5)

5. _Financial Environment_

Banks	% of domestic credit provided	Liquidity	Profit	Risk Premium	Degree x Weight = VAL (1,3,5) (1,3,5)

CHAPTER 5

THE SUPPLY CHAIN:
SUPPLY SIDE

In 1981 the U.S. Department of Commerce ran a dozen trade centers in strategic locations around the world. These fixed facilities put on shows in various industry sectors to offer U.S. companies avenues to exhibit their wares for export.

As a new, unseasoned manager, I had the unenviable task of coordinating the activities of these centers, which were coming under attack from Congress during the annual budget process for waste and inefficiencies.

Desperate for information and not understanding time differences, I called each center director, waking some in the middle of the night. Ralph Thompson, among others, was not pleased. "I can get you the data on each show for my region in the morning and I'll cable it to you," he said in a slumbering fog. "But that will take a week to type it all out and send it to Washington," I told him, frustrated. I had heard the same answer on four earlier phone calls.

"Well, what do you want me to do?"

"I should have all that information here every day so I can defend you guys out there," I said. "You know how management is here. With the sketchy info I have, I'll tell Bill, who'll pass it to the bureau, then it'll go to the administration, and up the line to the Secretary's people. And nobody'll believe it. And if they don't, do you think Congress will?"

"You know, we had 16 great shows last year," Ralph declared. "Doesn't anybody care what good we do?"

"You know the drill," I said. "Under cost recovery, we're supposed to do more than cover our costs. We're supposed to provide a tailor-made product for the customer and scale back expenses at the same time."

"Don't they know back there that to customize our exhibit booths costs money and the fancier we get, the more suppliers I need to hire? As it is I have eight on contract already, but since I don't use all of them regularly, I don't know if they're going to show up from one day to the next."

"Maybe we should get rid of the lot and hire four reliable ones full-time

instead," I said naively.

"Do you know what that would do to our costs? Plus then I'd have to manage them all." he screamed. "Listen, why doesn't someone back there ever talk to our customers. They love us and they would support us just fine on Capital Hill."

"I hear you, Ralph," I said "Just get those reports in as soon as possible."

Later that same day I had a call from representatives of the Pitney Bowes Corporation. After their sales pitch, I didn't believe half of what they said their product could do. "Now, let me see if I get this straight," I said. "With your machine, my 12 offices around the world can send me information, numbers, graphs, pictures as they happen. Instantly."

The men nodded, pleased at my astonishment: "As long as it takes to make a phone call."

"I need 12 of these today," I said. "But I'll have to get a few approvals up the line."

The men handed me their cards and told me to call them when I was ready to buy. The approval process only took six months; within eight, I had my thirteen facsimile machines.

Back then the international slice of the Department of Commerce was tiny, poorly connected overseas, and cylindrical in structure: Power rested inside the clogged tower of Washington headquarters. The supply chain was alive, if not well, but not clearly defined. Decisions were slow and rarely made with input from stakeholders. Employees were told to do their jobs but were burdened with weekly, monthly, quarterly, and annual reports; management back home needed piles of paper to prove the organization's worth. Back then we thought we were good—but we rarely asked our clients what they thought.

A company investing overseas should not operate that way. It enters a new realm and at the heart of that realm is a supply chain, not headquarters. Nearly 20 years ago Michael Porter said that a firm is a collection of activities that are performed to design, produce, market, deliver, and support its product. At each stage and in each activity, he claimed, a company had "value"; taken together all these activities constituted a firm's "value chain". Further, Porter declared, a company needed to look not just at its product or service but its entire value chain to determine its competitive advantage. Lastly, he said, the suppliers, distributors, and retailers that handled a company's product also had their own value chains.[1]

At the core of Porter's model lay the "focal company," the core firm that makes others in a supply change work toward a common goal. The concept assumes that this company is a stand-alone entity that controls and manages its own decisions and activities. Globalization, fierce price competition, and increasing emphasis on satisfying the customer has forced an evolution from the company-centric value chain to a process-centric supply chain where a family of companies take ownership to produce, deliver, and support products and services. Increasingly, competitive advantage comes not from individual value chains but from the synergistic linkages of a family of firms. This arrangement was labeled a few years ago the "extended enterprise" and more recently the "extended supply chain."

Any company looking to invest in foreign markets needs to understand the implications of the global supply chain and its evolution over the past 20 years. Because of the complexity of this concept, we will reluctantly break the chain in half, dealing in this chapter with the supply and production side of it and in the next with the distribution side. We will describe the stages involved as "decision areas." In chapter 7 we will explore an approach to strategy for a global or regional supply chain business and in chapter 8 we will examine how best to organize for it. In chapter 9 we will delve into the international financial implications and finally in chapter 10 we will lay out a step-by-step framework to work through the entire process.

The Global Supply Chain Forum describes management of the supply chain as "the integration of key business processes from end user through original suppliers that provides products, services and information that add value for customers and other stakeholders."[2] You will notice that the forum definition stresses *process* and *value to the customer.*

The stages of the supply chain include first-tier suppliers that interact directly with the focal company, second-tier firms that supply the first-tier suppliers, the focal company, distributors, and retailers. Each stage in the chain is linked to the next by processes,

---

[1] Michael E. Porter, *Competitive Advantage*, (New York: Free Press, 1985), pp. 33 – 66.
[2] Douglas M. Lambert, Martha C. Cooper, and Janus D. Pagh, "Supply Chain Management: Implementation Issues and Research Opportunities," *International Journal of Logistics Management*, 9 (2): 1.

activities, and tasks. For example, when a company buys raw materials for the production of a product, there are several tasks or activities involved in this seemingly simple process. Take a local company that sells only within its state. It needs raw materials or components to build its product or produce its service, so it has to identify one or more suppliers and negotiate an agreement with each. The suppliers have to produce and deliver the materials on time. The firm then has to pay for the materials and for holding inventory until it can be used. Assuming it has the materials it needs, the company can produce the product and package and ship it through a channel of distributors, where it might sit in one or more warehouses until it reaches a store where it can be sold. Many things can go wrong at each step or process.

Then imagine doing this with not one but several products or services. Add to that finicky customers who want something immediately; if they cannot get it, they will amble across the street and grab what they want elsewhere. Then spread this model across the globe and deal with suppliers, distributors, and customers that all think and act much differently from those in the parent company's home state.

While you consider all of things that can go wrong, think too of the numerous opportunities that can shape the firm's competitive advantages. In a perfect world the family of companies in the chain would work and communicate well with each other to identify and create such advantages. Unfortunately, we do not live in a perfect world, although working together toward perfection is precisely what the family of firms in a supply chain should pursue.

To build a strong international supply chain, a company must go abroad to explore decision areas and meet with potential partners. To show the range of this examination, Figure 5.1 depicts a supply chain with a focal company, such as a car manufacturer, and its suppliers, wholesalers, and dealerships, while Figure 5.2 shows various supply chain decision areas where firms can search for competitive advantages. Notice that stakeholders are an integral part of the supply chain. How a company leverages stakeholders to minimize problems and capitalize on opportunities can be a huge source of competitive advantage. All the elements depicted in the figure apply equally to both product and service providers.

Figure 5.1
Supply Chain With Focal Company

Figure 5.2
Supply Chain Decision Areas

Location/ Logistics	Suppliers	Production	Distributors	Stakeholders*
# of facilities integration	Vertical	Platform integration	Vertical	Customers
Facility type strategic partners	Specialized	Processes length	Channel	Shareholders
Facility configuration	Several suppliers	Standard-ization	Channel breadth	Employees
Transit time	Reliability	Customization	Reliability	Management
Transportation cost	Capacity efficiency	Inventory	Capacity	Government
Environmental cost capabilities	Automation/ innovation capabilities	R&D/Design innovation capabilities	Automation/ innovation	Competitors
Time cost	Responsiveness	Responsiveness	Responsiveness	Other

* Leveraging opportunities: how to maximize or minimize involvement or each stakeholder

In constructing a supply chain internationally, a company should weigh the following fundamental factors before exploring each decision area.[3]

- Is the GDP of the host country expanding or contracting?
- Is inflation controlled or heated (this will have an impact on prices and costs in the market)?
- Are interest rates likely to rise and fall? How will that affect financing of the investment?
- What political and regulatory issues will affect construction of the supply chain?
- What are the cost of living and the wage rates in the host country (to help determine price-cost differentials, margins, and consumer buying power)?
- What work skills exist in the market? What are the sources of supply?
- Are there local-content laws that require a certain percentage of labor and materials to be procured in the host country?
- What other requirements or restrictions will affect the supply chain?
- How will local holidays and economic changes influence operation of the local supply chain? How will that affect the global chain, if at all?

Having addressed these questions, a company can investigate the decision areas shown in figure 5.2 and make the tradeoffs necessary in trying to optimize them. Let's look closely at the first three areas, which make up the supply side of the chain.

Location – Logistics Decision Area

Since location affects both the value-added and the cost parts of a company's strategy, location decisions are all about tradeoffs. From a customer response point of view, having production facilities and distribution centers close to every sizable retail outlet would be ideal. However, brick and mortar facilities have both financial and environmental costs. Yet the farther the manufacturing and distribution facilities are from the retail market, the more expensive and time-consuming transportation becomes. Also, more facilities

---

[3] Jim Brimson, "The Role of Processes in the Supply Chain," *Think Tank* www.BetterManagement.com, 2003.

require more processes, complicating the supply chain and requiring additional management.

When such tradeoffs are considered in the broader international context, the problem becomes even more complex. Is local labor able and available? Are suppliers reliable? Do they have the quality materials needed or only inferior imitations? What are the business conditions in the host country: transportation, government policies and regulations, such as host country taxes and import duties, length of time goods are held in customs, and local content requirements?

A typical situation: Company A wants to invest in Malaysia to gain access to a cheaper source of raw materials or labor, but the government imposes a 20 percent duty on any imported component of the product Company A wants to make. The firm could use inferior components that would satisfy a 40 percent local content requirement, but this would cost Company A its high-quality competitive advantage in the regional market. Also, access to local raw materials or labor would save the company, say, 15 percent, but production would be only 90 percent as efficient so there would be additional time and money costs. Still, using imported components could cost up to 20 percent more.[4]

Companies also need to look at the configuration of suppliers, production facilities, distribution centers, and retail outlets to determine which combination works most effectively and efficiently for each target market. For example, how many and which distribution centers should service a given retail sector? The answer will depend not only on market size but also on how fragmented or concentrated the retail sector is. Similarly, a firm should consider positioning facilities in terms of lead-time, inventory control, and distance measured in terms of both transit time and cost.

Logistics on the supply side of the chain involves moving raw, semifinished, and finished goods into and through the company. It includes procuring and processing inventory in various stages of development. Problems arise when one or more processes backs up the workflow, resulting in delays. The system then is only as efficient as the weakest point. Such delays carry additional and sometimes protracted costs.

---

[4] "Logistics Costs Can Soar When Buying Abroad," www.Purchasing.com, March 3, 2003.

To minimize these bottlenecks, companies must analyze their causes, which usually stem from poor scheduling or plant utilization, inefficient flow of materials, absenteeism or poor worker performance, inadequate communications, or poor equipment usage. These are among the reasons firms are increasingly adopting automated materials flow. Automated systems now provide real-time information that allows not only supply side partners but all supply chain actors to share information. This allows the chain to be more responsive to customer needs, both pre- and post-sale.

On the supply side, specifically, holding inventories can cost between 20 and 40 percent of their value,[5] so trying to time inventories to coincide with demand is critical to minimizing costs. Starting with the Japanese-developed just-in-time and kanban inventory systems invented years ago, companies have tried constantly to better synchronize the movement of goods from supplier to production and from production to distribution on an as-needed basis.

The Partner Decision Area

Obviously, all its members make the supply chain effective and efficient, or not. That is why determining how much a company should do and control internally (vertical integration) and how much it should outsource is such a critical decision. Thirty years ago a typical firm spent about 30 percent of its revenue on outside supplies and services. Now that amount has doubled.[6]

Ideally, a supply chain would consist of strong, reliable, and capable partners who would be empowered to do their share of the work, all connected through automated, real-time communications. For this to occur, at least three stars in the collaboration constellation need to be aligned:

1. Company cultures, the way the partners operate and their values, have to mesh. In our context, this means the cultural values of the focal company must transfer well to foreign partners.

2. Partner firms must align their operational goals. If the focal company's goals and objectives are too ambitious for its part-

---

[5] Ram Ganeshan and Terry P. Harrison, "An Introduction to Supply Chain Management," Supply Chain Management, Penn State University, www.silmaril.smeal.psu.edu/misc/supply_chain_intro.html/ May 1995.

[6] Kevin R. Fitzgerald, "Best Practices in Procurement," *Ascet 4* (May 16, 2003).

ners, problems will arise. For example, what happens if at the height of seasonal sales in the focal company's country, its overseas suppliers are celebrating a weeklong holiday?

3. Partners must not only communicate quickly to meet the demands of the marketplace, they must be willing to share information as well. This is difficult to achieve among colleagues in the same firm, much less with suppliers that may provide materials to competitors of the focal company, or, worse, make specific components for them. Some partners may even be competitors serving, say, as a contract manufacturer for the focal company.

What companies look for in partners might vary but all should have some qualities in common. A supplier must be reliable, able to produce and deliver the amount of inventory needed on a just-in-time basis. It should have automated communication capabilities that are compatible with those of the focal company. It must be able to react and modify orders in real time to keep materials flow as cost-effective as possible. Finally, it must be able and willing to work on short notice with the focal company and other partners on specific projects, such as a particularly large order or redesign of an existing order. (In chapter 8 we look more closely at the qualities a company should look for in a partner.)

Alternatively, a company may decide to integrate vertically, making components that constitute a competitive advantage or contain proprietary technology. But to what extent would such integration disrupt normally efficient manufacturing? Would it be better to contract with a loyal, well-qualified supplier instead? But if the supplier is well-qualified, does it also provide components to competitors?

Generally a firm will want to manage or coordinate links with its first-tier suppliers and distributors, those in the supply chain that are closest to the production process. Likewise it may elect to monitor or audit links between first and second tier suppliers. For other relationships between nonmembers of the supply chain, box providers and the like, the company will delegate management to its suppliers[7] to manage.

---

[7] Keely L. Croxton, L., Sebastian J. Garcia-Dastugue, Douglas M. Lambert, and Dale S. Rogers, "The Supply Chain Management Processes," *International Journal of Logistics Management*, 12 (2; 2001): 13 – 36.

Production Systems

When production is discussed, typically it refers to manufacturing a product, not providing a service, though I see little if any difference between the two because both are increasingly affected by supply chain performance. In fact, many a service is nothing more than a good that is manufactured at the site of the customer. Consider for a moment a restaurant that produces a meal for a hungry diner. All aspects of the global supply chain are in effect: procuring raw materials, inventorying them, preparing semi-finished goods, taking and filling orders, delivering product, and providing after-sales service.

Or compare the automotive and the telecommunication industries. In both competition is intense, the product or service is comparable, and the competitive advantages rest in the workings of the extended enterprise. Neither a car nor phone service should be viewed as standing alone; each is but one link in its product or service chain. For example, when was the last time you went to a parking lot and had difficulty picking out your car? Cars have similar designs, colors, body styles, and even engines and accessories. Automotive companies exchange parts, like Honda providing General Motors with low-emission vehicle engines and automatic transmissions for diesel engines.[8] Then there are dealers that not only retail cars but service and even modify them.

The product itself bears a name and logo that tells the customer something about the reliability and quality of the product; it comes in different colors, one or two of which may just sell the automobile by itself. The car comes with instructions telling how to care for it. Can a consumer from the home country, much less a foreign market, understand them? There are accessories that can be added after purchase that may come from suppliers others than the car maker. How difficult is it to add something after the purchase? If the car does not live up to its sales pitch, there are warranty protections and after-sales service options.

Telecommunications providers similarly deal with more than telephone service. To access the service requires a telephone manufactured by a supplier that is not owned by the service company but is very much a part of the extended enterprise. When making a buying decision in this highly competitive industry, a customer

---

[8] Honda, "Honda Confirms Cross-Supply Engine Arrangement," December 1999. Press Release origin: Hondacorporate.com.

weighs the reliability and extent of the service; the customer service at point of purchase; the quality, variety, features, and cost of the phone; the difficulty of the instructions; and the after-sales service, warranties, and return policies. All these require not just one company but a well-functioning supply chain.

Whether it produces, products or provides services, a company's internal logistics functions are the stage for production. The more efficient the processes, materials, information flows, and worker performance, the smoother the production. But logistics and manufacturing are more than just static scenery upon which action happens; they are themselves a dynamic interaction of activities.

In seeking out the balance between reducing costs and adding value, firms are moving more and more toward production systems that are flexible, fast, efficient, and reliable. A production system consists of several processes that all must work in harmony to achieve efficiency. Modern systems also try to maximize standardization, while offering a certain amount of customization to respond quickly to customer needs. This evolving balancing process applies to both development of a new product or service and its production.

The following system and supply chain example deals with manufacturing a product because product elements are a bit more tangible than service elements, but the steps apply to both.

New Product Development

Rapid prototyping and manufacturing technologies are relatively new techniques for quickly producing solid parts from computer-assisted design data, regardless of the complexity of the shape. Traditionally, designers used foam and cardboard to make models fast. New prototypes in the product design and development process now include three-dimensional sketches, cosmetic prototypes, engineering and functional prototypes, marketing samples, and samples for safety approvals. These greatly enhance a firm's ability to bring new product to market faster.[9]

These technologies can also help bridge gaps among functions within a company and among partners within the supply chain. With Internet connection all members of the supply chain can use

---

[9] Wai Hon Weh, "RP&M in the Product Development Process," in *What Is Rapid Product Development* May 1999. "What is Rapid Product Development," The Hong Kong Polytechnic University, The Rapid Product Development Center (2000).

these prototypes and other computer-aided technologies to input into the design of products in real time to respond to demanding customers.[10] Information technology allows the group to accumulate technological knowledge that will enable them to identify an optimal set of variables affecting every work and operation involved in the complete life cycle of a given product or set of products.[11]

Product Production

On the production side, companies over the years have adopted flexible manufacturing systems geared toward better scheduling, worker utilization, and product adaptability. More recently, information technology has provided these systems with intelligent and sensor-based monitors that allow even more efficient flexibility.

For example, knowing each machine, process, tooling and machining task, the new Mitsubishi intelligent monitoring system can provide the machine-tool control system with information to optimize the machining process, ranging from execution of a simple feed stop to adaptive adjustments of a process. The system solutions cover a broad range of machining tasks, such as milling, grinding, and hard turning. This capability allows a company to create generic interfaces, systems, and algorithms portable to different processes, machine tools, and numerical controllers. Autonomous intelligent algorithms together with user knowledge enable machining systems to achieve higher accuracy and productivity with minimum malfunctions.[12]

In addition to intelligent manufacturing systems, companies are moving from strict platform manufacturing systems where a product is highly standardized to "architecture"-based systems. Shifting from what they call a "make-and-sell" approach to a "sense–and-respond" strategy, General Motors is trying to enter changing fragmented markets quickly with niche products that require less sales volume. To accomplish this, the company has designed a flexible global vehicle architecture that makes vehicles simpler to build, and allows for crossover products. The system maintains standard

---

[10] Martin C. M. Wong, "Business Driver Behind Rapid Prototyping and Manufacturing," in What Is Rapid Product Development 1999. "*What is Rapid Product Development*," The Hong Kong Polytechnic University, The Rapid Product Development Center (2000).

[11] ASD Products and Solutions, "Intelligent Manufacturing System – Virtual Production Enterprise Network" (2002). www.asdglobal.com/products/ims.html.

[12] Mitsubishi Materials Corporation, "SIMON – Sensor Fused Intelligent Monitoring System for Machining," February, 2003. www.ims.org/projects/project_info/simon.html.

attachment points while accommodating interchangeable pieces, thus letting a wide variety of products roll through the same assembly plant.

It is also interesting how GM sets up its production system. Manufacturing performance is constantly enhanced through five operating principles: people involvement, standardization, built-in quality, short lead time, and continuous improvement.[13] Workers are organized into small teams trained and empowered to use their skills and knowledge to solve problems and improve their work effort. The heart of the system is the operator and teams in the plant who build the product. They are fed through state-of-the-art materials-handling that calls for direct-to-the-line delivery of materials, eliminating the cost of maintaining inventory and improving safety by minimizing forklift activity in general assembly areas.

GM buys machinery and equipment as integrated systems, not piecemeal. This results in a leaner, more efficient plant structure and lower capital investment. Suppliers are encouraged to participate in the design and processing of a product, creating a very high level of trust between plants and suppliers. To help ensure that equipment and processes support operators, GM uses a 3-D math modeling to create a "virtual factory" that helps planners integrate the equipment, tools, fixtures, and machinery that will be used in the plant.[14]

With each new plant or renovation, the GM manufacturing system is refined through regional variations based on individual plant environment, supplier capabilities, vehicle architecture, and country culture. The firm rigorously collects worldwide competitive manufacturing practices to modify its common global manufacturing plants as needed to be more customer-responsive.

Since the Japanese taught the Americans many of these new supply chain initiatives, like just-in-time inventory, figure 5.3 shows how Honda, considered one of the most progressive extended enterprises in the world today, uses its supply chain to maximize its strategy.

---

[13] General Motors, "GM's Global Manufacturing System – A System to Build Great Cars and Trucks," *Automotive Intelligence News*, February, 2003.
[14] *Ibid.*

Figure 5.3
Honda's Supply Chain Strategy

Cut costs/Customer driven	Honda must devise ways to combine lean, essentially standard operations with the ability to respond to customer needs.
"Small born" manufacturing	Production starts small and is expanded as local demand increases. Honda has built 109 factories in 32 countries, producing at acceptable levels with room to expand.[15] This allows the firm to minimize its initial investment and grow with profit while setting up an efficient manufacturing system that uses fewer assets and parts, making products easier to build.
Digital manufacturing circle (DMC)	This is an e-business, intelligent system to increase the speed and efficiency of new model development. A computer network links Honda's R&D, manufacturing, and suppliers so that all three can work simultaneously, not sequentially as in the past, on the same 3-D drawings.[16] This system has resulted in the need for fewer prototypes, faster concept-to-production time, and less cost.
New manufacturing system (NMS)	This system reconfigures the assembly process to incorporate a highly efficient weld system to maximize flexibility. Together with DMC, it reduces the time needed to bring a new model to mass production and add an existing model at a different plant.[17] A typical

---

[15] Honda, "Glocalization," February, 2003. www.hondacorporate.com.

[16] Automotive Engineering Online, "E-Business: The New Game in Town," March, 2003, Automotive Engineering Online, www.sae.org/automat/features/ebusiness/eb3htm.

[17] Laurel Wright, "New Manufacturing System Gives Honda Flexibility," *Ward's Auto World,* September 2000.

Figure 5.3
Honda's Supply Chain Strategy (cont.)

	plant configuration is arranged in a five-zone global standard layout that lumps similar manufacturing processes into certain areas.[18] This has resulted in fewer assets tied up, more floor space, simpler operations, reduced inventories, shortened reaches–in effect, and more efficiency and adaptability at less cost. As a result of these production improvements, Honda is reducing the number of its motorcycle production lines in Japan while increasing the production capacity utilization ratio.[19]
Five-region strategy	With this flexible and rapid manufacturing system, Honda can pass decision-making responsibility for sales, manufacturing, and research down to each of its five main regional divisions: North America, Europe/ Middle East/Africa, South America, Asia/Oceania, and Japan. In each region products that best serve local needs are pushed to the forefront of the development and manufacturing process. Global platforms are adjusted to produce cars of varying sizes and engine types. Suppliers and subsidiaries throughout Honda's global network contribute to cost-effective solutions in each region.[20]
Competitive advantage	Honda believes this new integrated approach lets it start slowly and grow with demand, responding through-

[18] Katherine Zachary, "Not Done Yet," *Ward's Auto World*, November 2002.
[19] Honda World News, "Honda Launches New Motorcycle Production System in Japan," July 2000. www.hondacorporate.com.
[20] Honda Web Site, "Five-Region Strategy," March, 2003. www.hondacorporate.com.

Figure 5.3
Honda's Supply Chain Strategy (cont.)

out to customer needs. By being lean, fast, and responsive, Honda can concentrate on growth segments within each product line, e.g., motorcycles in Asia and light trucks in North America. Using a philosophy of manufacturing products where they are sold, Honda will combine its global manufacturing system with increasing local content of regionally produced product.[21]

While I have picked on the automotive industry in my examples, the supply side of the supply chain consists of similar stages for both services and products. Regardless of the line of business, companies expanding abroad are marrying globalization efficiencies and local customer needs through more creative supply chain elements and configurations.

The next chapter deals with the demand side of the chain.

[21] Wright, *op. cit.*, note 17.

CHAPTER 6

THE SUPPLY CHAIN: DEMAND SIDE

George Sterling had waited on the line for 10 minutes after wading through a series of taped messages (push 1 for this, push 2 for that). When a human voice finally picked up on the other end, he was irate enough to ignore the message that said his conversation would be recorded for training purposes.

"I bought this play set for my children and I can't figure out the directions," he roared. "You need to be a rocket scientist to figure them out."

"Sir, I can transfer you to a technical assistant, if you'd like."

"Well, what are you?"

"I farm out concerns like yours," the voice said politely.

I waited all this time for a farmer, George thought. "Fine," he harrumphed. "Transfer me."

"Very well, sir." After waiting another three minutes, filled with louder than necessary elevator music, another human voice said, "Sir, how can I help you?"

George repeated his problem. "If I could just get a little information from you first," the voice said. "Please verify your order number."

"Are you kidding me?" George shouted. "I just want to understand how to put this product together. Why does that require my order number?"

"Sir, we just need to follow certain procedures," the voice assured him. "It won't take a moment."

"It's already taken twenty minutes of my time," George bellowed. "Tell you what. Just tell me how to return this thing, because I can go to a half dozen other stores just as easily and get a better play set."

Customers worldwide can be categorized in two ways: those who are educated, sophisticated, and well informed about product selections and have the discretionary income to afford what they want, and those who ultimately will be like them. Both are subject to the great raging dichotomy of the day, "customization". On the one hand global companies are striving to standardize products and services to become cost-efficient. On the other, though, exposure to so many possible products lets customers choose as never before.

Customers are fickle, have short attention spans, and demand instant gratification, right? Most of us would not have waited the twenty minutes George did before demanding information on how to return the product.

In this chapter we consider the demand side of the supply chain and see how the customer increasingly controls it.

Many Ps and Leveraging Stakeholders

In today's global marketplace with demand-pull conditions in play, firms are learning that they do not create either the products or the marketing mix that they use to promote them. Customers do. Product and feature variety, together with fierce price competition, empowers the buyer to demand what he wants, when he wants it, and how he wants to get it. The object is not to sell goods but for the customer to want to buy them. Companies can no longer scream at clients; they must lure them.

A firm and a customer interact on the demand side of the supply chain in two real ways: marketing, which deals with reaching the customer psychologically, and distribution, which reaches him physically. Typically marketing is described in a barrage of Ps, from a company's promise to the packaging of its product. For now let limit the list to the classic four—product, price, promotion, and place—but add, since they are so important internationally, positioning of product and partner. Positioning is how a firm wants a customer to remember the product: high quality, easy to use, low-cost, convenient. While I don't ascribe it a separate "P", I stress it here because positioning a product in a different culture can be difficult and needs to be done carefully. *Partner*, though, deserves a separate "P" status because it relates to the network of local contacts a company relies on to help it penetrate the foreign market.

To appreciate the partner concept, a firm has to look beyond suppliers and customers to its entire web of stakeholders and determine how much leverage it can exert on each subset. Typical subsets would be creditors, suppliers, unions, management, special interest groups, the board of directors, retailers, distributors, suppliers, strategic partners, market personalities and sports figures, and, far from least, government.

A firm should study these groups for potential opportunities and threats. Yes, threats. As the list should make clear, all stakeholders do not necessarily want the company to succeed. GT Savage and others have classified stakeholders into four types:

1. Supportive – those that want the company to succeed
2. Nonsupportive – those that do not
3. Marginal – those that pose little threat or are sources of opportunity
4. Mixed blessing – those that pose either a high threat or a source of opportunity for success.[1]

Each firm must figure how best to neutralize or energize its stakeholders. How can a firm use its competitive advantages to leverage those stakeholders that can contribute positively to the business? What steps should the company take to minimize the negative potential of other stakeholders, or better yet convert them into positive contributors, as by getting a competitor to collaborate on a new product to benefit both firms? Leveraging examples are given below.

The International Customer Channel

To see how the 5Ps tie together, study figure 6.1. Like the gap analysis chart in figure 2.2, the "customer channel" presents an overview of the "5Ps" process. It lists many of the potential obstacles or factors a company may have to deal with as it works through the various "Ps". As a company considers these factors, it should look for possible competitive advantages that it may try to exploit.

[1] Mario I. Katsioloudes, *Global Strategic Planning*, Butterworth Heinemann, Oxford, UK, 2002, pp. 23 - 25.

Figure 6.1
The International Customer Channel

"5 Ps"	Obstacles	Gaps

Product	- Product fits market
	- Market conditions
	- Market size
	- Market segmentation
	- Market restrictions
	- Market elasticity
	    - buyer behavior
	    - buyer preferences
	    - buyer income level
	    - buyer needs
	- Product availability
	- Unique product features
	    - _____
	    - _____	

Price	- Price elasticity - Low-priced/standardized product - High-priced/customized - Competitor pricing - Product quality comparison - Discounts - Loss Leaders	

Promotion	- Message
	- Media availability
	    - TV, radio, newspapers,
	      billboards, etc.
	- Government restrictions
	  on advertising
	- Point of purchase
	- Brand recognition
	- Brand image
	- Product positioning
	  possibilities	

Place	- Market infrastruction
	- Government restrictions
	- Sources of supply
	    - Distribution channel and
	      configuration
	    - Retail configuration
	    - Level of corruption
	    - Feedback and after-
	      sales service	

Partner	- Availability of partners - Local leverage opportunities	

The Extended Product[2]

We begin with the product or service. As mentioned in the last chapter, I see very little difference between the two, especially if we look at both of them as a chain of elements. Internationally, though, cultural and language differences compound problems that may arise in the entire product or service chain. For example:

- Does the customer know the company that made the product or service and, if so, is its reputation positive or negative?
- Could the company logo or packaging in anyway offend the customer (wrong color, etc.)?
- Can the customer understand the labeling or instructions?
- Does the product work the same in another country (electricity wise, etc.)?
- What happens if the customer does not like the product or if it malfunctions?
- Are after-sales service, warranties, and return policies reliable and consistent?

The list goes on. What does it reveal? Clearly that a firm planning for overseas markets must weigh its total or extended product or service as is shown in figure 6.2.

Figure 6.2
Extended Product

Brand image   Financing Features/Options   Retail Service Accessories ⟶ Main product ⟵ Instructions Quality   Packaging Color   After-sales User-friendly/   service   comfortable   Returns

Demand Approach to Pricing
International pricing depends on several factors. As seen in chapter 2, a company venturing overseas normally will start with the cost of the product when it leaves the factory and add its domestic and international costs (the *cost-plus method*). Companies more experi-

---

[2] James B. Ayers, "A Primer on Supply Chain Management," *Information Strategy: The Executive's Journal*, Auerbach Publications, CRC Press (New York), Winter 2000.

enced overseas may use a flexible cost-plus approach, charging higher prices and gaining greater margins in certain markets while limiting their profits in others to be more competitive. Still others break into markets using the loss leader strategy, where they reduce and even subsidize prices to undercut the competition. Companies also run promotions, offer discounts on quantity sales, sell directly to retailers, or negotiate lower wholesale margins. Finally, if the market offers significant potential, a company will move from exporting to investing in the market to reduce the added costs.

Unfortunately, none of these approaches is customer-based, nor do they fairly assess the value of the company's competitive advantage. More sophisticated companies try to optimize their pricing, including their normal and markdown pricing. They do this by collecting intelligence on the consumer in order to anticipate demand and then balance those expectations with inventories downstream in the supply chain. They may price the same goods differently depending on market segment, buyer preferences, and distribution channel. For example, a sweater may be priced one way in an upscale store and another on the Internet. Just as the customer has different purchasing and venue choices, so too producers maximize their pricing by adjusting it for different market segments.

Given the vast diversity of foreign markets, this certainly holds true abroad, so exporting or newly invested companies should consider factors beyond cost-plus. If the price differential between local and foreign-made goods is minimal, that suggests that there is already foreign competition resident in the country. In this case a company needs to determine if it has a strong enough competitive advantage to attract buyers at a higher price, using competitor prices as a benchmark against which to assess the value of that advantage. If there is none, the company should either abandon the market or prepare to set a different price structure. It also needs to weigh its competitive advantages in terms of market elasticity: market conditions, demand factors, discretionary income levels, size of market segments, and the marketing costs of reaching those segments successfully.

Figure 6.3 presents a customer-driven pricing method. Chapter 10 also provides a way for companies to evaluate the compatibility of its product or service with both the market and local supply chain so that a firm can set pricing optimally.

Figure 6.3
Customer–Driven International Pricing Structure

Exporter	Investing Company
- Cost of changes amortized	- Cost of changes amortized
- Domestic cost	- Local costs
- Added domestic shipping and international costs	
- Distribution/retail costs	- Distribution/retail costs
- Input from agents/distributors	- Input from sales force/distributors

- Competitor prices as benchmark
- Market elasticity
- Cost of marketing
- Value of supply chain's competitive advantage

- Price differential justified	- Price Differential not justified
- Enter market	- Subsidize/Offer sales incentives
	- Seek alternative chain partners
	- Restructure pricing
	- Abandon market

Promotion

Promotion is the way a company projects its image, products, and services; it is ultimately captured through branding. Promotion starts with (a) an *idea* that is sent in a *message* to (b) an *audience* that receives the message and provides (c) *feedback* that goes to *improving* the product or service.

When a company takes its message international, complications may arise. Will the message translate well in a different language in a different culture? Does the company enjoy the same reputation abroad as it does domestically? Are the buying habits of the new target segments the same as of those in the home market? To answer these questions, companies should consult with a local marketing firm and observe competitor practices in the new market, both local and international, and see what works well. Beyond all this, a company new to a market but with a definite competitive advantage will want to:

- Establish its credibility.
- Leverage its uniqueness.
- Establish the brand.
- Promote and position the product.
- Interact with customers to confirm a promotional message and respond to customer feedback.

Establish Credibility

Although it may enjoy an excellent presence at home, a firm may be relatively unknown in the target market. To create the image it wants, it must assess its products and services relative to existing competition and at first discount the value-added it believes it has. Many a company makes the horrid mistake of thinking its product is so superior that it will succeed in a new market. Such companies should appreciate that their views are not necessarily shared by foreign customers. Overestimating local reaction has been the downfall of several well-intentioned firms. Firms that normally do well with new product launches get local help and do their homework before leaping into the market. Exporting before investing, of course, makes it easier to estimate demand.

Further, a firm has to gauge the reputation of its home country in the new market. I was riding in a car with an Egyptian acquaintance and his family in their native land. When we passed a familiar restaurant with golden arches, his youngest daughter barked, "McDonald's, McDonald's". In Arabic, her older sister chastised her. When I asked her father what the girl had said, he told me sheepishly, "That is an American restaurant and it is bad to go there." McDonald's has a worldwide reputation and is successful most places, but the company's image also reflects that of its home country, the United States, which is not so popular in many places.

Leverage Uniqueness

A new market entrant with a unique product or service enjoys a charmed existence for only a limited time, because if there is money to be made, competition will follow, even if it offers lower quality at special prices. From the outset a company should think of the launching of a new product as an iterative process: even before introducing it, the firm knows that a better one will follow when competition creeps in.

Especially if it lacks reputation or brand recognition, the firm must capitalize quickly on the uniqueness of its product, using it in lieu of reputation. The more unique it is, the more leverage a company has. With the help of the host country trade infrastructure or a network of contacts, the firm should seek endorsements from local sports heroes, movie stars, and public figures. Early endorsement helps build reputation and maintain the company and its product a notch above the rest when competition enters. An endorsement establishes the product as first among equals.

To the extent possible, early revenue gains should go to improving the product so that when competition does arrive, the firm is poised to launch a superior version, with more features or correction of initial problems. Staying a step ahead of the competition leads to a positive reputation and branding.

In addition to leveraging uniqueness, companies may use their domestic customers to carry their products and services overseas. Say Company A is somewhat cash-strapped but produces a unique IBM-compatible software product for data mining. Company B, a large multinational that enjoys a solid reputation and is located in several countries, buys the product and installs it in its IBM computers in headquarters. Pleased at how the software performs, Company B makes the product standard in all its subsidiary operations across the globe.

Two things have happened:

1. Company A has piggybacked onto Company B and Company B has moved the software product abroad. Rather than paying to expand internationally, Company A can build its reputation in other markets through Company B.

2. Customers and contacts in these markets become exposed to the new software and associate it with both IBM and Company B, companies with strong reputations.

By leveraging this way, Company A begins to gain international exposure, laying the groundwork for more costly market penetration later when the firm is hopefully in a better financial condition or has a sufficiently strong reputation.

Another form of leveraging is to combine forces with a competitor. Company Y wants to introduce its unique software abroad but lacks presence and reputation. Company Z, a competitor, is established in several key foreign markets. The two firms set up a joint venture where Company Y provides the new software and Company Z the market presence and reputation. Again, two things happen:

1. Company Y gains immediate market penetration and expo-sure.

2. It preempts a competitor. Through the joint venture, Company Z gains access to the new software without having to develop another version to compete against it.

Spinning this example slightly differently, Company Y can iden-tify a software company that is highly successful in a large regional market. If the local software firm has a reasonably sound reputation but an inferior product, Company Y can either acquire the firm for a good price or joint venture with it to help raise it to the next level.

In yet another example, the company can leverage by licensing the technology to a strong, reputable partner in another market. As we discussed in chapter 2, the downside of this is that the company has to share its technology. The upside is that a major local firm exposes the product to the local or regional market. The licensor not only saves on the expense of market penetration but it gains a license fee, typically paid at least in part upfront, and royalty income. The cost is minimal, except for the technology transfer. The revenue stream can also help the licensor develop new tech-nology—the iterative product.

Establish the Brand

Brand recognition is built in several ways. Companies with central-ized structures and global product divisions are more apt to have global brands.[3] These companies tend to be larger, well situated worldwide, with strong reputations in a number of regional markets.

Branding also allows a firm to standardize its products more. Some larger established firms use umbrella brands that oversee a family of smaller or local brands. Conversely, where localization is

---

[3] Susan Douglas, C. Samuel Craig, and Edwin J. Nijssen, "Executive Insights, Integrating Branding Strategy Across Markets: Building International Brand Architecture," *Journal of International Marketing*, 9 (2): 97-114.

needed for success, local rather than corporate brands are often used.

A market leader will tend to move successful domestic products overseas under the same brand names. The image has already been globally accepted and new products are relatively easy to fit into the product mix. On the other hand, if a company acquires a competitor overseas that has strong local acceptance, it may continue to promote the local brands and ultimately use them to introduce products of the parent. Or a parent company may lead with recognizable local brands and replace them over time with its superior products. Further, with the growth of global retailers, such as Walmart, companies can also gain brand exposure by having their products sold in these stores.

When it has a diverse product range, a company will see if a common brand can be applied to all or if different brands need to be used. If a company, like General Electric, makes products from television sets to aerospace equipment, it may retain the GE brand because it conveys hi-tech quality throughout. But if it adds financial services, which is now a large portion of GE's business portfolio, should it apply the GE name, which conveys strong engineering capabilities? General Electric has elected to use the same brand despite significant differences in the types of products and expertise it is marketing. But if the Mars Corporation, which has a solid reputation in the candy industry, were to buy a pet food company, would it sell the new product using the Mars brand? Perhaps not. Pet food and candy obviously do not convey the same taste preferences.

Some companies rely on an assortment of brand names to stress their variability and downplay their huge size and market dominance. Others use one brand name and image because they use mass production to keep costs as low as possible and rely on low prices and standardized packaging to succeed. Still others produce products geared to the very top end of the market and rely on quality, status and exclusivity to drive brand recognition.

In every case, the company is using its own added value to leverage and partner its way into a new market. When it has been relatively unknown, the firm has sought to partner with a medium that has a presence in the target market; when it is relatively well known and respected, it has led with its own brand or corporate image, modifying it only to project better to the local community.

Keep in mind, though, that as successful companies move farther from home, they should become more sensitive to customer
needs and market conditions and less concerned with moving large
quantities of goods. This is why international brand recognition and
promotion cannot be rushed, although many companies try to do
so. The process requires moving the passion of the firm to the customer. That takes time.

Promote and Position Its Product

To convey a message, a company needs to appeal to one or more of
the five senses in order to reach the customer's comfort level and
memory. The advertisement for a car race may be loud and full of
vivid color. The message for a sunburn cream may feature water,
something smooth, cool, and refreshing in blue or green. In short,
the message should suit the experience that leads to the purchase
of the item.

Yet while the message can capture the moment in one culture,
it may offend the potential customer in another. She may dislike the
colors presented, or the voice of the promoter may be grating, or
the message itself insults the customer's intelligence or leaves a bad
taste in her mouth. The customer's comfort level has been violated.
Worse, she does remember the product and perhaps even the company promoting it, but negatively. To send the right message, a company must learn the cultural sensitivities, buying behavior, and tolerance level of the target market. Only then can it construct a promotional message in terms of the customer, not the company, and
determine how it wants the customer to perceive or remember the
firm and its products.

Take the case of Nike and Tiger Woods. Historically Nike,
though well-known as a sports firm, has not been known as a golf
company the same way as, say, Titleist. To catch up to the competition, Nike used its brand reputation and deep pockets to sign the
best golfer in the world. The company leveraged its name to gain a
partnership that vaulted Nike over an otherwise cumbersome entry
process into a very competitive industry segment. The customer
wants to play golf better and admires people who play the game
well. Since Tiger Woods is recognized worldwide as the best player
in the game, what better vehicle could Nike have to bear its image?
Because Tiger uses Nike equipment and clothes, others want to use
them as well in the hope of playing better, or at least looking better

in the act of competing.

To capitalize on such exposure, Nike keeps its logo simple, attractive, recognizable, eye-catching, and memorable. When a golfer sees Tiger Woods hit one of his awesome, seemingly impossible shots, the potential customer not only remembers the swing but the brand on Tiger's shirt and hat, and says, "I want those." Nike's logic is that if Tiger Woods is the best, then Nike equipment and apparel conjure the best too and lure the customer to buy. The firm has positioned its product as top-of-the line among superlative products (see figure 6.4).

Figure 6.4
Positioning A Golf Product

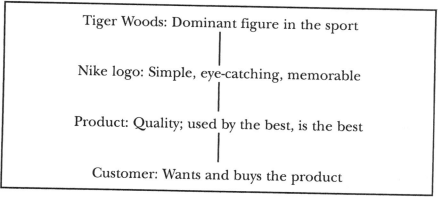

Tiger Woods: Dominant figure in the sport

Nike logo: Simple, eye-catching, memorable

Product: Quality; used by the best, is the best

Customer: Wants and buys the product

While every company cannot work with a Tiger Woods, the model illustrates the point, but while leverage is useful, do not overlook its underpinnings.

Leveraging, branding, and product positioning are reflections of the supply chain. The image a firm projects is only as good ultimately as the supply chain that produces and delivers its product or service; a company cannot promote one image and deliver another. A company that tries to capitalize on its uniqueness without ensuring the same quality in the execution of its business will lack staying power in the market. Firms, especially foreign ones, must create credibility in both product and process performance. In particular, they must always ensure against overcommitting.

Interact with Customers

We all know that business tends to become more difficult the farther a company ventures from home. To keep things simple, the company must focus on what it does best and transfer those capabilities to new markets as plainly and reproducibly as possible. In most cases the firm should similarly stay focused in its promotion and marketing, building from the bottom up, targeting a vulnerable niche that can be exploited to gain a mainstream foothold in the market.

The less leverage the firm has, as will be the case the farther it is from home, the smaller its initial target should be. A company far from home should concentrate on point-of-purchase marketing strategies that keep the firm close to potential customers. Mass marketing by unknown companies, especially in less wealthy markets, does not bring customers into retail outlets, much less get them to buy. To play on the customer's terms, a firm must appeal to them when they are in the mood to buy or seeking a similar product. The message can be heard better when the customer is listening rather than distracted by the competitive noise of related, or unrelated, things.

Point-of-purchase attractions, such as specials and discounts, samples, and other lures, can have an effect similar to that the image of Tiger Woods has on the golfer. By shortening and narrowing the promotion channel, a company saves money and puts the effort at the most critical point, where the customer is deciding to buy. This is where many of the marketing stars must be aligned to promote the firm's competitive advantage: signage, packaging, customer service, and superior message.

Similarly, an investing company should view customers on two levels: the retail outlet and end users. When the Swiss holding company, Ausag, first introduced the Swatch watch into the United States, it required that stores give it more space than they did for competitors, sell a limited number of watches, and accept a lower retail markup. What store would accept such an unappealing offer?

Almost all of them did—because Ausag promised to put not only a series of new watch designs into their stores every six weeks, but changing lines of apparel as well. New material draws new customers; by limiting the number of watches available for sale, demand stayed high. With the money that was saved on lower retail margins, Ausag threw very selective parties with key celebrities to entertain their loyal storeowners. This cost-effective approach intensified the marketing effort at point of purchase and proved widely successful for a company that had poor market feedback when it first introduced its new watch.[4]

Finally, with products changing and features increasing, companies need an effective way to capture customer feedback and use it to improve the product. Direct company or company-partner interaction is the most effective way to do this. It shows the personal touch, offers swift communication with suppliers and R&D, and provides speedy damage control when customers are unhappy. As customization intensifies globally, producers must be fast to respond without amassing large inventories. Sales persons, store clerks, and other point-of-purchase representatives have the opportunity to know the customer best; they can quickly transfer his likes, dislikes, and reactions to a product back down the supply chain. This downstream information flow is becoming increasingly critical to the entire family of firms in the chain.

Place

Place does not refer only to a specific location, such as point of purchase. It is the continuum within the supply chain from manufacturing to customer. This includes the distribution channel, that group of players that ensure the product gets to market, and the retail configuration or series of outlets that tie together the psychological and physical parts of the chain in the buying experience of the customer. While price might be the driver of the marketing mix, the distribution and retail tandem is its backbone. Just as a body has to adapt with a particular backbone or skeleton, the marketing mix must conform to place.

Within the channel, five activities normally take place, each with its own issues. These are presented in figure 6.5.

---

[4] This discussion is based on two cases from the Dardon Case Bibliography, Graduate School of Business Administration, University of Virginia.

Figure 6.5
Activities In The
Distribution Channel

1. Movement of goods from manufacturer to customer:

How many distributors are in the channel?
How many retailers are there and are they scattered or
   concentrated?
How many distribution centers are there?
Which ones serve which retail outlets?
Can incentives be given or alliances be made to compress
   the channel?
Are channel members compatible with the manufacturer?
Will the country infrastructure or geography inhibit the
   distribution channel?
Are there cross-border expenses, e.g., duties, transfer costs?

2. Price and ownership transfer:

What are the markup costs (number of distributors and
   retailers and their markup percentages)?
Is there corruption in the channel?
How is ownership transferred in the market (e.g., what
   government regulations are there)?

3. Transportation and storage:

What is the condition of roads, ports, and other
   transportation facilities?
What are product storage requirements?
Is there a need for climate control, refrigeration, or other
   product protection?
What is the inventory capacity?
Do the product and market conditions allow for intensive
   or selective distribution?
What obstacles may delay delivery?

Figure 6.5
Activities In The
Distribution Channel (cont.)

---

4. Customer interface, buying process, and delivery

What does the buyer expect at point of purchase?
Can the retail establishments meet the manufacturer's
expectations (educate/advise customer, provide friendly
service, etc.)?
Are there incentives the manufacturer can provide retailers?
Do retailers provide the right buying experience or aura:
ease, convenience, ambiance, variety, etc.?

---

5. After-sales service, warranties, and returns:

Who will provide after-sales service: manufacturer, supplier,
retailer?
Who is able to provide this service?
How will returns and warranties work?
How long will they take?
What communication links and capabilities must
intermediaries have to provide a quick response?

Internationally, these issues relate to host government policies, country conditions, the breadth and depth of the wholesale channel, and the retail configuration.

Host Government Policies

Companies should look at host government obstacles and incentives as they affect the entire demand side of the supply chain. Are there restrictions on advertising, such as local labor only or censorship? Are certain or all distribution channels closed to foreigners? Does the target market discriminate against foreign companies that are resident there? In terms of distribution, such discrimination usually takes the form of value-added taxes along the distribution channel that domestic firms may not have to pay. Countries may also impose standards, product specifications, or licenses that affect a company's ability to get the product to market.

Country Conditions

Next, a company must assess the country's infrastructure limitations. Can the product reach the market in a timely fashion? Can it be used in the country? The company has to evaluate electricity capacity, road and trucking systems, warehouse conditions, and ports and other cogs in the local distribution infrastructure.

Distribution Channel and Retail Configuration

The channels differ for an exporter and a subsidiary. The exporter normally ships goods overseas to its agent or distributor, who moves the product through customs and then the distribution channel to retail outlets or the ultimate customer. The subsidiary, assuming that it manufactures goods, works directly with customers or retailers or moves the product through the channel to the local marketplace.

The length of the channel refers to the number of agents or distributors that it takes to get the product from the manufacturer to market; the breadth is the configuration of wholesalers needed to reach that market. The fewer the number of parties, the shorter and thinner the channel. As the channel lengthens, costs mount and the possibility of things going wrong, such as theft, damage, or corruption, rises.

To some extent host government policies and market conditions dictate the type of channel a company must use. The type of channel will also depend on the retail configuration, whether stores are concentrated in well-defined urban areas or scattered across several cities and towns. If outlets are spread throughout the country in sprawling areas or hard-to-reach places, the manufacturer may have to work with several wholesalers to cover the territory. If the retail configuration is more concentrated, fewer wholesalers are likely to be required, or possibly, though not very likely, the manufacturer can sell directly to retail stores or even clients.

Some countries have closed distribution channels. The network of suppliers and distributors in the country is extremely difficult for foreign companies to penetrate. Still other countries may feature industry-based wholesalers who are the only ones that can distribute products in a particular industry. Certain countries also require that only specially licensed distributors that are 100 percent owned by host country interests can be employed. Several countries, as discussed in chapter 2, consider wholesalers under contract to be employees of the focal company with rights to severance pay and other benefits.

Not only should a company weigh these conditions when it adopts a distribution approach for the target market but the entire marketing mix may revolve around its channel choice. If a company produces a range of products from the high to the low end of the market, how the various products actually get to market may differ. For an expensive item targeted to an exclusive clientele, there may be only three stores in the country to be reached. Mass-produced, cheaper items might go to a number of perhaps totally separate retailers, requiring a different web of wholesalers altogether.

What is happening globally on the retail end of the distribution channel is interesting. Strategically, stores are pushing beyond pure sales to create a buying experience or aura for the customer, providing ambiance or dizzying the buyer with their overwhelming variety. Companies like Walmart are establishing super stores where customers can one-stop-shop for all their needs. These retailers may integrate vertically downstream or, because of the exposure they provide a producer, they may insist on a large portion of the profit under long-term contracts. Less scrupulous retailers even revert to tactics like bait and switch.

Consider two manufacturers working with the same retailer. Manufacturer A spends money to educate customers before they come to the store. Manufacturer B does not. Since A is spending money to attract customers, it may pay the store less margin per item sold than B, but when customers come to the store to buy, the retailer encourages them to buy B's product because the store receives more profit from that sale.[4]

In chapter 10, the five steps and the international conditions already described are presented in a way that will help a company evaluate how the conditions of the host country will affect its ability to distribute and sell there.

The Impact of the Internet

The Internet has given companies the ability to reach the customer in a totally different way while simultaneously cutting costs.

---

[4] Susan Douglas, C. Samuel Craig, and Edwin J. Nijssen, "Executive Insights, Integrating Branding Strategy Across Markets: Building International Brand Architecture," *Journal of International Marketing,* 9 (2): 97-114.

Improved communications and systems monitoring make it easier for manufacturers to sell directly to channel members and eliminate traditional intermediaries, such as distributors and other resellers. In fact, industry experts estimate that by 2005 the Web will influence 35 percent of all retail sales. [5]

These developments, coupled with profit pressures and shrinking gross margins, have led to consolidation of the distribution process, so that a manufacturer, retailer or even distributor controls more of the channel. This move toward vertical integration runs contrary to the rise in outsourcing and partnering as companies and supply chains hunt for innovative strategies. [6]

Whichever approach is used, improved Internet-based information flow is increasingly driving supply chains, making distribution channels more efficient. With real-time sharing of information, manufacturers and distributors can better understand what the other needs and is doing. Partners are slowly realizing that efficient chains need closer, more trusting relationships than was the case in the past.

Smaller firms can use the Internet to establish themselves as virtual offices, eliminating the confinement of space. In this way companies without much critical mass can represent themselves as being global and provide products through virtual warehouses. Because of the increased speed of communications and transportation, time from ordering to receipt can be greatly reduced, allowing smaller companies to compete in the global marketplace. That said, physical product sold over the Internet remains anything but virtual. A supply chain still provides the backbone to the sales mechanism.

As the world becomes a more sophisticated market, the power of the Internet will have a bearing on distribution channels across the globe. To reduce costs and respond to a more educated buyer, manufacturers will increasingly tinker with and reinvent their supply chains.

We will wait to do the gap analysis to help identify competitive advantages for not only the customer channel but the entire supply chain until we have explored ways to strategize and organize the chain.

---

[5] "Making the Most of Your Distribution Channels," MarketingProfs.com (February 2003), pp. 1–3.

[6] David Joseph, "Synchronizing Supply & Demand," sas.com Magazine, bettermanagement.com (2003).

CHAPTER 7

STRATEGIZING THE GLOBAL SUPPLY CHAIN

In 1492 a man named Christopher Columbus set sail to prove that the world was round. An avid sailor and reader, he decided to combine his two passions. While he did his research as thoroughly as he could at the time, what he read was not exactly accurate. Marco Polo calculated that Japan was some 1,500 miles east of China. Greek astronomers figured that Asia was significantly bigger than it really was and that the circumference of the world was much smaller. Given this faulty information, Columbus was convinced that Japan was only 5,000 miles west of Portugal. He was determined to sail west to Japan and prove the world round at the same time.

At first no one took him seriously. When he approached King John II of Spain in 1484, the King thought the sailor was daft. "Japan is at least 10,000 miles from here," the King declared for no particular reason. "There isn't a ship around that could successfully go that far."

Despite rejection Christopher persisted. Another monarch, Queen Isabella, and her husband, King Ferdinand II of Portugal, agreed to consider the idea, though six years later, they turned him down as all the others had before them. Yet a good friend of Columbus, Luis de Santangel, persuaded the king and queen to reconsider.

"You come to us with this crazy idea," Queen Isabella said.

"But, Your Highness, I have researched the situation well and, believe me, Japan is only 5,000 miles to the west," countered Columbus. "If you could just provide me with the funds, you will find that it will be well worth your investment. Japan offers this country substantial trade opportunities, especially in the area of spices, and I can prove once and for all that the world is indeed round."

The king frowned. "But what is your strategy? How do you know your research is accurate?"

"My strategy?" Columbus looked befuddled.

"Yes," the king insisted. "And do you have the resources to get the job done?"

"Oh, yes, sir," Columbus answered. "I can get the best of crews and ves-
sels today that can easily make the 5,000-mile journey."

Despite grave reservations, the king and queen financed the trek.
Columbus set sail on August 3, 1492. After a month and a half on the high
seas, the crews of the three ships began to question their captain. To convince
them of their progress, Columbus kept two logs, the real one and a bogus one
that told the crew they were closer to Japan than, of course, they actually were.
But in late September, the winds unexpectedly died and left the crews miser-
able. Disease began to set in and Columbus's plan began to disintegrate. By
the middle of October, the crews of all three ships had lost confidence in their
leader. On the verge of mutiny, they suddenly spotted land in the distance. It
was far indeed from Japan.

Inaccurate research, insufficient resources, surprises along the way, and
a strategy full of bogus feedback—how could such a plan possibly succeed?
Ironically, because they never reached Japan, Columbus did not achieve his
goal of proving that the world was round. But finding a new world was a
pleasant consequence of his vision, mission, and strategy.

Was his strategy successful?

Good question. Sometimes strategies that try to accomplish one
thing actually achieve another by accident. Yet why leave lofty expectations to chance?

Before discussing the supply chain, we looked at what companies need to do to trade with different countries. While technically
they may be entering foreign markets, they normally start out with
minimal exposure and risk. Essentially, exporting firms either use
the Internet as a virtual office or find partners abroad that do much
of the work for them: represent them, sell for them, even produce
and distribute for them. In every instance, these companies have for
all intents and purposes stayed domestic despite apparent expansion through international sales.

In a fast-paced and ever-changing global environment, many
companies, believing that further expansion is unnecessary, are
content to operate from home. As long as it works, this strategy is
fine. But many other firms find greater long-term success in building a working presence in overseas markets. To do this, as we have
seen in the past two chapters, they must make an investment abroad
and create a new supply chain, or at least enhance an existing one.
The complexity of their expansion demands an altogether different
type of strategy and execution, after the company thinks through its

organizational options and the financial implications of expanding across boundaries.

Motivation for Investing Overseas

Why would a company that is not already a global player want to move from exporter to investor? Many things can motivate a firm, but whatever the motivation it must rest on a solid foundation if it is to be converted into long-term success.

Key reasons for expansion are (a) leading the competition into new markets with new technology, products, or services; (b) matching the competition; (c) increasing market share through local production or a more permanent market presence; (d) deregulation, government incentives, or greater ease of operating in a target market; (e) access to cheaper factors of production; and (f) improving the global supply chain.

The Realm of Strategy

A good strategy should be designed to self-destruct. Since strategy is about change, those who shape a savvy strategy know that it will not last forever, it will simply move the company to another level. Then why go to all the trouble of strategizing? Many companies have a hard enough time keeping up with the proverbial in-box and fighting daily fires to spend time researching, analyzing, formulating, implementing, and monitoring a longer-range plan. Yet when all is said and done, firms need to strategize to maximize and sustain their competitive advantages. This is what separates above-average from below-average companies.

Michael Porter believes there are three generic strategies:[1]

1. *Cost Leadership:* This approach calls for broad distribution, low costs, maximum efficiencies in the supply chain, and good relations with host governments to minimize costs and barriers.

2. *Differentiation:* Here a company customizes the product or service to fit targeted market segments. A firm interested in this strategy should be an above-average performer in its industry and the price premium should exceed the extra costs to make the products unique.

---

[1] Michael Porter, *Competitive Strategy* (New York: Free Press, 1980), p. 36.

3. *Niche:* A firm concentrates on a few markets or market segments or on markets where the investing company and its products and services will be protected by host government restrictions, such as tariffs or local content requirements.

There are many ways of pursuing these strategies, among them reengineering, downsizing, merging with or acquiring other companies, joint venturing, product niching or horizontal or vertical product expansion, horizontal or vertical customer basing, and wholesale paradigm shifts. Although there are many approaches we will explore later, they all have at least one of the three generic options at their core. To stay focused, a company should keep that in mind from the outset.

No international strategy is easy to carry out. To evaluate options, firms have used opinions from experts, best and worst case scenarios, computer simulations, financial ratios, forecasting, and benchmarking techniques. They are all worthwhile, and they help to define a company's competitive advantages, in terms of both value and performance.

Historically, as might be expected, firms measured performance and value in financial terms only: growth, profitability, return on investment, earnings, and so forth. But as we mentioned in the last chapter, there has been a shift toward creating value for the customer as a means of achieving long-term economic value for the company. Indeed, many hold a hybrid view that tries to identify economic value that results in better employee performance, value to the customer, and wealth for shareholders.

The fact is that these models are not mutually exclusive but synergistic. A company needs to look for value, competitive edge, and strategic options not just throughout its entire supply chain and web of stakeholders but in the constant interaction of both.

The Strategy Process

How does a company determine its competitive advantages, much less craft and sustain a strategy to maximize them?

Not only strategies themselves but also the process of developing, implementing, and monitoring them has evolved greatly in today's ever-changing global environment. No longer is strategy developed in top management's ivory tower and imposed from above. The need for a company to be adaptive and flexible with its global supply chain prohibits such a rigid approach. Experts today espouse, quite properly, that formulation of strategy should involve all parts of the organization from the start, so that employees as well as managers take ownership in what needs to be changed, sensitivities and idiosyncrasies of staff from different countries are considered, and the strategy process stays dynamic, with constant feedback for improvement from the full range of stakeholders.

Strategy, then, is a process, dynamic and inclusive. To present it more clearly, I have broken down the process into the following six stages a company has to pass through or accommodate in order to implement strategy:

- Analyzing and testing the business: market and competitive positioning (industry and main competitors)
- Evaluating company capabilities against those of competitors to determine competitive advantages using the 4 Cs
- Establishing a strong base for strategizing
- Leading through action
- Formulating the strategy
- The strategy cycle

Leading through action deals with the first of the 4Cs: commitment. As the name suggests, it concerns the leadership that is necessary to create and execute strategy well. This is a dicey subject because in a company's self-examination, the top bosses do not necessarily like being put under the microscope. Still, this stage is critical: honesty must pervade the process and it has to start at the top. *The strategy cycle* shows the elements of strategy that need to be in place and "geared," if you will, to run smoothly. The other stages pertain to the background work that needs to be done to create an effective strategy.

Chapter 10 shows a framework for working through the stages. It allows a company to analyze all aspects of the firm and its business using an expanded 4C approach. All the areas covered from chapter 4 through chapter 9 are included in the framework: (a) assessing possible target markets; (b) examining a company's standing in its industry and comparing it to major competitors; (c) exploring the supply and demand side of the supply chain; (d) determining whether the company's organization and culture are compatible with supply chain needs; (e) assessing financial needs and capabilities; and (f) evaluating possible strategies.

After doing this analysis, a firm can synthesize its findings to determine its competitive advantages and weaknesses relative to the competition. In effect, the company is identifying gaps or targets of opportunity on which to base its international strategy. The firm can then test a variety of strategies to see which is most appropriate in different scenarios and how the competition is likely to respond. Once this is done, the company can back into its "company package": vision, values, mission statement, goals and objectives, as we did in chapter 2.

As we look at each of these stages more closely, evaluation charts elaborated on in chapter 10 will be featured.

Stage 1: Analysis and Testing of the Business

Generally, a company needs to know its business domestically before it can take it abroad. That means it must know its industry and where it stands within it, the market for its products and services, trends in both the industry and the market, and the likely long-term future direction of both.

Trends are like tugboats that can push an industry in a certain direction, but they may be at work only temporarily. The future direction of an industry may depend on several, at times conflicting, trends. Figuring it all out and creating a vision based on the ultimately right direction is key. Put another way, before a company can determine where it wants to go and how it wants to get there, it needs to figure out where it is.[2] This stage of the strategy process is only as good as the information and expertise that is gathered.

What does this analysis cover and where does it lead a company?

A company starts by collecting information on and monitoring its business. To do this effectively, it should track the current condition of both the industry (what are competitors doing, or are likely to do?) and the marketplace (what are the customers doing, or are likely to do?) to find "success keys," those actions or initiatives that tend to work well or on which the company can capitalize at that moment. Keys can be found in, among others, customer perceptions, price considerations, supply chain efficiencies, leading-edge technology, product quality or variety, mode of entering new markets, even consolidation or types of promotion.

Some are readily apparent, some are not, so a company should take care and dig deep to identify them. They may appear in the

---

[2] Mario Katsioloudes, *Global Strategic Planning* Oxford, UK (Butterworth Heinemann, 2002), p. 22.

trade press, at trade shows or conferences, or in the marketplace itself. A more difficult but often more rewarding effort is to devise success keys from what is not happening: those absences or gaps a firm observes that are contrary to popular belief or that the industry and customer do not realize they are missing.

Along these lines a company should also compare what is happening within the industry and market domestically and internationally. The movements here and abroad do not always mesh—indeed, they often differ—but eventually they may affect each other; or, better yet, one may provide opportunity when the other does not. Complicated? Not really. Taken together domestic and international trends often give clues on which long-term direction to take. Smart companies know how and when to capitalize on the combined signals emitted by the industry and the market.

Markets and industries send signals given their characteristics at the time, and these vary with each industry. Key market characteristics include the factors covered in chapter 4. On the industry side, indicators cover a wide gamut as well: consolidation, vertical integration, strategic alliances, costs of production, excess capacity, retail or supplier integration, technological innovation, product life cycles, and the industry cost structure. Smart companies analyze what is happening in each of these areas (they read the signals) to sort out which developments to avoid and which to capitalize on. The more perceptive firms can even turn apparent negatives into stellar opportunities. Figure 7.1 presents a number of possible variables a company would likely cull through.

Figure 7.1
Market-Competitive Assessment

Market/ Industry Grouping	Opportunity (+2)	Threat (-2)	Timing (+2, 0, -2)	Go/No Go (4 go now) (2 go later) (0 move on) (-4 no go)
<u>Target Market</u> Improved per capita GDP Increased buyer sophistication High energy costs Market liberalization High storage costs Free trade zone Pro United States goods Low-cost materials suppliers Poor intrafirm transfer record Good skilled labor <u>Industry</u> Consolidation Product life cycle: growth/maturing Limited innovation Influence leverage useful Low environmental risk Low-priced local competition				

Company A, a U.S. entity, has explored a target market and determined the items listed in figure 7.1 are key market and industry factors. A factor that provides an opportunity receives a value of +2; one that is a threat, –2. Timing on avoiding or exploiting the factor is critical to the task. If the timing is acceptable or of the essence now, it receives +2; if an opportunity is good but needs to be delayed, it scores +1; if no advantage can be gained, it registers 0; and if the risk is too great or the downside outweighs the upside, –2. The firm will then multiply the threat/opportunity number by the timing number to arrive at the go/no go number. Depending on the conclusion, a company will decide whether or not to take action.

There are many possible opportunities here but a few threats as well. The industry appears to be maturing and consolidating through mergers and acquisitions. Large companies consolidate to gain greater market access, but the target market may be too small for them so it offers promise to the smaller company analyzing the situation. Difficult intrafirm transfers and high storage costs may also discourage larger companies. But since GDP is rising with a more sophisticated customer base, the market may prove fertile for a smaller, more agile firm.

Given its demographics the country may also be a good place to introduce new technology or customize a product for a regional market since skilled labor is available and cheap. If the market is less traveled, competition will probably be light, allowing a new entrant the luxury of higher prices. On the other hand, if products in the industry are approaching the mature stage of their life cycles, perhaps the target market or its extended regional market is ripe for slightly aging technology that could sell at a relative premium. Even further, given its highly skilled yet inexpensive labor base, the market might become the incubator for new technology or products. The prospects of not only creating something new but launching it regionally could appeal to the host government, which in turn might give the company investment incentives.

Looking at the situation slightly differently, given that storage costs are expensive, perhaps a foreign firm interested in investing there could work a preferential deal with the government to give the company a competitive edge over late entrants. Or perhaps the firm could joint venture with a local partner to accomplish the same thing. Also, since the country is in a regional free trade zone, importing materials and processing them from around the region could have significant supply chain savings despite high-energy costs. Further, the firm might leverage the pro-American sentiment to bolster its lack of reputation.

Stage 2: Evaluating Company Capabilities Against Those of Competitors

Traditionally, companies have used SWOT analysis at this stage. SWOT stands for Strengths, Weaknesses, Opportunities, and Threats. Strengths and weaknesses generally relate to the company itself. What are its strong qualities or core competencies that can be capitalized on? What are the vulnerabilities it should either try to strengthen or avoid or eliminate altogether?[3] Opportunities and threats normally pertain to the environment that surrounds the company. What is happening within the industry and the marketplace that the company can exploit? What might it suffer from? Companies often think of these four areas in terms of what they can change or impact (their own strengths and weaknesses) and what they cannot (external events and competitor moves).

Given the competitive and far-flung nature of business today and the increasing importance of the total supply chain, the traditional SWOT analysis is not enough. While it may cover the gamut of factors that need to be analyzed, for instance, its structure may miss important elements, such as why one overseas market benefits a firm's global positioning better than another. The investment decision must be made not only in the context of the overall global strategy but also in terms of the stand-alone risks and advantages it poses. Country targeting and selection should be factored into this stage of analysis and SWOT analysis is not up to that task.

Moreover, since international business can change daily, a firm must track its progress against internal and external factors continuously, always in relation to the progress of the competition. In the end, the key to a successful strategy is for a company to maximize its strengths and strengthen areas where it is weak against those of the competition. As a company examines its global supply chain, it must look at every factor in terms of both itself and its competitors. Through continuous comparative evaluation, a firm can anticipate, neutralize, or preempt both internal and external factors.

A firm's competitors do not necessarily consist of all the companies in its industry.[4] A company should zero in on its own catego-

---

[3] Donald O. Clifton and Paula Nelson, *Soar with Your Strengths* (New York: Delacorte Press, 1992), pp. 15 – 18.

[4] Katsioloudes, *op. cit.*, note 2, pp. 23-25.

ry within the industry, that set of firms that exhibit similar behavior and sell comparable products and services. This is its targeted competitor group. If the company determines that a particular category best suits it, it should look at these competitors in its analysis. Otherwise, it has to decide which category it is likely to move toward in its new strategy and consider companies already operating there. Figure 7.2 lists different generic company types that may prove helpful.

Figure 7.2
Generic Types Of Companies

Type	Description
Vertical producer	Companies focus on a few core competencies or a narrow product or service area
Horizontal producer	Companies tend to offer a large range of complementary products
Trend setter	Firms innovate with rapidly changing technology or frequent product improvements, supported by strong advertising
Established monolith	Companies are well established and rely on global presence and standardization with little innovation, or because of their size can be out-maneuvered
Niche player	Firms explore small niches to expand rather than target the mainstream market
Mass market player	Firms target the largest possible market with low-priced products
Gatherer	Companies expand through mergers and acquisitions to gain market access and presence

Figure 7.2
Generic Types Of Companies (cont.)

Type	Description
Waiter and follower	Firms tend to wait for movement from others before acting themselves
"Perfect and expand" type	Companies like to perfect products domestically across industry lines, develop branding, and then expand abroad

Where can a company go to find out as much as possible about its competitors? University libraries and Internet sources are very helpful. Figure 7.3 shows a sample of the information available.

Figure 7.3
Sources Of Competitor Information

Field Data	Published Data
Sales force	Ward's Business Directory
Articles	WebLIUS
Engineering staff	Newspapers in competitor locations
Distribution channels	Competitor public relations offices
Suppliers	Government documents
Personnel hired from competitors	Speeches
Professional meetings	Press releases
Trade shows	Annual and quarterly reports
Market research firms	Patent records
Reverse engineering	Court records
Security analysts	Prospectuses
	Government filings
	Internet
	Value Line
	SIC industry data
	U.S. Department of Commerce
	Hoover's Online
	Mergent Online
	EDGAR
	NetAdvantage
	SIC manuals and codes
	Standard and Poors Industry Surveys

Source: Michael E. Porter, *Competitive Strategy*, New York: Free Press (Simon & Schuster), 1980, pp. 72-73. Expanded and updated by the author.

A company can compare itself against competitors by using an expanded 4C approach, expanded because of the complexity of going global: *Commitment* – leadership capacity; *Cash flow* – financial capability; *Capacity* – availability and adaptability of management, organization, and human resources; and *Competitiveness* – supply chain effectiveness and efficiency.

Moving from exporter to international investor requires a quantum leap in vision, leadership, and commitment, because without these the plan should stay in the bottom drawer (see *Leading through Action* below). With the right leadership a company should then test its cash flow resiliency, its ability to access capital and apply it in productive ways. Companies carry out this process by analyzing their past history, financial ratios, cost of capital, and capital budgeting. The last two topics are covered in chapter 9.

There is an old saying that many chief executive officers were never told or choose to ignore: "Horses for courses." If a company does not have the resources—human, financial, or otherwise—to implement change, it either has to get them or abandon strategies that call for them. A firm's capacity is not only about having the right resources but also about having the flexibility to fit itself into another market and transfer its values and culture there.

Competitiveness deals with a company's ability to outperform or outsmart the competition, not only in its product or services but, as I have reiterated, in the effectiveness of its supply chain. And, of course, a firm's competitiveness spans all 4Cs. Until it looks hard , a firm never knows quite where it will find its competitive advantages.

Figure 7.4 shows the Competitive Advantage chart used in chapter 10 to summarize the results of the company's analysis. It not only lets the firm see its strengths and weaknesses in each critical area, it also allows the company to ascribe a weight to each strength or weakness to reach a competitive number. Depending on its relative strength, the firm rates itself against competitors either as having an advantage (+2), draw (0), or disadvantage (-2). The firm then applies a weight of importance (1-Not important, 3-Important and 5-Very important) to arrive at a competitive number for each area. The more positive the result, the better it is for the firm; the more negative, the worse it is. Zero indicates that the factor is doable or affordable but offers no appreciable edge over the competition.

Figure 7.4
Competitive Analysis

Proposed Item to change	Company (+ 2)	Competitor (-2)	Draw (0)	Weight (1, 3, 5)	Competitive Number
Target Country					
Ind/Com Positioning					
Commitment					
Competitiveness					
Supply side					
Demand side					
Cash Flow					
Capital Access/ Availability					
Global Funds					
Capital Budget					
Capacity					
Structural					
Tolerance					
Compatibility					

Stage 4: Establishing a Strong Base for Strategy Development

A company is now ready to craft its strategy, starting with defining its competitive base.

What exactly is the competitive base? It often amazes me that company officials do not know the answer to this. The base consists of the core competencies, values, and vision of a firm and is articulated in its mission statement, goals, and objectives. How basic is that? Yet far too many companies, not just small ones, in service and manufacturing industries alike, operate without mission statements and fail to track progress against goals and objectives.

Why is this foundation important?

Vision and Values

The decision to go global takes the company on a quantum leap. To do it successfully requires strong corporate underpinnings, a solid grounding in fair and honest values. A leader who cannot convey the importance of practicing good values and ethics should keep her vision in the bottom drawer. Transforming a company and getting it to respond to change is incredibly difficult, especially when dealing with widely diverse cultures and strategic partners. If integrity and honesty are not the basis of the transformation, how can stakeholders be expected to perform or believe in the company's mission?

Corporate values, though, are not just about honesty and integrity and doing the right thing. While these characteristics are very important, they should be complemented with *motivational forces.* Values set the tone for how to do things; they should be intertwined with ways to achieve desired behavior. For example, Company X wants its sales force to be honest and friendly to clients. To preserve jobs, the company is also trying to find efficiencies in how it does things. If the staff understands that such efficiencies will not ultimately eliminate jobs but keep the company competitive and growing, they will perceive the efficiencies as something good, not threatening. When the sales force is rewarded for being honest and friendly, it should also be recognized for recommending operational efficiencies. In this way, the sales force makes building efficiency an integral part of their behavior, a motivational force that depends on ingrained company values.

While good values set the tone for the company, good vision provides it with unfailing direction. Vision transcends daily operations. It often takes a true leader to view things from an altitude to put temporary setbacks and challenges in their proper context. If nurtured right, vision and a good pilot can steady a firm in rough times.

The Company Mission Statement
The mission statement is the rudder that helps a company stay on course. It embraces values to set the right tone and vision to clarify the purpose and articulate the firm's business. According to Fred David, a good mission statement answers nine questions:

1. Who are the customers?
2. What are the firm's major products or services?
3. Where does and will the company compete?
4. What role does technology play?
5. What are the firm's economic objectives?
6. What are the firm's organizational philosophies?
7. What are its outstanding core competencies?
8. What is its public image?
9. What is its attitude toward employees?[5]

---

[5] Fred David, *Strategic Management,* 3rd ed. (New York: Macmillan, 1991).

Goals and Objectives

These track the vision and link to the mission to ensure that the steps taken are in logical sequence. How many times have we heard companies say they are going back to basics, their core competencies? The reason is that many companies as they grow tend to wander into marginal businesses and activities that distract them from their true purpose. Often these companies two, five, even ten years hence come back to what they do best. For instance, a company in the beverage business might frame its mission statement as follows:

> The company is in the soft drink beverage industry. It expects to achieve significant global market share with a superior quality product with an above average price . . .

However, as one of its goals it decides to expand in selected countries by complementing its beverages with high-end but local snack foods. An objective becomes to acquire snack food establishments in 20 countries over the next 5 years.

Fundamental questions arise immediately. How will snack food strengthen the company's mission? Is movement into the new subsector a logical extension of the core business? Or will snack food be so radically different that it will require different management strengths? And who is a foreign beverage producer to tell a host country snack food company how it should operate in that market? Will snack foods complement the beverage side or simply be a huge distraction involving conflicting corporate cultures? Goals and objectives should flow from the mission statement; any deviations, whether horizontal or vertical, should add value to the bottom line.

To stay the course a company needs a set of parameters for testing new initiatives against core tolerances and ensuring that unproductive wandering is held in check.

Stage 5: Leading through Action

Before we explore how to formulate strategy, let us look at the glue that is needed to hold strategy together and make it work. That is leadership. Traditionally, goal-setting and strategy development has been a top-down exercise where the chief executive officer, with or without the board of directors but certainly with a select group of top aides and senior management, has presented his view of where the company is and where it is going. Middle management, employees, even customers, were expected to accept this "vision" and dance to it with few, if any, questions asked. Though this scenario may seem simplistic, it is not far from the truth. But the complexity of the world marketplace and the inherent differences and difficulties in dealing in other parts of the globe has made the strategic process increasingly less dictatorial and more inclusive of the views of all company stakeholders.

If the process has changed, think how much leadership has had to adapt to guide it correctly. If leadership does not adapt to today's strategy requirements, the strategy will most likely fail. So what do company leaders need? In a word, balance.

With help from all stakeholders, a leader must identify problems, have a vision for fixing them that soars above operations, but know how to manage operations to work toward that vision. Does that sound contradictory? It should. A good leader may appear to be a walking, talking contradiction. In reality she must have balance to deal equitably with more than one side. For example, she must see the big picture while understanding and often getting down into the details. She has to control while allowing people room for growth and their own decision-making. And she must think globally and act locally. To do that effectively, she needs to have the experience and understanding of both.[6]

The whole purpose of strategy, especially when it spans a multi-national, multicultural supply chain, is to effect change to stay competitive. The strategic process includes gathering and analyzing information, creating something new from that analysis, and adapting the company to grow and survive. To be an effective agent for change, a leader must be an able worker and provider at each stage. But what exactly is change? Constant change is not dynamism but anarchy.[7] Yet as Gosling and Mintzberg point out, clothing still includes buttons, cars employ the basic technology of the model T, and even some people still use non-cellular telephones.[8] They argue that change has no meaning without continuity. Thus, unless a company confronts an incredibly new paradigm shift or has to radically pursue other business avenues to succeed, a leader has to focus on those things that need improving while holding steady the rest.

---

[6] Jonathon Gosling and Henry Mintzberg, "The Five Minds of a Manager," *Harvard Business Review*, Vol. 81)(11) (November 03): 59.

[7] *Ibid.*, p. 61.

[8] *Ibid.*

Another balancing act.

To be well balanced, a leader today must have the following attributes:

- *Thrives on Chaos:* There is nothing worse than when a boss enters the room, speaks, asks for questions, and is greeted with absolute silence. This suggests that he doesn't really want to hear concerns, only platitudes and adulation. Also watch out for the classic invitation of a new leader: "My door is always open." And it is, but it takes negotiating through seven minions to reach it. A good boss wants to know the situation in the trenches first-hand. He enters the room, takes off his jacket, rolls up his sleeves Bobby Kennedy-style, and listens with purpose. He cannot understand the problems throughout the supply chain or from a host of stakeholders – with lip service and a nod of the head. He must want to learn in order to improve.

- *Inspires Creativity, Is Not Threatened by It:* It is not enough for a leader to have a personality that connects well with the firm's web of stakeholders to get them to embrace proposed change. She must lead change by inviting it. A leader must be willing to include all stakeholders in the formulation of strategy and invite feedback from implementation of it. Before people can execute a strategy, they must buy into it, make it their own, and do their job well not because the boss wants them to but because they want to. This cannot happen unless workers, staff, and management are allowed to participate in change from the outset.

- *Is Flexible and Adaptable but Persistent:* For a leader to implement change, he must be flexible. How can he expect an organization to move to the beat of his drummer if he cannot bend when need be even after his plan has taken hold? He must be ready to adapt especially in international situations, where differences in culture, government, and customer tastes might dictate how things are done. On the other hand, though, he must not show weakness; he must not let the wind dictate his daily thinking but must accept honest criticism and use it when it improves the situation. He must know how to walk that fine line between flexibility and persistence, again with shrewd balance, to follow the course to success.

- *Can Create a Credible Vision and Stick to It:* When all is said and done, a good leader must decide what to do, and then do it. Plans, goals, and objectives can be modified, if not crushed by unexpected events, but a vision should transcend a stressful environment. Once all the analysis is done and converted into a plan of action, a good leader and the company around her must commit to where both are headed. This is not always possible. Some events can be genuinely catastrophic. But too many leaders buckle prematurely and sadly watch their visions crumble after just a few unexpected bumps in the road. To inspire those around her to follow, a leader must have a vision that not only takes the company forward but is achievable and shows progress along the way. If vision cannot tie to reality, it will lack credibility, and a leader above all must be credible. Commitment and sanity amid crisis enforces credibility.

Stage 6: Strategy Development

If a company has followed the strategy process, has the right leadership, and has a good foundation, the following will all be in place:

- Good information
- Rigorous analysis
- Competitive advantages identified
- Vision and values articulated
- Mission statement in place
- The right course chosen for this "horse"
- Ownership taken by stakeholders

If these parts are all properly in place, the strategy that results will be one that can be reasonably *achieved* and *sustained.* Yet no matter how solid the base, a new strategy carries with it change and uncertainty and it relies on specific things happening. At this point a company must build on assumptions and test scenarios for predicting the future. Say a company decides to enter into a joint venture in Indonesia. As it begins to ramp up, committing funds and manpower, its home government slaps the industry with stringent new environmental codes that must be complied with within a year. This spreads the management of the firm too thin to give proper attention to the project.

A month later, the government of Indonesia accuses the joint venture partner of financing terrorists and freezes the financial assets of the new venture. Meanwhile, competitors, reacting to the firm's strategy and seeing its problems, set up more cost-efficient operations in the Philippines and Malaysia, gain the much-needed regional market access, and succeed with far fewer growing pains. The competition has in effect usurped the firm's strategy and succeeded in snatching long-term market presence, while the originating company is stuck in a costly bureaucratic morass.

The more a company learns from doing a lot of homework in advance, the better it can appreciate what it can and cannot do, the more precise and accurate its assumptions and scenarios will be, and the more astute it will be in dealing with countermoves by competitors.

Assumptions and scenarios relate to the firm's business environment. They should be devised around four critical areas: industry, market, competition, and government and world events. Figure 7.5 presents a chart showing the inputs to the development of assumptions and scenarios.

Figure 7.5
Assumptions And Scenario Development

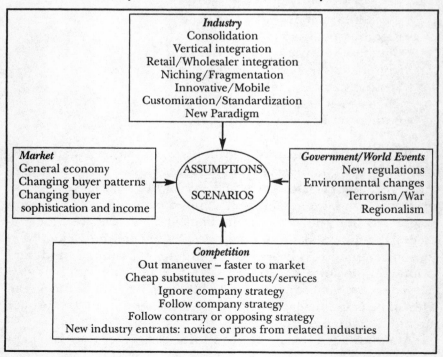

Within the context of credible scenarios, a firm can gauge the effectiveness of various strategies and see how well they will fit both the company and given scenarios. Figure 7.6 offers several possible options along with a way to evaluate them. A company lists a strategy within a given scenario, takes from its analysis of the 4Cs the strengths it possesses to succeed, and anticipates possible competitor responses. To simplify this exercise, a firm may want to label or number the scenarios developed.

Figure 7.6
Evaluating Strategies

Strategy/ Response	Scenario	Company Strength	Competitor
Downsize core competency only			
Enter untapped markets or market segments to establish niches abroad			
Customize while giants are consolidating/ standardizing			
Manufacture under private label for high-end boutique establishments, incur minimal marketing			
License for private label; license fees and revenue for R&D – lead tech curve			

Once a strategy has been selected, a company should put in place a means for evaluating and tracking it. Just as in the analysis stages, a firm will want to measure its progress relative to the competition. This calls for establishing benchmarks within critical areas, such as key supply chain processes, to ensure that the firm is carrying out the strategy well and making gains against competitors. These benchmarks are performance standards for success in, for example, product or service quality, cost efficiencies, customer services, and supply chain interaction. A company should not view benchmarking as a way to piggyback onto the competition,[9] but to beat it in the race.

The following is a good way to set up effective benchmarking:

Gather and Analyze Company and Industry Information

This step should not be reserved for one-time strategy development but should be done continuously. A company should set up one or more multidivisional teams made up of business unit managers, employees, and other stakeholders across the supply chain that should monitor and massage the information. Each team should communicate its findings regularly to trusted members of the supply chain and ask for input, making benchmarking part of the company fabric, like a value or motivational force. Again all stakeholders should not only be encouraged to contribute but come to expect it as part of their role.

Encourage Best Practices

Especially in companies that span several countries, smart ways of doing things may differ from one place to the next. This requires decentralizing the decision-making process, drawing it closer to the customer. Corporate management should not shiver at this prospect but embrace it. As we will discuss in the next chapter, allowing management and workers throughout the supply chain to find ways to improve their performance not only boosts their self–worth, it prompts them to buy into the company and what it is trying to accomplish. Firms should map the critical processes in the supply chain and urge staff at these points to think through how to improve performance there. Best practices should be submitted to the multidivisional team from all stakeholders but most notably those inside the supply chain.

Test and Select Best Practices

The multidivisional team should gather best practices regularly, evaluate them against certain performance metrics to determine which will enhance company operations, and cross-test them. Best practices in one area may work well in others or may be improved upon when shared. The search for best practices across a supply

---

[9] Katsiolides, *op. cit.*, note 2, p. 19.

chain not only encourages healthy competition, it also brings the various links in the chain closer together. Finally, the team should recommend to management certain practices for company-wide or regional adoption.

Reward and Publicize:
The best way to recognize a best practice is to reward the contributor and tell everyone what an important contribution she has made. Recognition makes employees want to buy into their jobs as much for themselves as for the firm and thus to perform better.

Benchmarking also sets a base on which a company can then forecast possible future events and trends that will likely shape the industry and market. Forecasting can take many forms, such as worst-case/best-case scenarios, computer modeling, and expert consulting—all of which look at the past and present to predict future direction based on certain assumptions.

Stage 7: The Strategy Cycle

A strategy fails if it cannot be executed successfully. To execute well a firm must create an environment for success, which is based, of course, on the stages that have led up to this point. At first blush, all appears to be in order. We have gone through the stages in their logical sequence. But there is a major problem. Traditionally, we have been taught to think exactly the way this sequence progresses: leadership, vision, mission, goals, and objectives. However, this progression implies linear thinking, a top-down approach. Yet the modern global marketplace is too fast and unpredictable to think that way; it calls for a different model.

Consider some of the defining features of a global company already discussed:

- Multinational
- Culturally diverse
- Strong supply chain partnerships and strategic alliances
- Global but customer-centric
- Stakeholder interests and input
- Rapid technology and efficiency improvements
- Decentralized decision making
- Continuous feedback, control, and modification

Looking at this list it is easy to see that traditional top-down management does not fit the new model. So how can a global strategy, stretching across a worldwide supply chain, succeed?

To answer that question, compare strategy execution to the golf swing. The swing is only as good as the setup that precedes it, and every good swing is a bit different to suit the individual golfer. The golfer is the company itself, defined by its leadership, mission statement, culture, and values. The set-up is its self-analysis, its industry, and the strategy it has created. The swing is the execution of that strategy.

We have dealt with the golfer and the set-up. Now the head and spine must remain still and let the arms, legs, and body revolve around them – the swing. In other words, let the various pieces of the total supply chain do their work. Strategy implementation is circular, not linear. It follows a core-based cycle, just like the supply chain itself, and not a top-down ladder. The measure of success lies in how well the golfer (core management) stays connected to the club head as it works its way through the swing (global operations), and strikes the ball (does business).

The actual swing is the activities surrounding it. If the cycle is set up properly, the following should happen:

- Stakeholders provide input at the beginning of mission and strategy development and continuously through feedback and best practices. A multidivisional team of stakeholders evaluates and tests their input and reports to top management.
- Management incorporates the input, articulates the mission, goals, and objectives, and communicates them throughout the supply chain. By so doing, it conveys what is critical for success and encourages input and best practices specifically in those areas. It also grants local latitude: maximum decision-making at the customer level. The leash can be long because the monitoring system rewards positive contributions, so it is in the best interest of local employees and management to do things well and improve operations.
- Based on what is considered critical for success, management works with the multidivisional team to set standards for comparing company progress against that of competitors and the industry and marketplace. These standards allow management to concentrate on critical process points in the supply chain.
- Based on best practices, benchmarking, and forecasting tools,

management can make credible predictions about the future course of the industry and what will be necessary for success. It can also test and apply near-term improvements.
- Finally, management can monitor and measure success, reward contributions, and make improvements or corrections to the strategy.

This cycle approach to strategy ensures that the process is dynamic, continuous, and inclusive, which allows the company to keep pace with the changing international environment. By implementing it this way, strategy stays manageably flexible.

A global supply chain is extremely hard to manage because of distance, players, and cultures, not to mention the range of unpredictability. For core management to micromanage this situation is not only impractical but foolhardy. Through the cycle approach, management does not have to control everything, only critical activities benchmarked against established standards. Control, like management, should be decentralized as much as possible, although fed routinely into the process as a whole. Stakeholders that need to have input can do so in several different ways.

Who really implements strategy? I strongly agree with Mario Katsioloudes, "Everybody does."[10] Taken literally, this means all members of the supply chain and contributing stakeholders. To maximize their effort takes more than just a reward system or their desire to perform well. The family of firms needs to internalize the supply chain strategy to the point where they are willing to execute it out of their own interests.[11] To do this the firms must align their goals and objectives. Morover, management must give staff and stakeholders time to adapt so that they gain an appreciation for the intended change and want it.

Finally, the cycle approach provides the momentum needed to keep operations vibrant and healthy. For example, Thomas Edison set the goal of having a major invention every six months but minor inventions every ten days. This kept his employees striving to do well and always creating something new. The result: his company amassed over 1,000 patents, a real display of accomplishment.[12] Not

---

[10] *Ibid.,* p. 224.
[11] *Ibid.,* p. 37.
[12] C. E. Shalley, "Effects of Productivity Goals, Creative Goals and Personal Discretion on Individual Creativity," *Journal of Applied Psychology,* 76 (1991): 179-85.

that this should be the goal of every company, but it does demonstrate how to encourage progress and achievement, energizing individuals to contribute continuously.

Does the cycle approach allow for operational control? Absolutely. It is built into the company's very fabric. Skeptics, though, might ask, "Well, now that we've empowered everybody and given them the ability to make decisions, how can we ever rein them in?" True, loss of control can have devastating ramifications, but too much control can cripple a company's progress and performance. What is the solution? Again, it rests in balance and tests the ability of management to lead: let the cycle work its course.

According to Erez and Kanfer, people accept change best when they understand the changes, have a sense of control over the situation, and are aware necessary actions must be taken to implement change.[13] Workers react well if they appreciate what is being done and why. And management has the responsibility not to change for the sake of change but to change within the right context, with continuity. Implementing strategy through the cycle allows for both. If everyone is on the same page, providing feedback as well as accepting it, the total effort is more cohesive, making it easier to apply controls and making the environment more conducive to superior results.

[13] M. Erez and F. Kanfer, "The Role of Goal Acceptance in Goal Setting and Task Performance," *Academy of Management Review*, p. 457.Vol. 8 (3), pp. 454-63, quoted in Katsioloudes, *op. cit.*, note 2, p. 245.

CHAPTER 8

ORGANIZING FOR THE GLOBAL MARKETPLACE

Over a thousand years ago foreign armies invaded countries in Europe continually. To protect themselves and their people, kings and nobles offered protection, land, and other assets to those lower on the economic ladder for services rendered, creating a chain of obligations stretching from kings to the poorest free man. This hierarchy linking man to man became the political, military, and economic system of medieval times. Kings and princes gave land and other assets to those beneath them. In turn, the recipients pledged undying loyalty, even homage, to their benefactors and paid them fees and services. Landowners became lords who could parcel out property to those lower than themselves, called vassals. Vassals then did the same with free men even lower, until even peasants could benefit from owning land.

Toward the end of the fourteenth century, though, land became more plentiful than good workers. Suddenly the peasant with a plough had leverage because he could get land fairly easily and work it to yield produce to keep the economy strong. One such peasant was John Freehope, who was invited to the castle of a powerful lord who possessed several thousands of acres.

"Welcome, kind sir," the lord greeted the ploughman as he entered a large waiting room in the castle. "Have a seat and I will tell you how you can become a wealthy man."

John peered at his rich host: "I understand there are too few men to work the land."

"Precisely," the lord acknowledged. "Good people are hard to find. But with your plough, you will fit in nicely."

The peasant felt confident. "My plough is not just any plough. I have saved up to buy the most up-to-date kind, and I expect to be compensated handsomely for it and my effort."

"And you will," the lord said. "I will provide you with protection from foreign armies and you in turn will work the land for me."

"With all due respect, sir, with my new plough I can do much more," said the peasant. "I have ideas that I want to explore."

133

The lord smiled. "Your obligation is to me. I will tell you what you can and cannot do."

"But, sir, my equipment can make you much richer than you already are," John told him. "We can create something new here. A farm, perhaps, that can generate enough produce for your domain and others as well. We can trade with other domains, which will gain for you great new wealth."

"You mean to trade with other lands?" the lord asked curiously.

"Of course. With our superior technology we can create a corporation that can do business not only across Europe but all the way to China."

"I admire your passion, my lowly friend," the lord said condescendingly, "but you forget your place. Remember I am head of the corporation and my castle is the site of all power. And the villages throughout my valleys are production units that work for me. I have many villages you know and my span of control is already too taxing and won't let me venture in ways you fancy."

"But, sir, if you would give me the power, I could do so much more for you. I could expand your domain into a kingdom unto itself."

"I won't hear of such a thing," the lord exclaimed. "You will do your job, pay me my due, and abide by my orders."

"But, sir, why won't you trust me?" John said. "You grant me land. Why not let me also take real ownership of it and your whole domain—?"

"You don't get it, do you?" the lord cut in. "You have your own bit of turf to worry about. The matters of the domain are mine and mine alone."

"But I have all these ideas. And working with others in your jurisdiction, I'm sure we could create a real vision for the future," John insisted.

"Keep your vision in your plough," the lord instructed, "and your place in the hierarchy, and all will be fine."

Given this brief look of feudalism, it is not surprising that late in the 1700s the entire system succumbed to private entrepreneurs with capitalistic ideals. At the top in feudal times was a manor, like the lord's castle, or a corporation. Vision was landlocked, work was compartmentalized, the castle ran the show. Vestiges of the feudal hierarchy exist in company structures today—which only goes to prove how hard it is to break such a rigid mold. But with the advent of a truly global marketplace, the need to recreate today's corporation has never been so imperative. It is not by accident that since serious globalization took off in the 1970s experts have urged firms to reinvent themselves, tear down bureaucratic silos, and embrace the new features of twenty-first century business.

Reinvention starts with a new strategy because strategy must drive company structure.[1] That sounds like energy shoving mass, the soul spearheading the body, the wind bending chimney stacks— truly not easy. Reorganization and personnel changes are by defini- tion disruptive, if not disastrous, depending on how they are done. So how can a new strategy succeed if the company has to endure shocks to its system at the same time?

The answer is, "It has to if it wants to survive." Change is hard, but unemployment is worse. Some say that it is easier to create a company from scratch, starting with a blank sheet of paper, than to change an existing one.[2] Why? Two reasons, actually.

First, reorganization tends to be incremental, not holistic, with the international side as the latecomer getting the proverbial short end of the stick. Too often international operations are treated as an appendage of the business rather than an integral part of it. This nat- urally leads to a heavy emphasis on corporate control, with less responsibility delegated to subsidiaries and insufficient attention paid to them. Traditional structures, aligned by function or product, rein- force a bureaucratic view when a panoramic one is called for.

From the outset in developing their expansion plans, compa- nies should consider international operations as a core part of their business. Hence the need for the blank sheet of paper. Think of it this way: If a company is expanding overseas, it must see its future growth in that direction. Why short-shrift the future? Recreate the business rather than simply adding to it.

Even if growth is through trade relationships, the company should have standard policies and incentives for all international operations. These policies should be inclusive from the start, with agents visiting headquarters regularly, interacting with one another, advising on planning and product development, and sharing best practices. This helps breed the trust and loyalty that drive empow- erment, the key ingredient in effective international management.

Second, something new should not be laden with old baggage. Rather it must be fresh to allow creativity to have its way. Many com- panies, because of their sheer size, think and act linearly. They are defined in terms of easily separable functions and business units, which in bricks and mortar parlance can be referred to as chimney

---

[1] Mario I. Katsioloudes, *Global Strategic Planning* ((Oxford, UK)Butterworth Heinemann, 2002), p. 123.

[2] Tom Peters, *Reimagine* (London, UK) Dorling Kindersly Ltd., 2003), p. 32.

stacks. Unfortunately chimney stacks hamper a firm's ability to recreate itself. Worse, they foster top-down bureaucracies where knowledge is clutched as power: "If I know something, I can't tell you because then I become expendable."

These companies are built on the turf of individuals, turf being a fundamental need we learn about when we first fight siblings and parents for our own bedroom. Thus, changing turf within a company is like pulling teeth because someone is bound to lose something quite painfully. But bureaucracy does not fit today's business environment. In the last chapter we concluded that strategy needs to be circular, not linear to meet the challenges of today. If strategy really drives structure, then organizations, and the management that runs them, must operate in a circular fashion as well.

In this chapter we will look at how the world dynamic has created new features that companies must contend with organizationally. We will describe the evolving company form, regional integrated systems (RIS), that is likely to drive future business. Finally, we will show what companies need to do to form a RIS and how to adapt to them.

Features of Global Organization
There are eight features that any firm operating in the global marketplace should consider in massaging or reinventing its organization.

Electronically, Not Chimney Stack, Based
The traditional global organization consists of a large corporate headquarters with tentacles stretching far and wide to 100 percent-owned subsidiaries. It is organized in top-down silos or chimney stacks that separate functions into near fiefs; communication between silos is not only discouraged, it can threaten the very existence of jobs and functions.

Enter the Electronic Age. Have you seen the ad where one employee, Jim, shares an idea with another, Paul? Paul smiles, compliments his colleague on his great ingenuity, and then runs down the hall to the boardroom to presents the idea as his own to the gathered leadership. As he does, though, Jim calls the CEO's secretary on his cell phone to tell her what is happening and asks her to keep Paul from entering the boardroom. He then e-mails the top management cloistered inside, all huddled around their computers, and shares the idea directly with them.

The story shows that turf and silos, and the fancy footwork they engender, are archaic ways of working. Electronics, especially the Internet, has torn away the bricks and mortar, giving way to a virtual presence marked by speed, availability, response time, quickness, and most of all superior communications among all parties, side to side and top to bottom. Given the need to cover global operations where time differences abound along far-flung supply chains, the Internet has proved up to the task. It has not only quickened communications but also has allowed several people to share communications at once. The instant involvement of all key parties eliminates the need for cumbersome layers of management. The premium now is on sharing information rather than hoarding it.

Flatter Organization with Management at the Core

The modern company structure is circular, like the strategy cycle, rather than top-down linear. Top management must descend from its ivory tower to place itself at the heart of the organization. It must shed its layers and tear down its chimney stacks by concentrating on core competencies and critical activities and managing through empowerment (see the next section). Only this way can managers get the panoramic vision they needs to run a global business.

Fewer layers of management not only require less overhead but give the organization the agility to react promptly to changing market conditions. Moreover, corporate management can focus on what matters most. Management does not need insulation but room to maneuver. What is not critical, either as a process point in the supply chain or proprietary technology in a product or service, can be outsourced or at least delegated throughout the chain. Management can direct instead of stifle and control, becoming entrepreneurial in addressing significant challenges. Removing the clutter also gives top management more time to listen. Instead of trying to oversupervise, it can initiate dialog with stakeholders, review and improve operations through feedback and best practices, measure results, and direct the future.

The flatter, management-centric organization can only work if it truly empowers the extended enterprise. The farther away headquarters is from operations, the more it will benefit by empowering staff close to the action. True, the risk of empowering them may be high because language and cultural differences are also greater. But varying cultures demand direct management skill sets that headquarters more often than not cannot provide.

Empowerment, built on trust and communication, is essential. Goals, objectives, values, core competencies and general direction must be communicated simply and clearly. Subsidiaries then need to translate these themes into local terms and share the results as feedback to headquarters. This way all sides can lock onto the same frequency, effort will go into developing best practices, and those practices will be adopted where they improve operations. This circular give-and-take improves performance because it is not micromanaged. Remember the golfer and his swing?

Stakeholder-Centric

In moving to foreign markets, a company's package—its culture, values, mission, goals and objectives—have to transfer well. Speaking another person's language is a sign of respect. Similarly, a company wants to show respect in the transfer of its package. Rather than being imposed, it needs to be presented in a way that new staff will embrace. To do this, the package must be flexible enough to invite comment and input. Such input is the first step not in relinquishing power but in giving and strengthening it. For long-term success headquarters has to empower its teams abroad, extending their ability to make local decisions—a long leash with measured tolerance for error.

But a company's package cannot just accommodate different work forces, it must deal with the differing political and business environments of target markets as well. Given some deterioration in the understanding of "globalization," a perception that is all about taking, not giving, expanding companies have to be prepared to offer something to the market that will appeal to all stakeholders there, from customers to host governments to shareholders in subsidiaries.

As markets become more sophisticated companies will continue to cater to customer needs and wants, but they will also come under the watchful eye of the host government, perhaps an unfriendly society at least to start, and local investors. All will look to the foreign subsidiary to do the right thing and be a good corporate citizen. Increasingly this will mean contributing to the local or regional market and keeping a higher percentage of profits there. What may be lost in the short term on the headquarters bottom line will raise the company's value over time. Not only will corporate headquarters have to empower the foreign activity, it may have to let it "go native" as well.

I once had a Filipino lawyer ask me if we had Coca Cola in the United States. When I responded, "Of course, it's an American company," the attorney was incensed, claiming that in fact Coca Cola was Filipino born and raised. When I had the opportunity years later to tell that story to the president for international operations for the firm (who happened to be Australian), he laughed and said that was exactly what Coca Cola wanted people to think—that the company was truly theirs.

Aware that Regionalization Is Here to Stay

Just as global companies tend to organize regionally, the move to form stronger commercial alliances on a geographically regional basis has too much momentum to be reversed. Europe's push for a central bank and common currency shows the strength in numbers and lets us glimpse a future with fewer currencies and more regional commonalities.

Companies agonizing over whether to standardize or differentiate will discover that the happy medium rests in commercial alliances. These country linkages not only offer seamless markets with customers of similar tastes and less diversity, but because of the reduction of import barriers many supply chain cost efficiencies as well. As we saw in chapter 5, automobile producers already do this, catering differently to the North American and Asian markets while using modified versions of the same worldwide manufacturing platforms.

Concerned with Process

In the past a product or service drove a firm's business; now process drives the product. As companies expand, do more of what they do best, and outsource the rest, this trend driven by supply chains and not individual firms will continue. Because most critical processes in a chain now contribute to the total buying experience, competitive advantages are becoming process- rather than product-based. A successful company has to view its business in terms of its entire supply chain, and as a company expands abroad, the chain gets longer, more complicated, and more diverse, requiring a more open structure and empowerment at the point of the customer.

That is why feedback from customer to supplier and at all points in between has to be *fast* and *inclusive* of all supply chain members (workers, management, suppliers, distributors, retailers, even customers and shareholders). Manufacturing and service systems have to be *flexible* to accommodate customer needs and product improvement. Suppliers have to be *timely* with just-in-time deliveries based on volume and rate of purchases. Managers with broader, system-wide views must ensure that processes run *interactively* as well as smoothly. Fast, inclusive, flexible, punctual, timely, and interactive—this is the new dynamic of global business.

The key to all this is automated communications systems. More and more firms are adopting these systems to streamline the chain, like putting grease on process joints. Such systems cover every aspect of the chain, including customer relationship management (CRM), enterprise resource management (ERP), and supply chain management (SCM).

Emphasis on the Customer

With their growing emphasis on meeting customer needs, companies are not just trying to improve and differentiate products and services, they are empowering the customer to dictate the product. The smart company increasingly turns to the customer to improve packaging, branding, price, place of purchase, ease of purchase, and the service that goes with it. Tom Peters, referring to the "buying experience," mentions Starbucks as providing not just coffee but a coffee-drinking experience from the time the customer leaves the car in the parking lot until she drives away.[3]

Gian Luigi Longinotti-Buitoni, president and CEO of Ferrari North America, claims that companies create products to stir customers to dream about products not yet envisioned but that someday will be demanded.[4] Ideas and desires of tomorrow become products and services. The client, not the engineer, now drives the innovation process.

Today's products and services have an aura to them that address all the senses of the customer: taste, desire, ease of use, ambiance, convenience of purchasing, instant gratification, and the promise of still more. Taken abroad, this aura offers the company both opportunities and challenges. Take any franchise: Its success comes from a one-size-fits-all formula, but abroad even the most successful franchises often have to modify not just their products and services but the complete buying experience. They have to adjust their sacred formulas. To make the right adjustments takes continuous on-the-ground intelligence.

---

[3] *Ibid.*, p. 143.
[4] Gian Luigi Longinotti-Buitoni, *Selling Dreams* (New York: Simon & Schuster, 1999).

Intense competition in the marketplace has enabled the customer. As we saw in the last chapter, too many options from too many places make customers believe that if they found what they were looking for in one locale, they can find something better and, yes, cheaper somewhere else. This attitude has shortened product life spans. Take computers, golf clubs, telephones, whatever: Just when you have the latest and greatest, wait a week, a day, an hour, and something greater still will emerge. Short product life cycles cause incredible pressures on the supply chain in design and production, raw materials and supplier inventories, and pricing and promotion. Further, as we saw in chapter 6, increased waiting on the customer has reinvented not only the retail sector but the entire supply chains, with retailers, suppliers, focal companies and distributors all jockeying for more control.

Branding and Nonfinancial Leverage
To move across borders today, a company must be known, and known favorably. Reputation and branding (see chapter 6) are not readily available for new entrants overseas. Knowing its leverage value and identifying value-added strategic partners are increasingly important capabilities for a global business.

Planning for Action
Some may be thinking, "Why spend so much time analyzing and formulating strategy only to let the organization loose in an ever-changing world marketplace?" The workings of the company will go more smoothly if the strategy driving it is solid and the people in place are ready and able to carry it out. Ironically, though, to execute strategy effectively calls for an organization that is ready to capitalize on opportunities that arise along the way.

Regional Integrated Systems
Recognizing the need for all eight of these features has already forced companies to question the effectiveness of their organizations and management styles. Not only are traditional structures top-to-bottom and ensiloed, but members of most supply chains, typically communicating by phone or fax, operate on a supply-push basis: They simply sell whatever they manufacture. In this fashion, they optimize demand by constraining production to control the business easier.

The evolving company and supply chain have entered a new dimension because of two key concerns: global competition and customer care. Corporate headquarters are shrinking as firms focus more on core competencies and move more mass closer to the customer to deal with diverse feedback and shorter product life cycles. To varying degrees, supply chains are changing from supply-heavy to demand-heavy, becoming structurally more innovative in the process. Real-time communications, the language that spans the supply chain, allows a family of firms to learn more about the customer, respond by providing product variety, and price strategically to maximize profit with differing customer segments and sales modes.

In the future companies will continue to refine globalization and customer care. Keys to this lie in business intelligence and a core competency focus. In its special report, *Consumer Nation: Retailing 2010*, PriceWaterhouseCoopers states that in a world of instant gratification, there is no substitute for having real-time knowledge about the customer at the point of decision-making.[5] David Joseph adds that business intelligence represents the last frontier for differentiation in the ultra competitive and over saturated retail market.[6] Given the increasing demand-pull on supply chains, this phenomenon cannot be restricted to retail establishments. All companies in supply chains will ultimately have to embrace this orientation; many already have.

Business intelligence involves measuring each vendor, each product or service line, and each group of customers and then determining an optimal combination of all aspects.[7] With real-time communications, the opportunity to accomplish this once seemingly impossible task is here. Industry analysts gauge that stronger collaboration and closer synchronization of supply and demand can reduce inventory levels by up to 25 percent.[8] By learning more about the customer, a company not only reduces its costs but gains happy customers: it has solved the basic strategy dilemma, the dichotomous challenge of customization.

Difficult as it may be to execute, this concept of keeping costs low and meeting varying customer expectations may be applied to

---

[5] PriceWaterhouse Coopers and *Retailing Magazine*, "The State of Retail Technology 2001."
[6] David Joseph, "Synchronizing Supply & Demand," *sas com Magazine,*, 2003.
[7] *Ibid.*
[8] *Ibid.*

all markets some day. Unfortunately, that is not the case yet. Supply chains and market differences preclude it from happening. In the market, wide ranges of buyer sophistication and purchasing power interfere. Supply chains function in a huge variety of different ways. In the make-to-stock (MTS) variety, the chain produces finished goods, takes orders, and delivers to the customer. In make-to-order (MTO), raw materials and semifinished subassemblies are staged until the customized order is taken, final assembly can be done, and delivery made to the customer. There is even engineer-to-order (ETO), where the customer not only has something made-to-order but adds product development, design and possibly some sourcing.[9]

Given these differences as well as the proliferation of products, market segments, channels, and regional markets, supply chains are finding they have to adapt. The family of firms needs several chain approaches each with a different strategy, a "mixed strategy supply chain".[10] To achieve this, firms must synchronize the supply and demand ends of the chain: ordering, producing, and forecasting sales. Some automated frameworks[11] today actually separate processes through what are known as point of postponement (POP), a process point triggered by a customer demand signal (either an order or a replenishment signal).[12] In such a mixed strategy, the POP is not fixed but floating.

In this age of the fickle buyer, to retain and satisfy customers long-term, a supply chain needs a segmented strategy, one that can not only predict customer needs and rate of purchasing but can do so for the range of products or services it provides. Viewed in an international context, where customer diversity and market variations are much greater, this strategy seems unattainable; if they are to come close, companies—and supply chains—have to thin down and focus on core competencies. Each firm in a supply chain can then do what it does best, allowing the chain as a whole, not a focal company, to address and respond to a larger range of customer needs. The extended enterprise no longer revolves around a core company but acts as a well-connected family of firms operating as a

---

[9] Vinay Asgekar, "Performance-Driven Enterprises Need Customer-Aligned Supply Chain Strategies," AMR Research, Bettermanagement.com, 2003.

[10] *Ibid.*

[11] Pierre Mitchell, "Purchasing Must Become Supply Management – Twenty Years Later and Counting," AMR Research, Bettermanagement.com, 2003.

[12] Jim Brimson, "The Role of Processes in the Supply Chain," THINK TANK, Bettermanagement.com, 2003.

dynamic web of interrelated processes, creating synergistic value that greatly exceeds the cost of losing independence.[13]

As gross domestic product strengthens around the world, regionalization will gather steam. As it does, efficiencies and customer commonalities will emerge. Subsidiaries will not only be integral parts of an extended supply chain, but for economic and political reasons these chains will conform to the region as well.

Concurrently, ties between headquarters and subsidiary and subsidiary-to-subsidiary will be strengthened, not in spite of increased subsidiary autonomy but because of it. Ownership and empowerment at both ends will be the measure of a firm's effectiveness. The functioning relationship will look like figure 8.1.

Figure 8.1
The Parent-Subsidiary Relationship

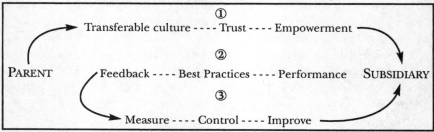

In this relationship the subsidiary, with parental guidance, takes greater control of its own destiny. Ultimately every subsidiary will earn the power to operate on its own so that it can make decisions with other partners that improve supply chain operations. Headquarters will not be shut out of the process but benefit from it. The subsidiary will function not as an isolated profit center but as a cog maximizing the capability of the total company worldwide. Each regional supply chain will consist of a web of subsidiaries[14] and regional partners, hopefully working seamlessly as a regional integrated system (RIS).

---

[13] What if each subsidiary is not a mini-version of headquarters? One might be a distribution or production center for many regions. The features of modern global business still apply. For any investment a firm will need to weigh the level of empowerment needed and whether it is possible, the regional supply chain, and the need to be a good corporate citizen in the host country. For any specialized subsidiary in a strengthening regional market, the potential to convert that entity into a full-fledged RIS will be strong. What better way to prepare for such an evolution than by instituting the right features from the start?

[14] C. E. Shalley, "Effects of Productivity Goals and Personal Discretion on Individual Creativity," *Journal of Applied Psychology*, 76 (1991): 179 – 85.

A firm expanding globally should start to think in these terms. This does not mean it should abandon the good management practices implicit in traditional organizational forms. It does mean, though, that in designing new ventures and modes of operation abroad, it may want to work with these concepts initially at least and put the classic organizational chart in the drawer for a while. Focal company, supplier, distributor or retailer—all are to varying degrees cogs in a chain. Every company is as unique as its supply chain. The companies in the chain may have varying, at times even conflicting, goals, strategies, cultures, and structures. Some firms are well positioned to adapt to the new global business model and some are not. Still others may fervently believe they do not have to change.

To help companies decide, appendix 8 describes most of the traditional forms of company structure and chapter 10 contains the tolerance index described below. The appendix lets a firm see where it is organizationally and the Index helps it to gauge its ability to change. A company then needs to determine its optimal mix, the balance of supply and demand factors that makes the most sense, and how much of the new model it wants to tackle.

Empowering the Extended Enterprise

To adapt to the new global model structurally, a company should begin by examining its human resources to find "horses for courses" and by reorienting its management team. No matter what strategy and structure it has, a company will not implement either successfully unless it has competent managers and workers who share the same attitude and work ethic. If management cannot become agile, flexible, and communicative and otherwise adapt to the evolving model for a global company, how can the organization and those that work for it?

Have you ever endured a reorganization? Anyone who has knows how difficult the experience is. Ironically, while people complain about the drudgery of their routine, they cling to it because of the comfort it provides. Comfort comes from understanding what needs to be done and being able to do it. In a reorganization, both understanding and ability may change; worse, people may lose their jobs.

Yes, the process is unsettling. The best way to get it done is for those affected to want the change. To want it, they need to understand why change is necessary, appreciate it for what it will do, consider it fair, and feel confident that they can not only contribute skills to it but benefit from it as well. How is all this possible? Through empowerment. Adopting the features of the new global corporation is not possible until corporate management can let go and truly empower not only their own staff but the extended enterprise as well.

Traditional hierarchal management assumes that the manager knows best and the employee needs supervision to perform well. The manager knows best because the manager presumably is more seasoned, more experienced, smarter, and knows more about what the company is trying to accomplish than the worker does. Employees need supervision because they lack an appreciation of their value to the organization and need to be motivated.

There are two fundamental problems with this logic. First, how can the manager know best when the employee, who is doing the job, is present at the point of action? Second, if employees understood the mission of the company and their vital role in it, wouldn't they better appreciate their contribution to the organization and be more motivated to do a good job?

If motivation is key to strong management, managers should strive to find the best means of motivating. To help them in their search, let's look at what drives motivation:

- Managers need to trust workers or they will never believe the job will get done effectively.
- Workers need to trust management or they will never believe in themselves.
- Both managers and workers need to act responsibly and communicate regularly to ensure the first two points.

How do these critical things happen? Management and workers need to earn each other's trust. They need to see and appreciate operations from each other's side. Does this mean that managers become workers and workers managers? If need be; whatever it takes for both sides to understand and implement needed changes. Appreciating roles from the perspective of the other side creates a credible base, which is the grist of a trust relationship. If both sides appreciate the other's viewpoint, there is room for listening. What a novel thought! This, in turn, allows for an exchange of ideas, more open and direct communication, and thus improved performance.

The best way to demonstrate trust is through empowerment. While I stressed this in the last chapter on strategy, I failed to say how empowerment happens. Figure 8.2 attempts to do that. You will notice that this process begins with an environment of trust conveyed through credibility. Leadership in action has to lead the way and show that the waters are maneuverable. Robert Trent Jones, the famous golf course architect, said once that he never designed a hole he couldn't par. Managers have to do the same. If they expect employees to cross the river, managers have to go first.

Figure 8.2
Empowering The Work Force

Management creates an aura of credibility throughout the company.

Management communicates the need for change and invites input, including:
1. Why there is a need?
2. How the company will benefit.
3. How the employee will benefit.
4. Why employees should provide input.
5. Incentives for their effort.

Management demonstrates sincerity by incorporating employee feedback wherever possible.

Management provides training so that employees understand the significance of changes and acquire new required skills to gain a necessary comfort level.

Employees buy into change and take ownership based on the perceived benefit to them.

Management encourages regular best practices and performance to enforce company values, such as communication, teamwork, sharing and responsibility, as well as key activities and goals, such as customer retention and product quality. Such contributions become commonplace, a part of every day work, a motivational force, a part of company culture.

Management regularly recognizes contributions.

Management reinforces contributions with greater delegation of authority and responsibility.

Employees are empowered to be creative and make decisions within the spans of their jobs.

Employees become passionate, more proactive and satisfied, boosting their effort.

Next management has to communicate not on its own terms but on those of the employees and other stakeholders. To motivate employees, management must show what is in it for them. Why should employees contribute to change, especially if they or their friends may possibly lose their jobs as a result?

Incorporating the ideas of employees and other stakeholders is the best way for management to be credible, but a manager should not ask for input unless she is prepared to use it. Regularly encouraging and recognizing contributions confirms employee value. Once they recognize their worth, employees will take ownership of what they are doing and will want to do more. They will, in effect, become passionate about what they do, pushing themselves to do better. Strong performance warrants greater trust and a longer leash to be creative and resourceful and make decisions. (For employees who cannot understand this simple concept, "upward mobility" is through the front door of the company.)

Does this mean that empowerment eliminates the need for management? Of course not. Rather, a company should shift the way it views management and how work gets done. People do not perform well because they are forced to; they perform well because they want to. One of my first bosses told me that he was a lazy manager and that suited him just fine. "I leave my people alone," he opined, "and they do the job." Certainly he underplayed his role, but I didn't miss his point.

A longer leash more often than not works better than a shorter one. That is why, in setting up an organizational structure, a firm should dole out management positions sparingly, placing managers only where they are truly needed, giving them the responsibility and authority to direct and coordinate, and allowing them to put enough velvet on the hammer.

One of the best ways to determine if the manager-employee ratio is set right is to see where management bottlenecks occur—where the interaction or inaction of managers impedes the business rather than moving it forward. For instance, in this age of Internet sharing, is a hierarchy of bosses necessary to move the word throughout the system and does that hierarchy help or hinder the decision-making process and the ability to get things done?

If this model works, and studies show that it does,[15] then empow-

---

[15] Michael E. Porter, *Competitive Advantage* (New York: Free Press, 1985), pp. 39 – 43.

erment flattens management and flexes the organization, readying it for global action. Trust, responsibility, and mutual ownership replace the need for stacks of supervision and control. Top-down communication gives way to four-way communication, vertical and horizontal. As a company broadens globally and has to rely more on extended supply chains, corporate management needs empowerment to cope with its expanded span of control. Hierarchal functions yield to greater use of cross-functional teams, replacing turf wars with synergy events.

Does this scenario ring true?

The chief executive officer gathers his board members and announces his new strategy and goal: to achieve a 20 percent increase in sales and a 10 percent increase in market share over the next five years. The marketing boss knows it will be difficult for the sales force, but after negotiating for a higher budget and commission rate, he assures the CEO that the goal can be reached. The production supervisor welcomes the increase to help boost the firm's lagging capacity. But the chief financial officer argues that the new marketing numbers are exorbitant and to attain higher production levels will require a huge capital expense in more modern equipment. The CEO beats the boardroom table: "Why can I always count on the line but always have a problem with my staff? Finance is supposed to support operations, not block them. Tell me how I can do it, not why I can't."

There are many possible problems here, such as the CEO announcing a new strategy without input from key stakeholders and preparation of managers, but, worse, the various units are out of whack, thinking within their own parameters and not in terms of the firm as a whole. Moreover, the CEO makes it clear that everyone is not equal. As Michael Porter explained years ago, a company's value chain has primary (marketing and production) and secondary (finance, accounting, human resources, etc.) activities.[16] Both of these lie at the heart of the problem in a traditional company structure—narrow perspectives, unequal partners, and we-they situations. For a company, much less its entire supply chain, to function

---

[16] Barry Saeed and Tom King, "Curing Supply Chain Indigestion," Boston Consulting Group, Bettermanagement.com, 2003.

seamlessly, it must view all operations as equally important and encourage the interaction of all in a synergistic whole. Cross-functional teams can only work if the players are respected as equals and their input, positive or negative, is seen as contributing to the general good.

The example shows that management, as much as strategy, determines the organizational structure of a firm. If the human relationships, vertically (manager to employee) and horizontally (across functional areas), cannot adapt, organizational changes will fail or worsen an already complicated predicament. The wider the gap between the parent and subsidiary, the harder it will be to transfer corporate values and ensure the proper execution of duties. By the same token, subsidiaries, local managers, and workers must buy into the corporate mission and values if they are to be empowered to do an effective job.

Finding the right people to empower in distant lands is critical but extremely difficult. Even foreigners who speak the language of the parent company and may even have been educated in the parent's country have different values and customs. Despite all the talk about "westernization," people from varying cultures act and behave and especially think differently from one another. Empowerment is not simply identifying competent people, becoming friendly with them, and delegating. Empowerment is something earned incrementally; it is a long process, one that is inexorably tied to strategy execution. Performance gains respect and trust. Trust and respect reciprocate by empowering, and the exchange is cultivated over time.

Restructure Outwards

Once a company can feel comfortable with management by empowerment, it can use that blank sheet of paper to organize outward. A global firm's structure should mirror its strategy if the strategy is to work well. An uncluttered center lets the firm focus on core competencies, leaving time to direct and coordinate a far-flung supply chain or series of supply chains. In its quest to stay competitive and provide products and delivery, with shorter cycles but geared to capture customers long-term, most companies will continue to outsource to stay nimble and responsive.

To organize outward a firm must (a) map out the new or existing supply chain and view it from an interactive 5V perspective; (b) decide the extent of outsourcing necessary and draw up criteria for aligning company packages among the strategic partners of the chain; and (c) determine the communications platform to be used in the chain.

Map the Supply Chain and View It from a 5V Perspective

To fully understand the extent of the new business, a firm should envision the proposed or existing supply chain as a series of tasks, activities, and processes. From there it should identify and map the key processes. Finally, it should view the entire chain from an interactive 5V perspective and determine its automated and collaboration needs. The 5Vs are volume, visibility, variety, value, and velocity. Each of these factors should be evaluated to see how it affects the supply chain[17] both separately and in combination with the others. *Volume* refers to how much product moves through the chain. *Variety* is the differences in those product choices. *Visibility* is the extent of one's view across the chain. *Value* stands for profit, the spread between costs and revenue. *Velocity* refers to the time it takes to move product from supply to customer. To test the interaction of these factors, typical questions a company should ask include:

- Does the company rely on large volume but little variety in its product or service mix?
- How fragmented is the supply chain? Does each firm in it have good visibility over all or part of it?
- How does fragmentation affect cost efficiency and speed of operations (velocity)?
- Does the company offer too much variety with little increase in volume?
- In differentiating, does the company slow operations down (velocity), underestimate the complexity of managing so much (visibility), and overlook disproportionate rises in costs, such as materials handling or warranties (value)?[18]

By examining the 5Vs in combination, a company can both measure the economic value of each V factor and decide on an optimal balance for all five. Further, this approach helps to sort out the critical and noncritical processes within the supply chain. For

---

[17] *Ibid.*

[18] Kevin R. Fitzgerald, "Best Practices in Procurement," Ascet 4 (May 2002).

example, a company should exert more control over those activities
that have a direct bearing on production and delivery than over secondary activities. After sorting this out, a firm can decide which
processes it should integrate, outsource, manage directly, simply
monitor, or let other supply chain members manage. In a more
extended supply chain especially, the family of key firms would work
together to balance the 5Vs and map the critical/noncritical
processes.

Extent of Outsourcing

If a a supply chain is to operate effectively, all members must be on
the same wavelength. They must all have a deep understanding of
the cost drivers within the chain, a spirit of cooperation, a cross-
functional approach, a culture of continuous improvement, and
common goals.[19] Can management styles from different companies
adapt and work together when the management and control of
operations are not centered under one boss? How will the interaction strain a member's organizational culture? Beyond this, in
international chains, distance and cultural differences create
greater room for error. Communications are slower the more players there are while time differences, transit times, and distortions in
market demand can exacerbate these communications. This can
lead to inventory excesses, idle manufacturing, and higher costs in
fixing problems.[20]

Determining how much to integrate or contract out becomes a
matter of balancing in as optimal a way as possible. In making the
decision to outsource, a company should draw up parameters for
negotiating the company package (values to objectives) with other
partners. If negotiations cannot fall within these parameters accept-
ably, a firm should look for other partners. To devise these parameters and to select the right partners, the company should ask the following type of questions:

- What is the cost to do something internally rather than externally?
- What are the company's quality standards? Can a supplier produce to those standards?

---

[19] Valdero staff, "From Planning to Control: Improving the High Tech Supply Chain", Valdero, Bettermanagment.com, 2003.

[20] David Ritter, Stuart Scantlebury, Michael Busch, and Anthony Datel, "From Toys to Tools: Using Web Services to Cut Business Costs," Boston Consulting Group, Bettermanagement.com, 2003.

- How smoothly will the task, activity, or process run with out-sourcing rather than vertical integration? Will outsourcing be disruptive to continuing operations?
- How much management is required from which partners for what activities and processes to make outsourcing cost-effective and add value?
- What are the production and communication capabilities of the supplier?
- How much trust is needed in the supplier relationship?
- Are the goals and culture of the company and supplier compatible?
- Does the company have the visibility across the supply chain to coordinate or manage the activities that the supplier will perform?
- All things considered, does outsourcing constitute a cost-effective way of getting the activities done in terms of cost, performance, and quality?

Communications Platform

Once partners concur on a consolidated company package and the 5Vs are balanced, they should agree on the communications platform to be used. Ideally, they would start with compatible hardware and software but after that they should not rush into just any automated system. They should first prioritize the areas with the greatest need by looking at supply chain processes that exhibit problems, including delays, excess inventories, redundancy, personnel frustration, poor decisions because of inadequate information, or inability to communicate to all key parties.[21] Then they should set a specific purpose for the communications and apply them to real projects.[22] Finally they should agree on a guiding architectural framework with consistent standards and continually monitor the effectiveness of the platform.[23]

Finally, in supply chain development we come full circle. Strategy is a cycle achieved by everyone. Similarly, in the end the members of the chain perform. With a strong consolidated company package and empowered parent-subsidiary relationships, the family of firms can operate in sync while each executes its own strategy cycle.

[21] David Ritter, Stuart Scantlebury, Michael Busch, and Anthony Datel, "From Toys to Tools: Using Web Services to Cut Business Costs," Boston Consulting Group, Bettermanagement.com, 2003.
[22] *Ibid.*
[23] *Ibid.*

The Tolerance Index

A company considering expanding abroad or changing strategy can now envision an ultimate structural form. The next step is to determine its ability to get to that point. Geared to help a firm do this, the Tolerance Index tests a company's capacity to adapt to the kinds of changes it will experience in international expansion. It helps target problem areas for change and determines how quickly or slowly a firm should move down the new path.

This tool is summarized in figure 8.3. It measures the company's (a) agility and flexibility, (b) organizational strengths and weaknesses in light of the new strategy, (c) symbiosis with the proposed new investment and supply chain, (d) management and labor requirements, and (e) the degree to which the firm needs and can reasonably take on modern organizational features. For each area a company can score the firm's ability (in terms of money, resources, and timing) to improve the condition of that area, scoring from 1 – 5, worst to best. A firm that scores low in one or more areas should estimate the impact of these weaknesses on its plans and strive to correct or minimize them.

Figure 8.3
The Structural Tolerance Index

Category	MC-CNC (a)	NC-CNC (b)	MC-CC (c)	NC-CC (d)	NCN (e)	SCORE
Company Characteristics						
Structure/ Strategy Alignment Needs						
Company/Investment Symbiosis						
New Organizational Features Compatibility Manpower Requirements						

MC-CNC: The company must change, but under the current situation, that change is impossible.
NC-CNC: The company needs to change, but it is not imperative to do so, and the price for doing so would be too great.
MC-CC: The company must and can change.
NC-CC: The company needs to change, but now it is not imperative to do so.
NCN: No change in this area is needed.

Figure 8.4 presents a tool included in chapter 10 for weighing the extent to which a company can expect to ingrain its vision, values, goals, and culture—the company package—into a new foreign supply chain. The firm should weigh the questions posed to shape the best way to transfer its package.

Figure 8.4
Applying Corporate Goals To A Supply Chain

To the extent possible a company needs to align its company package with supply chain partners and ingrain the package into its supply chain. The following is an approach to test the compatibility of the package with stakeholders and the chain.

Stakeholders and Supply Chain

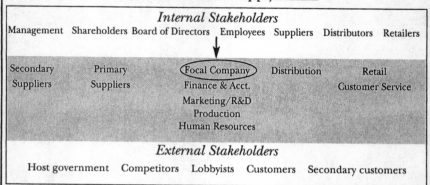

Internal Stakeholders

Management   Shareholders   Board of Directors   Employees   Suppliers   Distributors   Retailers

Secondary Suppliers	Primary Suppliers	Focal Company Finance & Acct. Marketing/R&D Production Human Resources	Distribution	Retail Customer Service

External Stakeholders

Host government   Competitors   Lobbyists   Customers   Secondary customers

Typical Questions to Ask to Apply the Company Package:

- To what extent can supply chain partners share and support the company package?
- To what extent can external stakeholders support the company package?
- How must internal stakeholders interact at each key point or process?
- Who should manage each key activity and process?
- How can the company best use a partner's strengths?
- What partner weaknesses must be corrected?
- What training is required?
- How quickly can empowerment progress?
- How can external stakeholders be neutralized, exploited, or made collaborators?
- How can friendly external stakeholders be involved?
- Where should stakeholders focus best practices efforts?
- How should internal stakeholders (company and supply chain) relate to external stakeholders?
- What performance measures should be applied to various process points and performance activities?

Together the tools in figures 8.3 and 8.4 can help a company to pinpoint where it may experience the greatest difficulty in reorganizing, how much of a problem changes will be, and which changes are essential to make.

CHAPTER 9

FINANCING THE
GLOBAL SUPPLY CHAIN

*In the early 1950s Ernest Hemingway[1] created a character named Santiago
and sent him on a long journey into the Gulf Stream off the coast of Cuba.
While this figment of Hemingway's imagination had caught big fish
before—as much as 1,000 pounds—they were nothing compared to the prize
beast that awaited him.*

*Santiago had the equipment he thought he needed: his skiff, of course,
harpoon and gaff, knives, sardines for bait, food, oars, rope, pencil-thick
lines, and other fishing gear. Now far out to sea, well beyond the sight of
land, the old man sought a great fish. He went about his business deliber-
ately, patiently executing his plan. But the effort took its toll. The fish, bigger than Santiago could have ever imagined, drained the man.*

*"I should have brought the boy," he said, bemoaning the fact that he
lacked the necessary resources to accomplish this project well. So huge was the
fish that it pulled the skiff with the old man aboard farther out to sea. But
after a brilliant performance, despite the calculated risk and the miles from
home, he managed to reel in the huge tuna and attach it to the skiff. Together
they sailed side by side toward a distant shore.*

*The challenge now was to get the great tuna to shore unscathed. The
project had so far proved successful, but it would mean nothing if Santiago
couldn't bring the prize home. He was in distant waters, "far beyond all
snares and traps"— tools that could help him against the dangers of the
open sea.*

*The first obstacle to surface was a mako shark, which took 40 pounds of
the great tuna and the old man's harpoon. Two shovel-nosed sharks followed
and took off with a quarter of the fish. Another two came presently, and
although Santiago beat them off with a club, half the tuna was gone when
they finally fell away.*

*"What can a man do without the necessary weapons?" the old man
moaned.*

[1] Ernest Hemingway, *The Old Man and the Sea* (New York: Charles Scribner's Sons, 1952).

That night a whole pack of sharks sped toward the skiff. Tired and dis-traught, knowing he had been beaten, Santiago pounded the waters with his club in hopes of salvaging something of the once grand prize. But by the time he reached home, he had only an 18-foot carcass " nose to tail" to show for his valiant effort.

"I went too far out and didn't have the right tools to cope with the situ-ation," he complained before he slept and dreamed of lions frolicking on the beach.

Up to now we have discussed strategy and the organization of the supply chain, but the discussion would not be complete without applying the glue to keep all the pieces in their proper place, the blood that keeps the body going. Poor Santiago. He had a plan and, despite a lack of sufficient resources and treading in waters too far from shore, he executed his plan successfully. He caught the fish just like companies earn revenue overseas. Unfortunately, once he had reeled it in, he didn't know how to protect the fish, any more than firms always know how to protect their offshore earnings. Many generate revenue but then fail to safeguard it against such lurking sharks as foreign taxes, government entrapment, and other obstacles, or do not let it grow in the best ways possible.

The thought of financing the chain should conjure up the same objective as strategy itself: minimizing costs and maximizing com-parative advantage to benefit both the company and stakeholders. Financing is integral to the structural discussion in the last chapter: chain configuration, partnerships, and ultimate business arrange-ments that define the links in the chain. While traditionally the domain of the focal company, financing is being spread to other partners in joint ventures, strategic alliances, and other business arrangements abroad. By sharing the cost burden, firms can expand affordably to more international markets.

Cost sharing is critical to today's supply chains, but each com-pany must weigh its own ability to tackle an investment abroad, either alone or with partners. A company must determine which projects with acceptable risk to finance, how to finance them, how best to position funds to maximize profitability and thus how best to use its capital.[2] More specifically, a company should begin its inter-national financial management with a three-pronged, interrelated

---

[2] Shafiq Jadallah, *Multinational Finance*, Chapter 21 – Repositioning Funds (Slide Presentation) (Harlow, Essex, UK) Pearson Education, Inc. 2003.

assessment process:

1. *International Money Management Assessment:* Does the project allow for optimal positioning of funds where they will incur the least cost and earn the greatest return?
2. *Impact Assessment:* How will any new investment impact the firm's cost of capital and capital structure?
3. *Risk Assessment:* Will the project generate a rate of return that will justify the investment?

Collectively, these three steps comprise international financial management. The three steps are interrelated because, to work through them, a firm must know the obstacles it will face in an off-shore investment and the tools it has at hand to counteract those obstacles. You may think that the order of these steps is wrong because the project must be up and running before money management kicks in. While this is true, the potential effectiveness of that money management should be weighed and its risk considered before doing the last two steps. How a firm can position funds optimally will affect its capital budgeting, cost of capital, and capital structure.

Obstacles to International Financial Management

Before exploring the three steps of the assessment process, let's look at possible obstacles to moving money across borders. The include: (a) access to capital; (b) subsidiary stakeholders' demands on equity; (c) host government blockage of funds; (d) tax considerations; (e) transaction risk and costs; and (f) financial requirements for subsidiary operations.

Access to Capital

Can the company raise the necessary capital either from domestic or international markets? Operating internationally allows a company to seek out different sources of funding. For example, raising money in international capital markets is less expensive than raising money domestically because the volume is usually larger and there are fewer country-based interest rates or reserve requirements. The very large multinational corporations with superior credit ratings have access to these markets.

A company should also assess its ability to raise capital in the

country in which it wishes to invest. Is debt financing available there
or elsewhere? If financing is available locally, does it cost less or
more than funds from other sources? If debt financing is cheaper
and accessible in another country, can funds borrowed elsewhere
be used to help finance the new investment in the host country?
What about equity financing locally? What are the credit rating, liquidity, and solvency of the local capital markets?

In evaluating financing options, a company should consider
these questions along with the relative cost of funds from one country to the next. A firm's access to capital will also depend on its international reputation and standing, the risk of its planned investment, and the relationship between local companies and financial
institutions. For example, under the keiretsu system in Japan, companies, especially for international expansion purposes, receive
preferential treatment from the financial institutions with which
they have close relations. Because of these ties, firms can limit their
risk and gain a substantial amount of debt financing while keeping
the use of more expensive equity financing to a minimum. Such
financing obviously favors indigenous companies while making
access to local capital problematic for foreign concerns.

Demands on Revenue by Subsidiary Stakeholders
*What restrictions will local investors put on the movement of funds from a
subsidiary to the parent or other subsidiaries?* Increasingly, as capital markets improve abroad, local shareholders are insisting on greater
returns on their investments. While these growing capital markets
provide increased funding opportunities to foreign firms, they also
add pressure to keep profits in the host country.

Host Government Blockage of Funds:
*What constraints will the host government place on the movement of funds,
either to protect the local economy or to penalize a subsidiary for legal infrac-
tions?* For a variety of reasons, the host government may restrict or
block the amount of funds a subsidiary may remit to the parent
company. For example, the country might be low on foreign
exchange reserves and will not let U.S. dollars leave the country
because the government needs them to pay off its debt. The government may insist that subsidiary earnings be reinvested in the
host country or that only a percentage of profit may be remitted to
the parent or another subsidiary. If local equity financing is used,

shareholders and the government will not want dividends remitted to the parent but will want them distributed there, so as a matter of policy the host government may limit the amount of dividend income that can be repatriated. Or the government can simply apply enough red tape to delay approvals for dividend and royalty remittances.

To reduce costs further, companies may try to buy and sell goods, parts, equipment, and components between subsidiaries in different countries for significantly discounted prices. Low-balling the cost of intrafirm transfers may undercut local import duties and thus such prices are discouraged, if not illegal in many countries. Claiming that the parent company is not dealing in good faith, the government may recalculate these transfer prices to make them market-based, effectively taxing the parent or the subsidiary on the imported goods.

Tax Considerations

What tax liabilities exist in the host country and how can payment of taxes be minimized worldwide? Countries can have very different tax systems and a multinational company needs to deal with these differences, constantly seeking ways to lower its tax liability. In contending with a variety of tax regimes, a firm may encounter double taxation from both home and host countries as well as a plethora of other taxes, including corporate, import, value-added, dividend, and royalty.

In viewing a country from a tax perspective, a company should consider the following:

- Is the corporate tax rate high or low?
- Does the company have high or low import duties? In moving money from one country to the next to pay for goods and services, there is a trade-off between taxes imposed on a subsidiary and import duties. If a country has a high corporate rate, it will probably have low import duties.
- Does the country have quotas on the amount (number of product units or dollar volume) that can be brought into the country. If there are quotas, a company may try to lower its transfer pricing to bring in larger quantities of goods.
- Does the country impose value-added, import license, or other indirect taxes?

- Does the country have a free trade zone where a subsidiary can be located to import, warehouse, or even process goods clear of normal customs duties and procedures? If so, duties can be lessened and foreign sourcing of parts and components facilitated.
- How are dividends, royalties, license fees, corporate overhead, and management fees taxed? Are they taxed at the normal corporate rate? Are there withholding taxes at the corporate or shareholder level through a tax imputation system (see below)?
- Does the host country impose "rules of thin capitalization" (see below) that limit the amount of debt versus equity that a company can use to finance a local subsidiary?

What are *thin capitalization rules and imputation systems?* Under the first, the host government may insist that a foreign subsidiary maintain a certain debt/equity ratio, usually 2:1 or 3:1. If this ratio is exceeded (too much debt capital), the subsidiary is considered thinly capitalized and the debt repayment becomes a dividend and is taxable as an equity payment.

Imputation systems have tax implications for a company's capital structure and cost of capital. If a company distributes its profit to shareholders, say as dividends, the tax responsibility is moved (or *imputed*) to the shareholders. The purpose of tax imputation is to eliminate double taxation at the corporate and shareholder level. Thus the company would not pay tax on distributed earnings, but shareholders would. Under an imputation system, shareholders receive a refund in the form of a *dividend tax credit,* but only on domestic earnings. Foreign-source earnings normally do not qualify because these funds have already been taxed in another country.

Transaction Risk and Costs

How can a multinational company minimize cash flows and exposure to fluctuating currencies and the fees associated with them? When dealing with different currencies, a company incurs foreign exchange risk. There are risks when currencies fluctuate against each other, and then costs to convert from one currency to another. These risks can show up in any transaction (*transaction exposure*) or over the long-term course of normal business operations (*economic exposure*). This risk can also rear its ugly head as translation exposure when multi-national firms have to consolidate their financial statements and must convert or translate foreign-source earnings and expenses into the currency of the parent company.

Business operations are based to the extent possible on the predictability of future cash flows, but if the exchange rate of the currency in the host country fluctuates relative to the currency in the home country, a company must worry about what the magnitude of those fluctuations means for future earnings. It must then address how best to deal with them. For instance, how would a sudden devaluation of one or more foreign currencies impact the company's consolidated balance sheet?

Financial Requirements for Subsidiary Operations

What much funding is needed to operate a subsidiary successfully and what is subsidiary profit target does the parent need to contribute to global operations?

This questions has many implications to a multinational firm. Not only do local shareholders want their due but the subsidiary wants to bask in its profits as well. If the parent or regional headquarters is constantly draining funds from the subsidiary, what incentive does it have to perform better? While contributions to parent and worldwide operations are important, the subsidiary increasingly is called upon to be a good corporate citizen. This imposes a greater financial burden. Likewise, the younger a subsidiary is, the more capital it will require to grow. In designing an overseas investment, financial growth requirements should be accommodated.

Before delving into the three-step financial assessment process, a firm should weigh the range and severity of these obstacles as they pertain to any new cross-border investment. Just as in strategy, once a company has laid out the constraints it will face, it can plan to deal with them as effectively as possible.

International Money Management Assessment

Consider again Hemingway's *Old Man and the Sea*. From a financial perspective, think of Santiago and his skiff as management and the company that has to navigate unknown waters. Think of the fish he caught as a new investment, a project or subsidiary that adds value to the company either by generating sales or reducing costs.

The key to financial success, then, is to ensure that the catch gets safely back to shore, that revenue earned by these investments is retained, safeguarded, and reinvested as well as possible. For this to occur, of course, management needs the right tools.

A firm must begin by determining how much revenue stays at the subsidiary or moves to headquarters or other subsidiaries to satisfy local stakeholders and optimize the use of capital. Figure 9.1 illustrates how funds can be moved internationally and the obstacles they may encounter along the way.

Figure 9.1
Ways And Obstacles For Transferring Funds

Payment to Parent or Other Subsidiary	Possible Obstacle
Profit from Sales unhappy stakeholders	Parent share too large/ Blocked funds Foreign exchange risk Tax considerations
Reimbursement from Cost of Goods	Transfer payments need to be "arms-length," market value
General Overhead Fees	Tax considerations Foreign exchange risk
Technology and Management Fees (license fees, royalties, payments for transferred technology)	Tax considerations Foreign exchange risk
Interest on Debt to Parent/Other Subsidiaries	Tax considerations
Dividend remittances	Tax considerations Blocked funds Local shareholders' demands

Once the means of transferring funds is well understood, a company must decide where to put the funds to keep them safe and productive. In short, the firm needs to best position those funds. To do so, it will likely employ a combination of the following tools: (a) tax instruments; (b) bundling and unbundling of funds; (c) transfer pricing; (d) fronting loans; (e) hedging; and (f) minimizing cash reserves.

Tax Instruments

A company needs to compare the tax regime of the host country with the home country tax structure. Do tax credits or tax deferrals apply? Is there a tax treaty between the two countries? How are dividends and royalties taxed? Do income taxes apply? If the home country corporate tax rate is higher or lower than that of the host country, how will the difference affect cash flows?

Home country tax credits, tax treaties, and tax deferrals help lessen the tax burden. A *tax credit* lets a company subtract the taxes it pays to the home country from the tax it pays to the host country for subsidiary operations. A tax *treaty* between the home and host country is usually an agreement that income will be taxed where it is earned. A tax *deferral* lets a parent company pay tax on foreign-source income when the parent actually receives it, which is not necessarily in the year it is earned.[3]

A company must work out the ramifications of these three tools in deciding how best to treat income generated by subsidiaries. For instance, the company can usually deduct interest expense on debt in both host and home countries, so it follows that to the extent possible the interest on this debt should move from the country with the lower tax rate to the country with the higher rate. Say the host country of Company ABC's subsidiary has a tax rate of 30 percent. ABC's country of domicile has a rate of 40 percent. The subsidiary should transfer interest payments to the parent because the after-tax cost of debt will be lower.

Conversely, if the tax rates are reversed, the parent should give funds to the subsidiary as dividends for investors, which are taxed first in the subsidiary country, where the tax rate is lower. Under a tax treaty between the two countries or as a tax credit, this income can be taxed in the parent country as well but only by the *difference*

---

[3] Charles W.H. Hill, *International Business*, Competing in the Global Marketplace, Postscript: 2000, 3rd ed. (New York: Irwin McGraw-Hill, 2001).

between the rates of both countries. Under a tax deferral, this incremental tax can only be levied if and when the funds return to the parent as dividends.

Because of the variability of these factors, most overseas subsidiaries, whether they are joint ventures, alliances, or Greenfield investments, should probably be debt-financed. Nevertheless, a company needs to consider other factors as well. If debt is used, can it be properly serviced? What are the implications if a subsidiary fails to generate profit? In which country, host or home, will the company be best able to take advantage of a tax-credit loss?

Let's not forget, either, about the thin capitalization rules. Where they apply, parent companies may use preferred stock to help finance subsidiaries because the instrument could be viewed as equity in the market with thin capitalization rules and as debt in the home country without such rules.

A hybrid security, like preferred stock or convertible debt, can be used in the following case as well: Company XYZ capitalizes its subsidiary with a certain amount of preferred stock. The parent company receives a dividend payment on the stock from the subsidiary. Since the stock is seen in the subsidiary's country as a debt instrument, the interest is tax-deductible. Because in the parent's country the payment is seen as a foreign-source dividend, the parent can claim a tax credit for the implied taxes that the subsidiary would have had to pay. If the payment to the parent were considered an interest payment, the parent could not make that claim.[4]

Finally, where there is an imputation system, a company can finance subsidiary operations more through debt than equity and shift foreign taxable income into domestic income to maximize the advantage of the dividend tax credit.

Bundling and Unbundling the Transfer of Funds

Companies may "bundle" funds leaving the country or "unbundle" them into separate cash flows to take advantage of tax effects and to avoid upsetting the host government with excessive repatriation of profit.

Assume that Subsidiary A can repatriate funds to the parent company in the form of dividends or royalty payments or fees. While they are the most popular way to transmit funds from a sub-

---

[4] Roger Conlon and Gina DeConcini, "Choose Your Instruments Carefully," *International Tax Review* (April 2000).

sidiary to the parent, dividend remittances face several obstacles: tax, foreign exchange risk, and whether the subsidiary needs to keep the funds for growth purposes or to distribute to local investors. Royalty payments for the use of technology or management fees for general overhead, research and development, and the like also carry transmittal costs and risks.

But there are differences. Royalties and fees tend to be tax-deductible in the host country whereas taxes normally must be paid before dividends are distributed. Dividends may also incur an income tax, though because they are distributed after host country taxes, the parent can add them back for tax credit purposes. While the parent can apply a tax credit, if host country taxes exceed those of the home country, the parent could suffer a net loss.

David Eiteman[5] gives a good example: A subsidiary earns $10,000 before remitting funds to the parent and before host country taxes. The host country corporate tax rate is 50 percent, the home country's is 34 percent, and both countries allow for a tax credit. After taxes, the subsidiary has $5,000 to send to the parent company. In a bundled situation, the subsidiary lumps royalty fees and dividend income into one remittance of, say, $4,000 to the parent company, leaving $1,000 in the subsidiary for reinvestment. Since taxes have already been paid in the host country, 80 percent of the host country taxes are added back under the tax credit for a total of $8,000, which is then subject to home country tax at 34 percent, or $2,720. However, the tax credit negates this amount because the foreign tax has already been paid, leaving a tax balance due of zero. The parent receives $4,000, the subsidiary contributes a total of $5,000 to the company's worldwide earnings, and total taxes are $5,000, all collected in the host country.

In an *unbundled* situation, the subsidiary sends the parent a royalty of $2,400 and a dividend of $1,600, for a total of $4,000. The host country tax is 50 percent of $10,000 minus the $2,400 tax-deductible royalty. After deducting host country taxes and the $2,400 royalty, $3,800 is left as a possible dividend. The $1,600 represents 42.1 percent of that amount. When the parent company receives the dividend of $1,600, it adds back 42.1 percent of the host country taxes (another $1,600) and is thus taxed on $3,200 at 34 percent, or $1,088. Again, the tax credit cancels this amount since

[5] David K. Eiteman, Arthur I. Stonehill, and Michael H. Moffett, *Multinational Business Finance*, (Reading, MA, et al.) Addison-Wesley Publishing Company, 1992).

the foreign tax already paid exceeds this amount. Consequently, home country tax is eliminated. The royalty, though, is taxed at the full 34 percent, or $816. Thus the parent receives $3,184, the subsidiary contributes $5,384 to company-wide income and the total tax paid (all to the host country) is $4,616.

Figure 9.2 shows how these two examples break out. While some of the factors in the figure are blank, the company should consider them when making the decision to bundle or unbundle remittances. Key considerations are: the need for cash locally; the tax rates of home and host countries; and whether or not royalties and fees are tax-deductible, dividends carry a withholding tax, the host government blocks funds, and a tax treaty exists between the countries.

Figure 9.2
Bundled Versus Unbundled Remittances To Parent

	Bundled	Unbundled
Subsidiary Statement		
Subsidiary pre-tax income	$10,000	$10,000
Less royalties and fees	- - -	$2,400
Taxable income (Host Country - 50%)	$10,000	$ 7,600
Less 50% host country tax	$5,000	$3,800
Available for dividends	$5,000	$3,800
Dividend withholding tax	NA	NA
Dividend to parent	$4,000	$1,600
Reinvested locally	$1,000	$2,200
Parent Statement		
Dividends received	$4,000	$1,600
Add back foreign tax	$4,000	$1,600
Grossed up dividend	$8,000	$3,200
Home country tax (34%)	$2,720	$1,088
Less credit for host country tax	$4,000	$1,600
Home country tax on dividend	- - -	- - -
Royalty received	- - -	$2,400
Home country tax on royalty (34%)	- - -	$816
Royalty after tax	- - -	$1,584
Cash to parent	$4,000	$3,184
Tax to host government	$5,000	$3,800
Tax to home country	- - -	$816
Contribution to worldwide income	$5,000	$5,384

Source: David K. Eiteman, et al, *Multinational Business Finance 6th Ed.*, (New York: Addison-Wesley Company, 1992). Modified by author.

Transfer Pricing

Another tool to counteract tax and blocked funds is the way companies price goods, materials, and components that move among the subsidiaries of a company and the parent company, the intrafirm transfers discussed above. A company or subsidiary will try to set lower prices for goods going to another subsidiary in a country where import duties or value-added taxes are high or based on a percentage of the value of the goods. Conversely, it will try to raise prices for goods when host country taxes are high or currency devaluation seems likely, or when dividends are limited or funds are blocked. The higher prices will help move money out of the country to avoid these restraints or excessive tax liabilities.

Nevertheless, transfer pricing can be a disincentive to a subsidiary when higher-priced transfers lower its profit-making ability. The pricing can also alienate the host country, which in turn can recalculate the price of imported goods to market levels, essentially taxing the parent or subsidiary. For this reason companies are encouraged—or in many markets required—to charge transfer prices that are arms-length or the same as they would charge an unrelated party. Nevertheless, there is ample evidence that companies still indirectly manipulate transfer prices to reduce their worldwide tax liability.[6]

Fronting Loans

A company may also give loans to subsidiaries, using large international banks as go-betweens instead of dealing with the subsidiaries directly. Firms employ this technique because some host governments are more willing to allow foreign subsidiaries to repay loans from international banks than to remit funds to the parent company and may even block such funds.

Charles Hill[7] gives a good example. Subsidiary A in Bermuda, which is a tax haven, deposits $1 million at 8 percent in a London bank for Subsidiary B, which is located in a country that has a 50 percent corporate income tax rate. The bank lends the money to Subsidiary B at 9 percent interest. The net result is:

a) Subsidiary B pays $90,000 interest on the loan and deducts

---

[6] Hill, *op. cit.*, note 3, p. 679, citing D.L. Swenson, "Tax Reforms and Evidence of Transfer Pricing," *National Tax Journal*, March 2001: 7–26.

[7] Hill, *op. cit.*, note 3.

this amount from its taxable income, leaving an effective after-tax cost of borrowing of $45,000.

b) The bank receives $90,000, keeps $10,000 for its services, and pays $80,000 interest on the deposit to Subsidiary A in Bermuda.

c) Subsidiary A receives $80,000 interest on its deposit tax-free.

d) Because Subsidiary B's after-tax cost of borrowing is only $45,000, the parent has moved another $35,000 out of B's host country.

In this case $80,000 in cash has moved from a high-tax country to a tax haven. Had this been a direct loan from Subsidiary A to B, the government of B might have disallowed the deduction of the interest, saying that it was actually a dividend to the parent disguised as an interest payment.

Hedging

Companies use a number of hedging strategies to reduce foreign exchange risk. Hedging balances the risk so as to minimize it: In the game of roulette, if I place a wager that a red number will come up, I can also bet that a black number will be the winner. I have a 49 percent chance that it will be red and a 49 percent chance it will be black. I have minimized my risk by betting on both possibilities. This may appear to be a silly bet, as if I were betting against myself, but companies hedge similarly in order to better predict future cash flows.

A company might hedge by borrowing money in a country where it has made a sale with delivery in, say, six months. Let us say Ford Motor Co. sells $1 million of automobiles to Japan, payment to be made in yen at time of delivery in 180 days. To hedge the exchange risk between the dollar and the yen, Ford borrows $1 million in yen for six months, also payable in yen. When in 180 days the firm receives the yen from the car sale, it uses it to repay the debt. The yen-to-yen exchange eliminates financial exposure. This is a form of natural hedging where a firm hedges its normal business operations.

Alternatively, Ford could sell $1 million of automobiles to Japan, payable in yen in six months, and buy parts from suppliers in that country, also payable in yen in six months. The company can then use the currency received in the sale to pay for the parts.

A variation of natural hedging is the *lead/lag strategy*, where a company can play with payables and receivables. In a *lead* strategy a company tries to collect receivables denominated in a foreign currency early, before that currency weakens, and pay payables in a foreign currency early, before the currency can strengthen in value. In a *lag* strategy, a company tries to do the opposite: It will wait to collect receivables in a foreign currency if the currency is expected to strengthen and wait to pay payables if the currency is predicted to weaken.

A company can also use *contractual* hedging, where it locks in an exchange rate for a currency at a point in the future when the company expects to be paid. Say a U.S. firm buys components from a French supplier with delivery in 120 days and payment in euros at time of delivery. When the two negotiate the sales agreement, the exchange rate (*spot* rate) is $1.25:1. To predict its exchange rate risk in four months, the company can buy a *forward rate contract* from a bank. Essentially, the bank agrees to provide the company with euros for dollars in 120 days at a specified rate, the four-month forward rate. In this way the company knows how many dollars it will need for the future transaction. Forward rate contracts, though, are not available in many currencies that are considered too volatile. Alternatively, then, a company can buy futures contracts or currency swaps, although these are usually reserved for hedging in smaller amounts and can be much riskier. Finally, a firm may find that it needs to negotiate with suppliers and distributors to hedge so that all parties can share the foreign exchange risk.

Minimizing Global Cash Reserves

To avoid excessive currency transfer and other fees, a company tries to reduce its international cash balances. At what point can the company stay sufficiently liquid to have cash when needed and still maximize its return on earnings? The balancing gets particularly tricky when a host country restricts the amount of funds that a subsidiary can send to the parent company or insists that a percentage of the subsidiary's profit be reinvested in the subsidiary. Transfer pricing and fronting loans are in part designed to circumvent some of these problems, but companies also employ the following tools to manage fund flows more effectively:

Multilateral Netting

Parents and subsidiaries, and subsidiaries themselves, engage in many transactions, as both buyers and suppliers. Thus they will have balances due to one another. The practice of netting basically allows the parent and subsidiaries to reduce the number of cash flows needed between the entities. They net the flows and transfer the differences from the indebted entities to those that are owed. For example, during one quarter Subsidiary A owes $75,000 to Subsidiary B for various intrafirm transactions and Subsidiary B owes A $50,000. Rather than each paying for each transaction as they go along, they settle up at the end of the quarter, and Subsidiary A sends the $25,000 net to Subsidiary B.

Now imagine if a number of subsidiaries and the parent company all have transactions with each other. If there were no system to control the payment process, all of these entities would be transferring funds in different currencies constantly. More cash flows generate additional foreign exchange and transfer fees that negatively affect the focal company. What a costly mess that would be!

Alternatively, the company can put some order into the process. Regularly, say once a month or a quarter, subsidiaries and parent settle up. They net their expenses to one another and the indebted entities pay those that are due payment.

Figure 9.3 illustrates the multilateral netting process. For simplicity's sake, the unnetted cash flows are limited to four subsidiaries, although six different flows are possible. Before netting, various subsidiaries owe funds to each other. If all payments were made as indicated in the "before netting" diagram, $3,180,000 would flow among the subsidiaries; the foreign exchange commissions and the transfer fees would equal about 1 percent of that. But if the cash flows are netted, the following occurs:

a) The German subsidiary owes the Brazilian firm, on balance, $100,000.
b) The Mexican owes the German, on balance, $500,000.
c) The Canadian, on balance, owes the Mexican $600,000, and the Brazilian another $100,000.
d) Rather than reimbursing the Mexican subsidiary, the Canadian can cover the Mexican's debt to the German, and

the German's debt to the Brazilian. Thus the Canadian subsidiary sends $400,000 to the German and $200,000 to the
Brazilian.

e) Rather than incurring transaction costs of over $31,000, the
company as a whole pays just $6,000.

Figure 9.3
Cash Flows Before And After
Netting And Currency Conversion: Four Subsidiaries

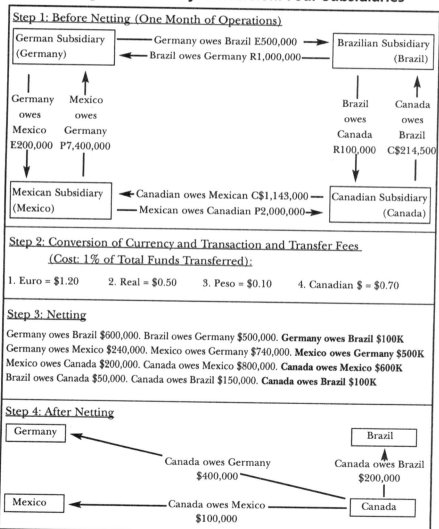

Step 1: Before Netting (One Month of Operations)

German Subsidiary ——— Germany owes Brazil E500,000 ——▶ Brazilian Subsidiary
(Germany)   ◀——— Brazil owes Germany R1,000,000 ——— (Brazil)

Germany Mexico   Brazil   Canada
owes   owes   owes   owes
Mexico   Germany   Canada   Brazil
E200,000 P7,400,000   R100,000 C$214,500

Mexican Subsidiary ◀— Canadian owes Mexican C$1,143,000 — Canadian Subsidiary
(Mexico)   ——— Mexican owes Canadian P2,000,000 ——▶ (Canada)

Step 2: Conversion of Currency and Transaction and Transfer Fees
        (Cost: 1% of Total Funds Transferred):

1. Euro = $1.20   2. Real = $0.50   3. Peso = $0.10   4. Canadian $ = $0.70

Step 3: Netting

Germany owes Brazil $600,000. Brazil owes Germany $500,000. **Germany owes Brazil $100K**
Germany owes Mexico $240,000. Mexico owes Germany $740,000. **Mexico owes Germany $500K**
Mexico owes Canada $200,000. Canada owes Mexico $800,000. **Canada owes Mexico $600K**
Brazil owes Canada $50,000. Canada owes Brazil $150,000. **Canada owes Brazil $100K**

Step 4: After Netting

Germany ◀   Brazil

                   Canada owes Germany   Canada owes Brazil
                   $400,000 $200,000

Mexico ◀———— Canada owes Mexico ———— Canada
                   $100,000

Centralization vs. Decentralization

Financial management covers a wide variety of activities. A company or subsidiary needs money for daily business activities, such as receivables and payables, overhead costs, and business-related fees. It needs funds to pay interest expense and dividends. Overseeing and monitoring all these cash flows requires organization and management. A company has to decide if it is better to let the cash balances stay with individual subsidiaries or be centralized regionally or even globally, depending on the size and complexity of its worldwide structure.

Increasingly, these functions are being centralized for efficiency and cost-control reasons. For example, *cash pooling* is on the rise. Rather than maintaining their own cash reserves, subsidiaries centralize them in one location where a financial manager controls currency exposure, makes payments for the contributing subsidiaries, or deposits the pooled reserves so that they remain liquid; because of their increased volume, the pooled funds earn more interest, and the financial manager can shop for better rates with banks or move some funds into higher-growth opportunities while maintaining needed liquidity at lower rates.

A variation of this is where one subsidiary assumes ownership of invoices and payments for several subsidiaries. This *reinvoicing* center is typically located in a country with low taxes and few income restrictions. The center buys from one subsidiary, taking title to the goods, and then sells to a second subsidiary. Once the center has taken ownership, currency from the sale or purchase can be converted into another currency, netted against other payments, or repriced in accordance with the potential tax benefits of the center's host country.[8] Knowing the financial obstacles of the target or host country and the tools available to it, a firm can determine how it wants to position the funds the investment is expected to generate. Now the company can focus on impact and risk assessment.

Impact Assessment

Generally, a company has three ways to finance an investment: debt, such as bonds; equity, such as retained earnings and common stock; and preferred stock, a hybrid[9] of the first two. Determining the

---

[8] Michael R. Czinkota, Ilkka A. Ronkainen, and Michael H. Moffett, *International Business*, 5th ed. (Fort Worth, TX: Dryden Press, 1999).

[9] Preferred stock is considered a hybrid by some and equity by others. For our purposes, we will refer to it as a hybrid.

weighted cost of each of these sources of financing is a company's overall *cost of capital.* The mix of these sources is its capital structure.

To grow a company requires continuing evaluation of current and potential capital projects and how the company will pay for them in terms of debt and equity financing. In each case the company has to show that it can generate a return on investment that can either service the debt with interest and principal payments or satisfy the expectations of equity shareholders.

Debt in the form of bonds tends to be less expensive than equity because bonds pay a specified yield before any distribution to equity; if a company declares bankruptcy, the debt holders get paid before shareholders. Thus, firms incur debt to help lower their cost of capital. By paying less for debt, a company can actually raise returns to shareholders if return on assets is positive. This is a form of *financial leverage.*

But as a company borrows more and increases its leverage, the cost of debt—and the perceived risk of the company—is likely to rise as well. Thus a company must determine its optimal mix of equity and debt at the corporate level and see how each potential investment will impact that mix. In other words, if a company wants to maintain a corporate debt-to-equity ratio of 30:70 percent, it needs to see how each new project will impact that balance.

We will discuss this dilemma later on. First, let's look at the cost of the various debt and equity instruments:

Debt

For discussion purposes, assume a company's debt takes the form of bonds.[10] A bond is a contract in which a company guarantees to pay an investor a certain amount of interest as well as return the principal, usually denominated in $1,000 increments, at a given time. Say AT&T issues a bond for $1,000 face value at an interest *(coupon)* rate of 7 percent and a maturity date of November 2006. AT&T would have to pay $70 in annual interest payments to the bondholder, besides returning the face value of $1,000 in November 2006.

The *cost* of debt is the amount of interest creditors demand when buying new bonds. A company would figure the cost of a bond as follows: First, it would compute the interest paid during the life

---

[10] A company's current liabilities, which are a form of debt, bear a cost as well, but this "debt" is expensed in the normal accounting process, as is interest on bonds.

of the bond.[11] Second, since the interest on bonds is tax–deductible, the firm would deduct the tax savings from the yield rate. In the AT&T example, if the S corporate tax rate is 40 percent, AT&T would reduce the 7 percent by 40 percent (= 2.8 percent) to reach an effective bond cost of 4.2 percent.

Retained Earnings

These are the earnings that a company does not distribute to the shareholders as cash dividends but keeps to reinvest into the firm. Technically they belong to the shareholders, but the shareholders in effect allow the company to use them to help grow the company. The shareholders entrust these funds to the company. They expect the company to invest them as if the shareholder had actually received them and used them to buy more company stock.

If a company uses retained earnings to help finance a capital investment, it must ensure that the investment will generate a return equal to what the shareholder would have received from the purchase of additional stock. One way to gauge the cost of these earnings is to apply the Capital Asset Pricing Model (CAPM) method discussed below, or to use the bond yield plus risk premium approach, with the firm starting with its long-term interest rate and adding another 5 to 7 percent.[12]

Common Stock

The cost of a company's common stock is the expected return that will attract investors. In other words, what does a stockholder expect to gain when she buys a share of stock? It will be more than the return on a bond because the risk is greater. Stockholders are not guaranteed a return. They have to wait until bondholders and other creditors take their pound of flesh if a company fails.

To compensate for the greater risk, a company has to offer a rate of return that is high enough to get investors to buy the stock. Domestically, companies might determine a surrogate for this cost of equity capital by using the *risk-free* rate, usually the rate guaranteed on a U.S. Treasury bond, and the *market-risk premium*, which is the difference between stock performance as a whole (the market) and the risk-free performance of Treasury bonds, plus the quirki-

---

[11] This does not include the administrative costs of issuing a bond or preferred stock.
[12] Teachmefinance.com, "Cost of Capital," December 2002.

ness of a company's performance as it relates to the entire market, called its beta.[13]

What does this all mean? Start with the risk-free rate, the U.S. Treasury bond rate. The market risk premium normally exceeds the risk-free rate by 7 percent. The beta is a statistical estimate of whether a company's stock is riskier or less risky than the stock market as a whole. Theoretically, a firm with a beta of 1 tracks the movement of the S&P 500 Index.[14] For example, if a company has a beta of 1, it has risk equal to the market or portfolio of companies in a particular industry. If the beta is more than 1, a company is considered riskier than the market as a whole, and if the beta is less than 1, it is considered less risky than the market.

Assume that the high-tech company K-X Corporation has a beta of 0.9. The risk-free rate is 7 percent. The expected rate of return on hi-tech companies is 14 percent. What is the required rate of return (R) for K-X stock? Using the CAPM method, we get:

R(KX) = Risk-free rate + (Beta x Market Premium)
R = 7% + [0.9 x (0.14 – 0.07)]
R = 13.3%

So one estimate of the cost of K-X common stock is 13.3 percent. If this is a new issue of common stock, flotation costs should be added.

Preferred Stock

This financing mechanism is considered a *hybrid* security because it combines characteristics of both common stocks and bonds. It resembles common stock in that it has no fixed maturity date and dividends are not tax-deductible. But, as its name suggests, if a company fails, preferred stock investors receive compensation before common stockholders do. Because of this feature, preferred stock pays a lower return than common stock, but because bondholders are first to get paid when a company is liquidated, preferred stock normally produces a higher yield than bonds.

The cost of preferred stock is figured essentially by dividing the

---

[13] These are the factors used in the Capital Asset Pricing Model (CAPM), a formula used to determine the required rate of return from an investment in common stock.

[14] Anne Farrelly, *Invest Without Stress: What Successful Investors Know* (West Los Angeles, CA: Camden Press, 1996).

stock dividend by the price of the stock.[15] For example, if the annual dividend is $3.00 on preferred stock currently selling in the market at $35, the rate of return would be 8.6 percent. There is no tax adjustment for the company because preferred dividends are not a deductible expense like bond interest.

No matter what financing means it uses, a company must be prepared to provide a return that will compensate an investor for the investment. The amount of that return is based on the amount of risk the investment carries. The higher the risk, the greater the expected payoff.

Every company uses a mix of instruments to pay for capital assets worldwide and to generate the necessary returns to attract investors; this mix is the company's capital structure. Say a company uses common stock to finance 15 percent of new projects. The company would then calculate the cost of common stock (13.3 percent from the example above) and multiply it by 15 percent. It would do the same for each financial instrument and total these percentages to arrive at its *weighted average cost of capital (WACC)*. **The weighted average cost of capital is the average of the after-tax costs of each of the sources used by a company to finance a project. The weights reflect the proportion of total financing raised from each source.** (See figure 9.4.)

Figure 9.4
Calculating The Weighted Average Cost Of Capital

Financing Instrument	After-tax Cost to Firm (%)	Percent of Total Captial Structure	Percent of Total Financing
Bonds	4.2	40	1.7*
Preferred Stock	8.6	15	1.3*
Common Stock	13.3	15	2.0*
Retained Earnings	12	30	3.6
WACC			8.6
* Rounded up from 1.68, 1.29, and 1.995.			

The WACC in this case is 8.6 percent, meaning that a company would have to generate this return on average for every dollar it

---

[15] This does not include the costs of issuing a bond or preferred stock.

employs.

In international investments, though, investors may require a much higher rate of return than for a domestic investment because of country risk, international currency fluctuations, tax differentials between countries, and similar factors. What is an optimal WACC that allows the firm to grow internationally?

An underlying issue in finding the answer to this is whether, as a matter of policy, a company elects to maintain a company-wide capital structure or delegates the choice to its subsidiaries. If the parent has an optimal capital structure, say 30:70 debt to equity, should it allow the new venture to be structured independently or as part of the company?

The answer normally lies in how risky the venture is. A firm should grow its budget in proportion to its optimal capital structure, but as it expands internationally, its incremental cost of capital will eventually rise[16] unless diversification of projects can lower the market risk.

Risk Assessment

For most well-run companies, capital budgeting is the ultimate test for evaluating the validity of cross-border investments. In this process the company uses the analysis it has done to measure potential market success against risk and cost to see whether the venture is likely to generate an appropriate return. On the one hand, the company predicts its future revenue streams based on the projected performance of the investment. On the other, it weighs the returns against the risks of doing the venture and adds them to a risk-free rate of return, which results in a hurdle rate, the rate of return required to make the project viable.

A company then looks at the present value of future revenue streams, say five years out, and discounts them by the hurdle rate. The result lets the company estimate reasonably whether the investment will generate a positive or negative return. If the *net present value (NPV)* flows are positive over time, the investment should be undertaken; if they are negative, the project should be abandoned.[17]

---

[16] Eiteman, et al., *op. cit.*, note 5.
[17] A capital budget can have a positive accounting return, positive net income, but a negative net present value.

Essentially, net present value is:

NPV = Present value of estimated annual cash flows – Initial investment

NPV is based on the understanding that money is worth more today than tomorrow; it is the opposite of compounding. For example, if I have a U.S. dollar, I can spend it, save it, or invest it. Because of inflation, if I save or invest it, the dollar will be worth less in the future unless I can grow the money. If I put the dollar in the bank earning 6 percent interest compounded annually, the dollar will grow at a rate of 6 percent per year. If inflation grows at 2 percent, my real rate of return would be approximately 4 percent per year. But if I stuff the dollar into my mattress, it would actually lose value to inflation.

Thus an investor wants his money to grow at the highest possible rate, but only as far as his risk level will let him venture. If he wants a return greater than 6 percent, he needs to find an investment that will earn him a greater return, but for that greater return he must expect to incur more risk. He has the opportunity to place his money in a low-risk, low-return instrument or a high-risk, high-return investment.

If compounding interest tells us what the future value of today's U.S. dollar will be given a certain rate of return, NPV takes a future cash flow and discounts it back to today's worth, also using a certain rate of return. In capital budgeting a company estimates revenue streams based on the likely performance of an investment or subsidiary and then converts these streams back to present-day dollars using the discount or hurdle rate. That rate should include the company's cost of capital plus an additional factor that reflects the estimated risk of the venture. Again, the greater the risk, the higher the rate. A company uses capital budgeting to determine what it will have to pay to attract debt and equity financing.

The capital budgeting process works as follows:[18]

Step 1: Determine the Initial Investment

A company has to figure how much capital will be needed to make the investment successful. This includes primarily money for facilities, labor, and working capital. The rule of thumb, of course, is "you get what you pay for". A company that tries to cut corners, perhaps by hiring less-qualified personnel and paying them less, or buy-

---

[18] This case is based on one given by Jeff Madura in *International Financial Management* (St. Paul, MN: West Publishing Company, 1995).

ing old equipment when state-of-the-art is critical, is estimating for failure, not success.

Step 2: Determine the Venture's Perspective

Capital budgeting will produce different results depending on how success is measured: by the parent company or a subsidiary. Should the parent let the subsidiary function as an independent profit center? Or should it weigh its value in terms of how it impacts company-wide operations and contributes to overall performance? If a parent company uses high transfer pricing or fronting loans to counteract host country policies and drain the subsidiary of funds, the revenue streams from the subsidiary will appear low to the subsidiary, resulting in negative NPV cash flows for that entity. On the other hand, from the parent's perspective, draining money from the subsidiary may generate strong cash flows for the parent and show positive returns in the capital budget.

Step 3: Estimate Demand

The firm needs to determine likely total demand for each product to be produced by the new venture or find some other way to estimate its annual contribution to the company to arrive at its net value. The company does this by (a) setting a competitive price; (b) allocating overhead (OC) and variable (VC) costs to each unit; and (c) subtracting costs from sales:

(Price x Number of units sold) − [(OC + VC per unit) x Number of units sold)]

This gives the projected net revenue streams for a period, although these revenue streams will probably vary as time goes by and the venture achieves better market penetration.

Step 4: Determine the Life of the Venture or Investment

The company should consider a definite life span for the venture, say four or five years, though of course, many ventures last much longer while some die sooner. The company needs to figure the value of the venture after its projected lifetime, its salvage value. This estimate should be based on the probable success of the venture and the projected risk in the host country at the time of liquidation, an estimate that should be highly conservative.

Step 5: Estimate Host Country Blocked Funds, Tax Structure (Including Depreciation Allowance), Inflation, and Exchange Rate Differentials

Assuming that the capital budgeting process is done from the viewpoint of the parent company, these items must be determined because they affect cash flows to the parent. If the host government is expected to block a percentage of the remitted funds, the company would subtract this from the venture's projected earnings.

As we saw, tax laws of the host country will also negatively affect funds transferred to the parent. Depreciation as a non-cash expense should also be deducted. Finally, the firm should approximate the volatility of the host country currency based on the country's history of inflation, long-term interest rates, and fiscal and monetary stability. Assume, for instance, that a U.S. company plans to invest in Mexico. Over the five-year span of the venture, the Mexican peso may be expected to depreciate 2 percent per year against the dollar.

Step 6: Estimate Home Taxes

The parent company should explore how remitted funds will be treated by its home government. Is there a tax treaty between the countries? Does it eliminate double taxation? Are tax credits or tax deferrals available? What is the home corporate rate and are there withholding requirements? A company should subtract annual tax loss from its projected revenue.

Step 7: Set the Hurdle Rate

The required rate of return for the project or subsidiary will include the company's cost of capital, plus an added percentage for venture risk, including host country risk. The more risk, the higher this additional factor will be. Just as it is important to estimate initial investment and demand well, it is equally important to set an accurate hurdle rate.

Capital Budgeting Example

The Jackson Company manufactures a wide variety of sports gear in the United States. It wants to move into Mexico to penetrate a potentially large market and take advantage of labor and overhead cost efficiencies there. The firm is considering a Greenfield investment or joint venture with a large sports equipment supplier in Guadalajara. To prepare for either scenario, it has collected as much information on Mexico as it can and has asked several people both in and outside the company for advice. The peso dollar exchange rate is 9 to 1. From what they have learned, the firm posits the following:

Initial Investment

To do a Greenfield investment properly, Jackson calculates that it will take $9.5 million. If the investment were a joint venture, the amount could be half as much, but having a partner could adversely affect the company's expected return, lessen its control over the venture, and potentially raise other problems.

Venture Perspective

Jackson wants to look at present value cash flows from its corporate perspective, regardless of whether it does a Greenfield investment or a joint venture.

Demand, Price, and Costs

The company has 10 products, all with approximately the same market projection. The average price of similar Mexican products is $80 or P720, but the firm is confident, because of its higher quality, that it can charge an average of $100 or P900 per product. Even at that 25 percent price differential over local competition, Jackson expects to sell 70,000 units in each of the first two years and 100,000 units for the next two.

Based on these projections, variable costs will be $50(P450) per unit, annual overhead including the parent's contribution will be $280,000 (P2.52 million), and annual rent for the Mexican facility will be $290,000 (P2.61 million).

Venture Life and Salvage Value

The tentative venture life period is four years with a calculated salvage value based on similar project liquidations of $6 million (P54 million). The likely sale price at that time is 85 percent of the initial investment. If the venture succeeds, its value could be much greater, in which case Jackson would probably continue operations.

Blocked Funds, Tax Structure, Depreciation, Inflation, and Expected Exchange Rate

In Mexico the government will not block funds but the subsidiary or joint venture will be taxed at 25 percent with 5 percent with-holding on dividends remitted to Jackson. Mexico will allow all equipment and facilities of the venture to be depreciated at $750,000 (P6.7 million) annually. Despite a rocky decade, the peso has leveled at 9 to 1 to the U.S. dollar and is projected to be relatively stable for the next four years.

Home Country Taxes
The U.S. Government will allow a foreign tax credit on taxes paid in Mexico but the marginal corporate tax rate in the United States is 40 percent. Remittances to the U.S. will be taxed separately at 10 percent. However, since no funds will be blocked, Jackson wants all net cash flows sent to headquarters at the end of each year.

Required Rate of Return
Jackson has calculated a 15 percent hurdle rate.

Based on all these analyses, figure 9.5 shows how the capital budget for this project would look.

Figure 9.5
Jackson's Capital Budget for Its Mexican Project

Item	Year 0	Year 1	Year 2	Year 3	Year 4
1. Demand (Units)		70,000	70,000	100,000	100,000
2. Price (P)		P900	P900	P900	P900
3. Total revenue (U x P)		P63,000,000	P63,000,000	P90,000,000	P90,000,000
4. Total variable cost (U x VC per U)		P31,500,000	P31,500,000	P45,000,000	P45,000,000
5. Overhead		P2,520,000	P2,520,000	P2,520,000	P2,520,000
6. Rent		P2,610,000	P2,610,000	P2,610,000	P2,610,000
7. Depreciation*		P6,750,000	P6,750,000	P6,750,000	P6,750,000
8. Total expenses (4 +5 + 6 + 7)		P43,380,000	P43,380,000	P56,880,000	P56,880,000

Figure 9.5
Jackson's Capital Budget for Its Mexican Project (cont.)

Item	Year 0	Year 1	Year 2	Year 3	Year 4
9. Before-tax earnings (3 – 8)		P19,620,000	P19,620,000	P33,120,000	P33,120,000
10. Host government tax (25% of 9)		P4,905,000	P4,905,000	P8,280,000	P8,280,000
11. After-tax earnings		P14,715,000	P14,715,000	P24,840,000	P24,840,000
12. Net cash flow (11 + 7)		P21,465,000	P21,465,000	P31,590,000	P31,590,000
13. Blocked funds		0	0	0	0
14. Venture remits (100%) to parent		P21,465,000	P21,465,000	P31,590,000	P31,590,000
15. Tax withheld on remittance (5%)		P1,073,250	P1,073,250	P1,579,500	P1,579,500
16. Amount remitted after Mexican taxes		P20,391,750	P20,391,750	P30,010,500	P30,010,500
17. Salvage value					P54,000,000
18. Peso: dollar exchange rate		9-1	9-1	9-1	9-1
20. Pretax cash flows to parent		$2,265,750	$2,265,750	$3,334,500	$9,334,500
21. Cash flows net of additional U.S. tax (10%)		$2,039,175	$2,039,175	$3,001,050	$8,401,050
22. Present value of CFs** at 15%		$1,774,082	$1,541,616	$1,974,691	$4,805,401
23. Initial investment		$9,500,00			
24. Cumulative NPV***		-$7,725,918	-$6,184,302	-$4,209,611	$595,790

Notes to Chart:

* Depreciation is a non cash expense and thus will be added back when funds are remitted to the parent company.

** From Net Present Value tables, the percentages for the four years are Year 1: .870; Year 2: .756; Year 3: .658; and Year 4: .572.

*** Take the initial investment and subtract the present value cash flows (line 22) from it. If the cash flows more than cover the initial investment over the project span of the venture, resulting in a positive cash flow on a present value basis, the venture is viable. If not, the venture is not viable.

In this example the difference between the cumulative discounted cash flows to the parent company and the initial investment is positive, meaning that the venture is acceptable. However, capital budgeting is only as good as the analysis that goes into it. What about the demand projections? Are they optimistic? What if Jackson has overestimated the number of Mexicans that have the discretionary income and are willing to pay more for its sports products? Would they pay $5 more on average but not the projected $20?

How would these projections look if Mexico imposed a 15 percent reinvestment requirement? Or insisted that 20 percent of earnings had to stay in country? What if local shareholders demanded dividends? Or the corporate tax rate were higher than 25 percent? These are some of the reasons why factors discussed earlier in this chapter and the tools to mitigate them should be considered before doing the capital budget.

Large companies more than small ones tend to use NPV or internal rate of return to calculate their capital budgets. To adjust for risk, both large and small firms also tend to raise the hurdle rate rather than change projected cash flows.[19] Both of these points suggest that, especially for smaller firms, estimating cash flows and hurdle rates is not very precise. Obviously, the accuracy of this process depends on the rigor of the analysis that precedes it. Certainly, if performance estimates are overstated and the hurdle rate is understated, actual cash flows could fall well short of projections.

Because the capital budgeting process should take into account all significant perceived risk and strategic analysis, the process,

---

[19] S. Block, "Capital Budgeting Techniques Used by Small Business Firms in the 1990's," *Engineering Economist*, 42 (4) (1997): 289 – 301.

though quantitative, needs qualitative input from experts both in the host country and inside the parent company.

To better grasp all this, chapter 10 contains a chart to test cross-border investment flexibility. This matrix lists the obstacles, asks if any of the tools can be applied to them, and then lets the company give each obstacle a numerical weight for risk of "high," 5; "medium," 3; or "low," 1. To complete the chart, a company needs information about the targeted host country as it relates to each obstacle. If the company cannot complete the assessment, it needs to do more homework. Following the matrix is a brief description of the financial tools that may be applied to minimize the impact of obstacles.

To simplify the financial discussion, we have dealt with a parent company and its wholly-owned subsidiary, which implies that the parent has sole control over all operations. In a joint venture or strategic alliance, with one or more partners from other countries trying to form a seamless supply chain, how effectively would all the financial tools work? Quite well if all the financial implications can be harnessed early on and made part of negotiations. They matter as much as the alignment of partners' company packages; in fact, financial strategy should be part of the combined supply chain package.

In the final chapter we bring together all of the pieces we've discussed since chapter 4. Using the framework provided, you can work logically through the concepts and analyses that are critical to preparing well for international business through investment. Happy planning.

CHAPTER 10

A FRAMEWORK FOR DEVELOPING INTERNATIONAL BUSINESS STRATEGY

"Have you read Taft's new book?" said Betsy Matson, VP International for Dubi Sciences.

"What does that have to do with anything?" asked Larry Kane, president and CEO of the company. "Besides, you know I don't have time to read."

Kane's management team sat round the large mahogany table in the company's boardroom, discussing how best to move the company forward.

"Well, he talks about just the things we're tossing around now," Matson went on. "Going from exporter to a multinational company is a big step, and, frankly, we need help."

"I agree," concurred Mary Williams, CFO. "I'm not sure we have the funds to begin investing in our five best markets, or can get them. The risk of these new ventures is going to hurt our WACC and attracting investors in this down economy is going to be rough."

"We still have enough domestic capacity to feed most of our overseas markets," Bill Riley, chief production manager, said. "Why not just try to open in one place instead of five?"

"Because the competition is on the move," noted Harry Nichols, right hand aide to Kane. "Jerome Ind—"

"Jerome Industries has far more products than we do," Jim Sloan, VP domestic, interjected. "They have almost 50 percent of the market in our bread-and-butter product areas. And their volume lets them produce for far less than we can. That's why we're a niche, a special-customer player."

"Maybe we could piggyback onto their expansion," suggested Judd Wilson from Planning. "Maybe we can leverage our customized products with their mass-produced ones. After all, going it alone will cost us big bucks."

"Not to mention the risks," Williams said.

The group turned to Larry Kane.

"Perhaps we should read Taft's book," he said.

Companies have different approaches to global business strategy. Some use computer-generated models and algorithms that involve qualitative and quantitative inputs; others just take a finger-in-the–air approach to see which way the wind is blowing.

The framework presented here is geared to help representatives in both types of companies—and those in between—to grasp the concepts and steps to sound strategy. The material discussed in chapters 4 to 9 is presented here in a series of charts to help you lay out development in a workable, logical fashion. The seventeen charts cover the following areas:

- Target Country Assessment: The Country Profile
- Competitive Positioning
- C 1: Company Commitment
- C 2: Competitiveness
    - Supply Chain – Supply Side Analysis
    - Supply Chain – Demand Side Analysis
- C 3: Cash Flow
    - Capital Access/Availability and Global Funds Management
    - Risk Assessment
- C 4: Capacity
    - General
    - The Tolerance Index
    - Company Package Compatibility
- Competitive Advantage Analysis
- Strategy Testing
- Strategy Framework: Vision, Values, Mission, Goals, and Objectives

In completing these charts try to be as inclusive as possible, gathering input from people both in and outside the company and target markets.

Chart 1
Target Country Assessment

This chart is based on the information discussed in chapter 4, which should be used to select new markets. It includes country risk factors as well as population, political, infrastructure, economic, and financial aspects of a market. Use this chart with the target assessment methodology described in chapter 4 and summarize your findings in Chart 3. (All the information you need is available in the World Bank's annual *World Development Indicators*.)

Country Profile

1. Population/Market Size

	Size	Fertility Rate	Mortality Rate	Under-Nourishment	Degree x Weight = VAL (1,3,5) (1,3,5)
Population Index					

Age Composition		0 - 14	Years 15 - 64	65+	Degree x Weight = VAL (1,3,5) (1,3,5)

	Popu-lation (M)	GDP/ capita	1st 20%	2nd 20%	% of Income per 20 Percentile 3rd 20%	4th 20%	5th 20%	Degree x Weight =VAL (1,3,5) (1,3,5)
Income Distribution								

Country Profile (cont.)

1. Population/Market Size (cont.)

					Degree x Weight = VAL (1,3,5) (1,3,5)
Education Level	Primary	Secondary	Tertiary		Degree x Weight = VAL (1,3,5) (1,3,5)
Employment	Unemployment rate	Skilled labor Sci/Eng/Tech	% in Ind.	Value Added	Degree x Weight = VAL (1,2,3) (1,2,3)

2. Political

Stability	Leader entrenched	Nationalization likelihood	Bureaucratic red tape	War	Degree x Weight = VAL (1,3,5) (1,3,5)
Law/Order	Law enforced	Judiciary strength	Int'l arbitration	IP protection	Degree x Weight = VAL (1,3,5) (1,3,5)

3. Infrastructure Development

Information Technology	News papers	TV/Radio	PC's	Internet	Tech Expertise	Degree x Weight = VAL (1,3,5) (1,3,5)

Country Profile (cont.)

3. Infrastructure Development (cont.)

Power and Communication

Retail Est. per 1000	Energy per 1000	Internet per 1000	Phone per 1000	Degree x Weight = VAL (1,3,5) (1,3,5)

Transportation

Roads	Rail	Seaports	Airports	Degree x Weight = VAL (1,3,5) (1,3,5)

Privatization

Telecommunications	Water Sanitation	Energy	Transport	Degree x Weight = VAL (1,3,.5)

4. Economy

GDP/Industry

Industry by GDP					Degree x Weight = VAL (1,3,5) (1,3,5)
Food/ Bev	Textiles/ Apparel	Machinery/ Transp	Chemicals	Other	

Balance of Payments

Trade Export/Import	Investment Capital Flows Abroad/Home	Change in Exchange Rate	Foreign Cash Reserves	Degree x Weight = VAL (1,3,5) (1,3,5)

Country Profile (cont.)

4. Economy (cont.)

				Degree x Weight = VAL (1,3,5) (1,3,5)
External Debt	Debt Classification (Lo/Mod/Hi)	% of GNI	% of Exports	% of Total Debt Short-term
Foreign Direct Investment	Amount	Risk Ratings S&P Others	Gov't Restrictions	Aid to GDP
Business Environment	Entry Regulations	Contract Enforcement	Insolvency Time/Cost to Resolve	
Tax Policies	Tax % of GDP	Exp Duties (% of taxes)	Imp Duties (% of taxes)	Tax Rate Ind/Corp
Prices/ Exchange Rate	Real Int. Rates (IR – Inf)	Consumer Price Index	Real Exchange Rate	Exchange Rate Change

Country Profile (cont.)

5. Financial Environment

			Degree x Weight = VAL
			(1,3,5) (1,3,5)
Stock Market	Market Capitalization	Number of Firms Listed	
Banks	% of Domestic Credit Provided	Liquidity	Profit	Risk Premium	Degree x Weight = VAL (1,3,5) (1,3,5)

6. Market Receptivity

			Degree x Weight = VAL
			(1,3,5) (1,3,5)
Trade Relationship	Imports from Target Country	Exports to Target Country	% Change (3 years)	

Chart 2
Competitive Positioning

This chart explores the company's standing within the industry and among its main competitors in order to establish a good analytical base from which to work further.

	Yes				No
	1	2	3	4	5
Industry Status and Trends					
Fragmented					
Stagnated					
Mature					
Mobile					
Innovative					
Saturated domestically					
New markets available					
Growth by merger/acquisition					
Fast-paced/changing					
Global industry liberalization					
Standardization					
Customization					

	Percent of Total Budget							
	0	5	10	20	30	40	50	60
Industry Cost Structure								
Production								
Marketing								
Support functions								
Wholesale markup								
Retail markup								

	Company	Competitors
Company Type		
New and aggressive		
New and untested		
New and mobile		
New and innovative		
Critical mass		
Small and flexible		
Vertical producer		
Horizontal producer		
Large and inflexible		
Large and flexible		
Low-cost producer		
Trendsetter		
Follower		
Niche player		
Preemptive striker		
Established monolith		
Customizer		
Standardizer		
Perfect and expand type		

Chart 3
Summarized Market Competitive Assessment

This chart is designed to summarize the first two. It looks at the key factors regarding market and competition and allows the firm to view them in terms of strength (opportunity) or weakness (threat), timing of taking action, and decision to proceed or not, and when.

Market/ Industry Grouping	Opportunity (+2)	Threat (-2)	Timing (+2, 0, -2)	Go/No Go (4 go now) (2 go later) (0 move on) (-4 no go)
Target Market Population factors Political factors Infrastructure factors Economic factors Financial factors Overall risk				
Competition Industry status/trends Cost structure Company type			.	

Chart 4
C 1: Commitment

This chart attempts to compare the leadership qualities of a company with those of competitors. Put a (+) for factors where the company excels and a (−) where the competition does. Even if the truth hurts, here is where a firm should confront it most.

	Company +	Competition −

Motivation
  - Lead competition
  - Follow competition
  - Increase market share
  - Company restructuring
  - Gain broader reputation
  - Access cheaper resources
  - Improve supply chain		

Leadership
  - Structured policies and strategy framework
  - Risk level
  - Payback period
  - Vision
  - Credibility/persistence
  - Communication
  - Inclusive management		

Chart 5
C 2: Competitiveness

Supply Chain – Supply Side Analysis

This chart allows a company to consider aspects of the supply side of the supply chain. It starts by helping a firm determine what it wants to achieve in the supply chain and then leads into decision areas. It also lets a company look at what it has or needs to succeed against key competitors and evaluate the factors using the 5 Vs (volume, visibility, variety, value, and velocity). Each factor should be evaluated to see how it affects the supply chain, both individually and together. Volume refers to the amount of product that moves through the chain. Variety is differences in product choices. Visibility refers to how far a firm can see across the chain. Value stands for profit, the difference between costs and revenue. Velocity refers to the time it takes to move product from supply to customer. Once a company has determined what it has and needs and examines impact from a 5V perspective, it can compare its capability to that of the competition. While it may not appear so, most of the aspects of competitiveness on both the supply and demand sides of the supply chain pertain to services as well as products.

	Company						Competitor
	Has Needs	V1	V2	V3	V4	V5	(+ -)
Company/Product Type Good innovation/supply chains Everyday products, sharp competition, supply chain innovation Superior product, poor supply chain Ordinary products/inadequate supply chains							
Location Decision Area # of facilities Configuration of facilities Facility type Transportation Transit time Environmental costs Time cost							

Chart 5
C 2: Competitiveness (cont.)

	Company						Competitor
	Has Needs	V1	V2	V3	V4	V5	(+ -)
Production Decision Area							
Standardization							
Customization							
Make and sell system							
Sense and respond system							
– Agile: Flexible manufacturing system							
– Lean: efficient manufacturing system							
Rapid prototyping, CAD/CAM, etc.							
Intelligent system design							
Communication capabilities							
Continuous improvement							
Process coordination							
Equipment usage							
Absenteeism							
Plant utilization							
Inventory efficiency							
Time							
Cost							
Logistics Decision Area							
Ordering/payment process							
Scheduling							
Absenteeism							
Performance							
Inventory-carrying costs							
Processes (efficiency/number)							
– Raw							
– Semi-finished							
– Finished							
Information flow							
Time							
Cost							
Suppliers Decision Area							
Vertical integration							
Many suppliers							
Specialized suppliers							
Strategic alliances (1)							

(1) See Chart 6: Qualifying Strategic Partners – Supply Side

Chart 6
Qualifying Strategic Partners – Supply Side

	Excellent			Poor		Total Score
	1	2	3	4	5	
Supplier						
Quality standards						
Capacity						
Fill rate/delivery record						
Return capability						
Service reliability						
Value added:						
– Innovative						
– Customer-driven						
– Responsive						
– Timely						
– Technological						
– Informational						
Profitability						
Growth prospects						
Company-loyal						
Competitor interaction						
Accessible, easy to work with						
Provide JIT:						
– Volume too much						
– Volume too little						
– Volume just right						
Conditions in supplier's home country						
Communications capability						
Supply Chain Effect						
Smoothness of process						
Level of management required						
Level of trust required						
Impact on operations						
Impact on quality, product and service						
General						
Internal cost						
Outsource cost						
Overall cost-effectiveness						

Chart 7
C 2: Competitiveness

Supply Chain – Demand Side Analysis

This chart is a continuation of the supply chain analysis. This one allows a company to determine what it has and what it needs in the customer channel and compare its capabilities with those of the competition, starting with target market type and buyer capacity. This profile is a basis for creating an appropriate marketing mix and identifying competitive advantages in the customer channel or demand side of the supply chain.

	Few or Strong			Many or Poor	
	1	2	3	4	5
Market Type					
Underserved					
Local competition					
International competitors					
Entrenched international and domestic competitors					
Niche possibilities					
Partner(s) required/preferable					
Buyer Capacity					
Condition of local supply chain					
Company reputation					
Product universally accepted					
Market conditions					
Disposable income:					
- Widespread – middle class					
- Top 5 – 10 percent					
Market segment well defined					
Cultural sensitivity: few – many differences					
Consumer tastes: few – many differences					
Competition:					
- Domestic					
- Foreign					
Constraints on product use: few? many?					
Regionally accessible					

Chart 7
C 2: Competitiveness (cont.)

	Company (+)	Competitor (-)
Product		
Unique features		
Additional features		
Everyday item		
User friendly:		
Instructions		
Heavy, cumbersome		
Easy to use		
Difficult to learn		
Saves time		
Multiple uses		
Electrical compatibility		
Comfort/styling/colors		
Service friendly:		
Customer service retail		
Availability		
Selection		
Accessibility		
Packaging		
Brand recognition		
Warranties/Returns		
After-sales service		

	Elastic		Inelastic
	1	2	3
Price			
Price in local market			

	Percent of Total Price	Company Price	Competitor Price
Domestic cost			
Domestic shipping			
Export documentation			
Channel member markups			
Input from agents/distributors			
Competitor prices as benchmark			
Cost of local marketing			
Company's competitive advantage			

Chart 7
C 2: Competitiveness (cont.)

Price difference justified?	Yes Not Needed Low/ Few/little	Needed/ Not possible OR	No Needed/ Possible High/ Many/much
	1	2	3
Promotion			
Internet use			
Establish credibility and reputation			
Establish brand			
Promote and position product			
Degree of leveraging:			
Strong local figures			
Institutional customers			
Local established competitors			
International competitors			
Degree of customer interaction			
Access to:			
Television			
Radio			
Newspapers			
Billboards			
Marketplace			
Word of mouth			
Place			
<u>Movement: manufacturer to customer</u>			
Infrastructure-friendly			
Number of distributors in channel			
Number of distribution centers needed			
Number of retailers			
How scattered are retail establishments			
Channel member compatibility with manufacturer			
Channel corruption			
Possible incentives for distributors			
Possible channel compression			
Channel cost			
Channel time			
Ownership of goods transfer difficulty			

Chart 7
C 2: Competitiveness (cont.)

| | Not Needed | Needed/ Not possible OR | Needed/ Possible |
	Low/ Few/little		High/ Many/much
	1	2	3
<u>Transportation and storage</u>			
Product storage requirements:			
- Climate control			
- Refrigeration			
- Other			
Inventory capacity			
Country conditions restrictions			
- Governmental			
- Infrastructure			
- Geographic			
<u>Customer Interface</u>			
Buyer expectation at point of purchase			
Retail ability to provide service			
Incentive possibilities for retailers			
Competitor noise at point of purchase			
<u>After-Sales Service</u>			
Ability to provide it			
Returns needed			
Warranties needed			
Time involved in returns			
Supply chain member – customer communication required			

Chart 8
C 2: Competitiveness

Summarized Supply Chain Assessment

Like Chart 3, this one summarizes findings from the previous two. It allows the firm to view key factors regarding market and competition, and in terms of strength (opportunity) or weakness (threat), timing of action, and decisions to proceed or not, and when. As in Chart 3, a company is encouraged to specify key findings under the more generic ones listed below.

	Opportunity (+2)	Threat (-2)	Timing (+2, 0, -2)	Go/No Go (4 go now) (2 go later) (0 move on) (-4 no go)
Company/Capacity				
<u>Supply Side</u>				
Location decision area				
Production decision area				
Logistics decision area				
Suppliers decision area				
Buyer Capacity				
<u>Demand Side</u>				
Product				
Price				
Promotion				
Place				
— Manufacturer to customer — Transportation and storage — Customer interface — After-sales service				

Chart 9
C 3: Cash Flow

Capital Access/Availability and Global Funds Management

This chart allows a company to evaluate its ability to attract the necessary capital and isolate financial issues in target markets to determine how they will impact not only operations there, but worldwide. The financial obstacles covered in chapter 9 are included, followed by a list of tools that can be applied to them.

	Strong			Weak
Capital Access/Availability				
Credit rating				
Financial ratios				
Access to capital				
Market share				

	Risk Level			How obstacle
	High	Medium	Low	can be mitigated
Global Funds Management				
Taxes: Host Country				
Corporate tax rate				
- High				
- Low				
Import duties				
- High				
- Low				
Quotas				
Import license fees				
Free trade zone				
Thin capitalization				
Imputation system				
Interest tax deductible				
Taxes on:				
- Dividends				
- License fees				
- Management fees				
- Royalties				
- Retained earnings				
- Distributed earnings				
- Withholding tax on remitted dividends				
Depreciation allowances				

Chart 9
C 3: Cash Flow (cont.)

	Risk Level			How obstacle can be mitigated
	High	Medium	Low	
Host government incentives				
Taxes: Home Country				
Tax treaty with host government				
Corporate tax rate				
- High				
- Low				
Imputation system				
Interest tax deductible				
Taxes on:				
- Dividends				
- Royalties				
- License fees				
- Retained earnings				
- Distributed earnings				
- Shareholder withholding tax				
- Corporate withholding tax				
- Tax credit allowances				
- Tax deferral allowances				
Blocked Funds				
Poor currency exchange				
Reinvestment requirements				
Government approvals needed				
Limits on transfers of foreign exchange				
Limits on transfer of funds (royalties, dividends)				
Local dividends required				
Poor convertibility of local currency				
Foreign Exchange Costs				
High conversion fees				
High currency volatility				
Currency depreciation expected				
Currency appreciation expected				

Chart 9
C 3: Cash Flow (cont.)

	Risk Level			How obstacle can be mitigated
	High	Medium	Low	
Financial Risk				
Financial markets in target country:				
- Rating				
- Liquidity				
- Solvency				
Securization of payments and transfers				
Availability/accessibility of local debt financing				
Availability/accessibility of local equity financing				
Subsidiary Risk				
Local shareholders required				
Debt financing needs				
Liquidity needs				
Earnings power				
Local labor pool				
- Skilled				
- Nonskilled				
- Local management				
Parent ownership restrictions				
Land ownership restrictions				

To determine whether or not a tool may apply to an issue, the following shows generally how the tools are used:

Tools	*Application*
Transfer funds bundling/ unbundling	Tax savings; avoids excessive exodus of funds from host country; can move blocked funds; exposes financial breakdown to competitor
Transfer pricing	Tax savings; transfers funds to countries with less risk or lower taxes; can move blocked funds but this may cause problems in host country
Fronting loans	Tax savings; moves blocked funds or money from high-tax to low-tax country; parent shielded by international bank intermedi-

Continuation

Tool	Application
	ary; host government may be more inclined to let subsidiary pay bank to maintain good credit than to pay parent company
Hedging	Avoids foreign exchange risk
- Natural	Hedging through normal business operations: sell to one party, payable in its local currency, and buy from another, payable in the same currency; payment on both is due at the same time
- Contractual	Forward rate or futures contract that locks the company into a certain rate in the future; comes with a cost
- Negotiated	Foreign exchange risk shared with partners (e.g. importers, distributors, suppliers, customers)
- Leading/lagging	Avoids foreign exchange risk; allows company to time collections and payments to exploit the strengthening and weakening of the host country currency; can move blocked funds
Multilateral netting	Minimizes cash flows and transfer fee expenses; can move funds to safer, low-tax countries
Centralized depositories/ cash pooling/reinvoicing center	Positions funds in high-yield, less risky environment where return on the funds can be maximized and operating cash balances for each subsidiary minimized
Local borrowing	Can borrow money cheaply; avoids foreign exchange risk; may also be used to help finance projects/investments in countries where financing is more costly
Unrelated exports (e.g. R&D facility)	Used for blocked funds
Special dispensation	Frees blocked funds

Chart 10
C 3: Cash Flow

Capital Budget Format

This is a net present value method for capital budgeting. If the NPV flows are positive over time, the investment should be undertaken; if they are negative, it should not. Note, though, that a company can have a positive accounting return (positive net income) but a negative capital budget return (a negative NPV).

Item	Year 0	Year 1	Year 2	Year 3	Year 4
1. Demand (Units)					
2. Price					
3. Total revenue (U x P)					
4. Total variable cost per unit					
5. Allocated overhead					
6. Rent					
7. Depreciation					
8. Total expenses (4 + 5 + 6 + 7)					
9. Before-tax earnings (3 − 9)					
10. Host government tax					
11. After-tax earnings					
12. Net cash flow (11 + 7)					
13. Blocked funds					
14. Remits to parent (%)					
15. Tax on remittance withheld					
16. Actual remittance after taxes					
17. Salvage value					
18. Foreign exchange rate					
19. Cash flows to parent					
20. Present value of cash flows					
21. Initial investment					
22. Cumulative NPV					

Chart 11
C 4: Capacity

Structural

This chart helps a company compare its own structural strengths and weaknesses with those of the competition. For factors where the company excels, put a (+). Where the competition excels, put a (–).

Capacity Category	Company +	Competitor –
Resources – Home Organization/Management Flexibility Domestic strategy International strategy Domestic plus Multiproduct domestic strategy Global strategy Transnational strategy Specialized Geographic Functional Customer Project Hybrid Matrix Open/flat/communicative organization Bureaucratic Centralized decision-making Decentralized decision-making Best practices Core competence-focused Open-minded management Agile/demand-driven		
Resources – Target Market Local management talent available Local skilled labor available Local labor cost Training needed One product/region focus More than one product/region focus Supports other subsidiaries Full service facility Better access to production factors		

Chart 12
C 4: Capacity

The Tolerance Index

This chart helps a company measure (a) its structural agility and flexibility; (b) organizational strengths and weaknesses in light of a new strategy; (c) its symbiosis or compatibility with proposed new investments and supply chains; (d) management and labor requirements; and (e) the degree to which the firm needs and can reasonably take on modern organizational features. The lower the score, the more difficult necessary changes will be.

Category	MC-CNC	NC-CNC	NC-CC	MC-CC	NCN	SCORE
	(1)	(2)	(3)	(4)	(5)	
Company characteristics						
Structure/ Strategy alignment needs						
Company/Investment symbiosis						
New organizational features compatibility						
Manpower requirements						

MC-CNC: The company must change but in the current situation, change is impossible.

NC-CNC: The company needs to change but it is not imperative that it do so, and the price for doing so would be significant.

NC-CC: The company needs to change but it is not yet imperative to do so.

MC-CC: The company must and can change

NCN: No change in this area is needed.

Chart 13
C 4: Capacity

Applying Corporate Goals to a Supply Chain

A companion to chart 12, this one helps a company weigh the extent to which it can expect to ingrain its company package into a new foreign supply chain. The questions help to isolate areas that may prove most problematic.

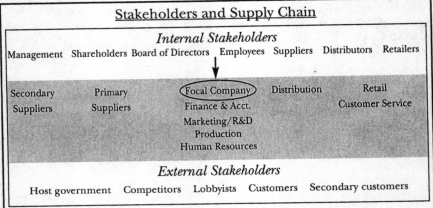

Stakeholders and Supply Chain

Internal Stakeholders

Management Shareholders Board of Directors Employees Suppliers Distributors Retailers

| Secondary Suppliers | Primary Suppliers | Focal Company
Finance & Acct.
Marketing/R&D
Production
Human Resources | Distribution | Retail
Customer Service |

External Stakeholders

Host government   Competitors   Lobbyists   Customers   Secondary customers

Typical Questions to Ask to Apply the Company Package:

- To what extent can supply chain partners share and support the company package?
- To what extent can external stakeholders support the company package?
- How must internal stakeholders interact at each key point or process?
- Who should manage each key activity and process?
- How can the company best use a partner's strengths?
- What partner weaknesses must be corrected?
- What training is required?
- How quickly can empowerment progress?
- How can external stakeholders be neutralized, exploited, or made collaborators?
- How can friendly external stakeholders be involved?
- Where should stakeholders focus best practices efforts?
- How should internal stakeholders (company and supply chain) relate to external stakeholders?
- What performance measures should be applied to various process points and performance activities?

Chart 14
Competitive Advantage Analysis: First Chart

This chart lets a company look at its strengths and weaknesses against those of the competition in each of the areas previously analyzed. It also helps to identify areas where a firm can likely develop competitive advantages. For each subheading, list a key advantage and disadvantage to work on. Discuss all possible advantages and prioritize them in terms of their value and achievability. Finally, summarize the findings in Chart 15.

	Company +	Competitor -
<u>1. Target Market Assessment</u> Market advantage(s): _____ _____ _____ Market disadvantage(s): _____ _____ _____		
<u>2. Industry/Competitor Positioning</u> *Industry Status and Trends* Advantage: _____ _____ _____ Disadvantage: _____ _____ _____ *Company Type* Advantage: _____ _____ _____ Disadvantage: _____ _____ _____		

Chart 14
Competitive Advantage Analysis: First Chart (cont.)

	Company +	Competitor -
C1: Commitment Advantage: _____ _____ _____ Disadvantage: _____ _____ _____		
C2: Competitiveness **Supply Chain – Supply Side** *Location Decision Area* Advantage: _____ _____ _____ Disadvantage: _____ _____ _____ *Production Decision Area* Advantage: _____ _____ Disadvantage: _____ _____ _____ *Logistics Decision Area* Advantage: _____ _____ _____ Disadvantage: _____ _____ _____		

Chart 14
Competitive Advantage Analysis: First Chart (cont.)

	Company +	Competitor -
Supplier Decision Area		
Advantage: ———————————		
Disadvantage: —————————		
<u>Supply Chain – Demand Side</u>		
Market Elasticity/Type		
Advantage: ————————		
Disadvantage: ———————		
Product		
Advantage: ————————		
Disadvantage: ———————		
Price		
Advantage: ————————		
Disadvantage: ———————		

Chart 14
Competitive Advantage Analysis: First Chart (cont.)

	Company +	Competitor −
Promotion Advantage: _____ _____ Disadvantage: _____ _____ *Place* Advantage: _____ _____ Disadvantage: _____ _____		
C3: Cash Flow Capital Access/Availability Advantage: _____ _____ Disadvantage: _____ _____		
Global Funds Management *Taxes: Host Country* Advantage: _____ _____ Disadvantage: _____ _____		

Chart 14
Competitive Advantage Analysis: First Chart (cont.)

	Company +	Competitor −
Taxes: Home Country Advantage: _____ _____ _____ Disadvantage: _____ _____ _____ *Blocked Funds* Advantage: _____ _____ _____ Disadvantage: _____ _____ _____ *Financial Risk* Advantage: _____ _____ _____ Disadvantage: _____ _____ _____ *Subsidiary Risk* Advantage: _____ _____ _____ Disadvantage: _____ _____ _____		

Chart 14
Competitive Advantage Analysis: First Chart (cont.)

	Company +	Competitor -
C4: Capacity *Structural* Advantage: _____ _____ Disadvantage: _____ _____ *Tolerance Index* Advantage: _____ _____ Disadvantage: _____ _____ *Company Package Compatibility* Advantage: _____ _____ Disadvantage: _____ _____		

Chart 15
Competitive Analysis: Second Chart

This chart lets the firm summarize the findings in Chart 14. Notice there are fewer categories. This is done purposely to force a company to pinpoint its strengths and weaknesses so that it can focus on the few that are most important in designing its strategy and company package. Compare each item against competitors by assigning either a +2 to favor the company, a –2 to favor the competition, or 0 to indicate a draw. Multiply each number by a weight of relative importance (1, 3, or 5). The resulting number or product will be the competitive number for that item. The goal is to maximize strengths and minimize weaknesses against those of the competition.

Proposed Item to change	Company + 2	Competitor -2	Draw 0	Weight 1, 3, 5	Competitive Number
Target country					
Industry Positioning					
Commitment					
Competitiveness					
Supply side					
Demand side					
Cash flow					
Capital access/ availability					
Global funds					
Capital budget					
Capacity					
Structural					
Tolerance					
Compatibility					

Chart 16
Evaluating Strategies

Once strengths and weaknesses have been identified, they can be tested against various strategies. This chart provides a few strategies and shows how a company should test them. As discussed in chapter 7, companies can use computer-simulated "what-if" scenarios and possible outcomes. They should then try to anticipate possible competitor responses to the firm's strategy, given its competitive advantages.

Strategy	Scenario	Company Strength	Competitor Response
Downsize/core competency only			
Enter untapped markets or market segments to establish niches abroad			
Customize while giants are consolidating/ standardizing			
Manufacture under private label for high-end boutique establishments; incur minimal marketing costs			
License for private label; license fees and revenue for R&D – lead tech curve			

Chart 17
The Company Package

The company is now ready to "back into" its company package. This chart sets up the package in the order it should be organized.

Vision

Values

Mission Statement

Goals	Objectives
1.	
2.	
3.	

APPENDIX 1

QUESTIONNAIRE FOR ASSESSING A COMPANY'S EXPORT READINESS

The following questionnaire can help a company evaluate its ability to do international business using the 4Cs formula. It is not designed to be an absolute measure but should indicate whether a company is ready to explore international possibilities.

Representatives from all levels and functions of a company should fill out this form and the results should be disseminated to the entire workforce, as described below. To do this exercise, a company should have performance and financial data on hand for at least the past two years.

Respondents should answer each question by circling one of the numbers 0 to 5, choosing the answer that comes closest to the firm's actual situation. Using the scoring system at the end of the appendix, a company should total scores separately for each of the following groups: (a) top management, (b) middle management, and (c) employees. The scores of each group should first be compared to one another, then averaged. The tabulated results should be shared with company members and then the company should come together to discuss the results and findings. Questions that show significant differences of opinion especially should be reviewed.

There are no magic formulas or exact target numbers. Each company will vary, with different strengths and weaknesses. However, an overall score between 169 and 294 indicates that the firm is export-ready; between 127 and 168, the company is close but needs to work on certain areas; below 127, the firm is not ready and much work still needs to be done.

Questionnaire

I. Commitment

A. Does the company spend time on international business?

1. 50% or more
2. 25 – 49%
3. 10 – 24%
4. Less than 10%
5. Zero

B. Why does the company pursue international business?

1. It is the lifeblood of the company and at least as good as the domestic market.
2. It helps especially during slow periods in the domestic market.
3. The domestic market is becoming saturated and growth overseas is the only way the company can survive.
4. Domestic market share is low; and overseas business is needed to shore up domestic operations and sales.
5. To sustain long-term growth, the company needs a combination of domestic and international business.

C. What is the status of your business?

1. In business less than five years, $500,000 - $1million turnover.
2. In business less than 5 years, $1 million - $10 million or more turnover.
3. In business 5 to 15 years, $500,000 - $1 million turnover.
4. In business 5 to 15 years, $1 million – $10 million or more turnover.
5. In business over 15 years, $1 million – $10 million or more turnover.
6. In business over 15 years or more, $10 – $100 million or more in turnover.

D. How much time will the company spend on international business over the next five years?

    1. 50% or more
    2. 25 – 49%
    3. 10 – 24%
    4. Less than 10%
    5. Zero

E. How much time does top management spend on international business-related matters?

    1. 50% or more
    2. 25 – 49%
    3. 10 – 24%
    4. Less than 10%
    5. Zero

F. How much time does middle management spend on international business-related matters?

    1. 50% or more
    2. 25 – 49%
    3. 10 – 24%
    4. Less than 10%
    5. Zero

G. How much time do employees spend on international busines-related matters?

    1. 50% or more
    2. 25 – 49%
    3. 10 – 24%
    4. Less than 10%
    5. Zero

H. Will or should those percentages change over the next five years?

  1. Yes, by more than the rate that international business grows in the company.
  2. No, expansion can be handled well enough at the current rate.
  3. Yes, management's time will increase, but not so much for employees.
  4. Yes, management and employees will increase their time on international business at the rate that business grows.
  5. No, but additional international business experts will be hired to handle that side of the business.

I. Should the company increase the amount of international business the company does?

  1. Yes, because the capacity is there.
  2. No, because the ratio of domestic to international business is already correct.
  3. Yes, because business overseas can generate needed income.
  4. No, because more international work would hurt the company financially.
  5. No, because international business is too insecure, risky, or difficult.

J. The company does international business mainly to:

  1. Increase sales because domestic sales are below average.
  2. Increase global market share.
  3. Reduce operating costs and use excess production capacity.
  4. Even out seasonal domestic sales.
  5. Avoid domestic market saturation or keep up with the competition.

K. If the company were to expand internationally, what percentage of total current business would you expect the new international business to achieve for the company after one year?

  1. 50% or more
  2. 30 – 49%
  3. 10 – 30%
  4. 5 – 10%
  5. Less than 5%

L. If the company were to expand internationally, what percentage of total business would you expect the international operations to achieve for the company after five years?

  1. 50% or more
  2. 30 – 49%
  3. 10 – 30%
  4. 5 – 10%
  5. Less than 5%

M. If the company were to expand internationally, what percentage of the overall operating budget should be used on this expansion?

  1. The same percentage as the international business growth rate in the company.
  2. Expansion can be handled well enough at the current rate of domestic and international spending.
  3. A flat 10 percent because the company budget cannot accommodate more.
  4. More should be spent on international business because it is new or more complex.
  5. A flat 5 percent because the budget cannot accommodate more.

N. Should the company make modifications in its products in order to adapt to overseas markets?

  1. Yes, up to $1 million if the projected market is $3 – 5 million over five years.
  2. Yes, up to $500,000 if the projected market is $1- 3 million over five years.
  3. Yes, up to $100,000 if the projected market is $500,000 – 2 million over one year.
  4. No, unless costs are below $25,000.
  5. No, the risk and expense of modifying the products would be too great.

O. If the company expanded overseas, would it:

1. Work only through agents and distributors and be paid in dollars under letters of credit?
2. Consider licensing its technology if the opportunity were right?
3. Work only through agents or distributors but, after time, consider working on an open account basis if the relationships with these partners were strong?
4. Invest overseas either in a 100% company-owned subsidiary or a foreign company acquisition to gain permanent market presence?
5. Form a joint venture to gain permanent market presence?

P. How much would your company be willing to spend to explore and penetrate overseas markets?

1. $5,000 – $10,000
2. $10,000 – $25,000
3. $25,000 – $50,000
4. Less than $5,000
5. Over $50,000, or whatever amount is necessary

Q. If it were to expand internationally, would the company need to change organizationally?

1. Yes, and management is prepared to make whatever changes are needed, including hiring new personnel.
2. No, the company is already organized to do effective international work.
3. Yes, a key person would be hired to handle the international side of the business.
4. No, reorganization would be too disruptive and expensive.
5. No, but current staff would be trained to do international business.

R. What is the company's risk profile?

  1. It takes no risks.
  2. It will take risk when the return on investment (ROI) is 80% certain and the payoff is substantial.
  3. It will take risk when the ROI is 60% certain and the payoff is substantial.
  4. It will take risks when the ROI is 60% certain and the payoff is 10% to 50%.
  5. It will take risks if the ROI is 30% certain and the payoff is 10% to 25%.

II. Competitiveness

A. How many competitors does the company have for its products domestically?

  1. 50 or more   2. 25 – 49   3. 15 – 24
  4. 7 – 14   5. Fewer than 7

(If the company produces more than one product or service, answer this question for each one.)

B. What is your domestic market share for each product or service?

  1. 50% or more   2. 25 – 49%   3. 15 – 24%
  4. 7 – 14%   5. Less than 7%

C. What is your international market share in the countries where the company is already operating?

  1. 50% or more   2. 25 – 49%   3. 15 – 24%
  4. 7 – 14%   5. Less than 7%

(Answer this question for each product or service.)

D. What makes your product or service competitive domestically?

  1. Price   2. Quality   3. New/different features
  4. Advertising/packaging   5. Superior supply chain

(Answer for each product or service sold domestically.)

E. What makes your product or service competitive internationally?

    1. Price   2. Quality   3. New/different features
    4. Advertising/packaging 5. Superior supply chain

(Answer for each product and service sold abroad.)

F. What is the company's understanding of the competition domestically?

    1. Knows all competitors and their products or services well.
    2. Knows key competitors and their products or services well.
    3. Knows the key competitors but does not know their products and services well.
    4. Does not know key competitors or their products or services.
    5. Knows the key competitors and that their products or services are not as good as those of the company.

G. What is the company's understanding of the competition internationally?

    1. Knows the local and international competitors in each target market and their products or services.
    2. Knows the local competition and their products or services in each target market but not the international competition and their products or services.
    3. Knows the local and international competition but their products or services are not competitive compared to those of the company.
    4. Does not know either the local or international competitors, but knows that the target markets have competitive products or services.
    5. Does not know the competition in the target markets.

H. Are product or service modifications necessary to be effective internationally?

1. No, people worldwide like the product as is.
2. Some, but the expense is too great.
3. Some, but the company has made or is prepared to make the necessary changes.
4. Yes, but too few or insignificant to bother making.
5. Yes, but where they are excessive, the company will forego the business in that country.

I. What business arrangement would make the company most successful internationally?

1. Selling directly through an agent or distributor.
2. Selling directly to retailers abroad.
3. Licensing the product in selected markets.
4. Management contract or strategic alliance to have better control of operations and stronger market presence.
5. Forming a joint venture or investing abroad; the company will do so if appropriate.

III. Cash Flow

A. Describe the current volume and profit of the company in the domestic market.

1. 100,000 units or more with 3% – 15% overall profit
2. 100,000 units or more with 16% – 50% profit
3. 50,000 – 99,000 units with 3% – 15% profit
4. 50,000 – 99,000 units with 16% – 50% profit
5. 20,000 – 49,000 units with 3% – 15% profit
6. 20,000 – 49,000 units with 16% – 50 % profit
7. 10,000 – 19,999 units with 3% – 15% profit
8. 10,000 – 19,999 units with 16% – 50% profit
9. 5,000 – 10,000 units with 3% – 15% profit
10. 5,000 – 10,000 units with 16% – 50% profit
11. 1,000 – 4,999 units with 5% – 15% profit
12. 1,000 – 4,999 units with 16% – 50% profit
13. 1 – 999 units with 5% – 15% profit
14. 1 – 999 units with 16% – 50% profit

B. Describe the company's financial situation.

1. Has a healthy profit margin with ample room for international expansion.
2. Has a good profit margin with some room for growth.
3. Has maintained a minimal profit margin for at least 3 – 5 years.
4. Has operated at a loss for 1 – 2 years with significant liabilities.
5. Has operated at a loss but with no substantial liabilities.

C. Describe the company's debt situation.

1. There are no major debt requirements outside normal business operations.
2. There are significant debt requirements due in the next two years, but they are well budgeted for.
3. There are significant debt requirements for which the company will seek revenue from new international operations.
4. There are tolerable debt requirements which the company will finance internally or with borrowed funds.
5. There are debt requirements as the company is currently expanding domestically but there are funds available for expansion.

D. When the company introduces a new product into the domestic market, what is its expected payback period?

1. 6 months   2. 1 year   3. 1 – 5 years
4. Immediately   5. Over 5 years

E. In international sales, does the company reduce its price structure to be competitive?

1. No, the product price is increased because per unit profit is greater in overseas sales.
2. Yes, the product has to be sold for more overseas to accommodate added costs, e.g. shipping, duties.
3. No, but additional costs from doing business internationally make it difficult to be competitive.

4. Yes, the product is sold for less and domestic sales can help finance overseas sales.
5. No, the cost of doing business domestically and abroad are about the same.

F. When entering a new market, what is the company's payback period?

1. 6 months   2. 1 year   3. 1 – 5 years
4. Immediately   5. Over 5 years

G. Does the company have access to capital for expansion?

1. Yes, up to $50,000.
2. No, it is very difficult to get even working capital.
3. Yes, up to $500,000.
4. Yes, up to $1,000,000 or more.
5. Yes, but less than $10,000

IV. Capacity

A. Describe the company's production facilities.

1. Owns or leases one production facility or produces all products or services from one headquarters operation; because of the complexity of the product outsourcing is not available or is very difficult.
2. Has multiple production facilities or offices, all company-owned and domestically located, and produces all products from these facilities.
3. Subcontracts or outsources all production overseas or domestically.
4. Does a combination of internal production and outsourcing.
5. Does most production from its own facilities, but can outsource if necessary

B. Describe the condition of the facilities.

1. Are less than 5 years old and can accommodate some product modifications.
2. Are 5 – 10 years old and in excellent working order but cannot accommodate product modifications.
3. Are generally more than 10 years old and need some repair.
4. Are well over 10 years old and need repair.
5. Can accommodate existing orders but cannot handle product modifications.

C. The utilization rate of the facilities and equipment is:

1. 95% or more   2. 75 – 94%   3. 55 – 74%
4. 45 – 54%   5. Less than 44%

D. Describe the equipment.

1. New and can be used for existing orders and for many product modifications.
2. Five years old or more and can be used for some product modifications.
3. Ten years old, needs repair, and cannot accommodate product modifications.
4. New but cannot be used for product modifications.
5. Old and needs repair but too expensive to be replaced at this time.

E. Can the company expand or increase capacity if needed?

1. Yes, has the space and financial resources to do so.
2. Yes, but expansion would be costly and take months to accomplish.
3. No, incremental costs would be too great; outsourcing is not an option.
4. Yes, but the company may not be able to secure the funds to do so.
5. No, but outsourcing would be an option.

F. How does the company currently manage its supply chain?

1. It sources materials domestically and produces, packs, and ships from its own facilities.
2. It sources materials from various places around the world but produces, packs and ships from its own facilities.
3. It sources materials from various places, produces product, and handles internally or outsources packaging and shipping.
4. Sourcing materials is completely integrated or just-in-time delivered and production, packaging, and shipping is automated and monitored for quality control.
5. Materials sourcing, production, packaging, and shipping are slow and not well coordinated.

G. Describe the company's relationship with its international freight forwarder.

1. Does not have such a relationship.
2. Uses several, all well qualified and reliable.
3. Uses several, but some, if not all, are of questionable ability.
4. Uses one because the company currently does business in only two or three countries.
5. Currently interviewing freight forwarders.

H. Are there delays in delivery?

1. Yes, on average 50% or more of deliveries are late.
2. No, delivery is done regularly in a timely fashion.
3. Yes, but delays are minimal.
4. Yes, on average 10% of deliveries are late.
5. Yes, on average 20% or more of deliveries are late.

The Company Assessment Questionnaire
Question (Q)/Scoring (S)

Q	S	Q	S	Q	S	Q	S	Q	S	Q	S	Q	S

Commitment

Q	S	Q	S	Q	S	Q	S	Q	S	Q	S	Q	S
1.A.1	7	1.B.1	7	1.C.1	3	1.D.1	7	1.E.1	7	1.F.1	7	1.G.1	7
A.2	6	B.2	4	C.2	5	D.2	6	E.2	6	F.2	6	G.2	6
A.3	5	B.3	3	C.3	2	D.3	5	E.3	5	F.3	5	G.3	5
A.4	2	B.4	0	C.4	6	D.4	2	E.4	2	F.4	2	G.4	2
A.5	0	B.5	6	C.5	5	D.5	0	E.5	0	F.5	0	G.5	0
				C.6	7								

Q	S	Q	S	Q	S	Q	S	Q	S	Q	S	Q	S
1.H.1	7	1.I.1	5	1.J.1	1	1.K.1	0	1.L.1	5	1.M.1	4	N.1	7
H.2	1	I.2	4	J.2	5	K.2	1	L.2	5	M.2	0	N.2	7
H.3	3	I.3	3	J.3	4	K.3	3	L.3	5	M.3	2	N.3	7
H.4	5	I.4	0	J.4	4	K.4	4	L.4	3	M.4	7	N.4	3
H.5	3	I.5	1	J.5	3	K.5	5	L.5	1	M.5	1	N.5	0

Q	S	Q	S	Q	S	Q	S
1.O.1	2	1.P.1	3	1.Q.1	7	1.R.1	0
O.2	4	P.2	4	Q.2	7	R.2	2
O.3	3	P.3	5	Q.3	2	R.3	4
O.4	7	P.4	1	Q.4	0	R.4	5
O.5	7	P.5	7	Q.5	3	R.5	0

Competitiveness

Q	S	Q	S	Q	S	Q	S	Q	S	Q	S	Q	S
2.A.1	1	2.B.1	7	2.C.1	7	2.D.1	5	2.E.1	5	2.F.1	7	2.G.1	7
A.2	2	B.2	6	C.2	6	D.2	5	E.2	5	F.2	6	G.2	5
A.3	3	B.3	4	C.3	4	D.3	5	E.3	5	F.3	1	G.3	4
A.4	4	B.4	3	C.4	3	D.4	5	E.4	3	F.4	3	G.4	5
A.5	7	B.5	1	C.5	1	D.5	5	E.5	3	F.5	3	G.5	0

Q	S	Q	S
2.H.1	3	2.I.1	3
H.2	0	I.2	2
H.3	7	I.3	4
H.4	2	I.4	6
H.5	3	I.5	7

Q	S	Q	S	Q	S	Q	S	Q	S	Q	S	Q	S

Cash Flow

Q	S	Q	S	Q	S	Q	S	Q	S	Q	S	Q	S
3.A.1-14	3.	B.1	7	3. C.1	7	3. D.1	2	3. E.1	7	3. F.1	1	3. G.1	3
**		B.2	7	C.2	6	D.2	3	E.2	1	F.2	2	G.2	0
		B.3	6	C.3	5	D.3	6	E.3	2	F.3	5	G.3	5
		B.4	4	C.4	4	D.4	1	E.4	1	F.4	0	G.4	7
		B.5	2	C.5	3	D.5	4	E.5	5	F.5	7	G.5	1

Capacity

Q	S	Q	S	Q	S	Q	S	Q	S	Q	S	Q	S
4.A.1	2	4.B.1	7	4. C.1	1	4. D.1	7	4. E.1	7	4. F.1	5	4. G.1	0
A.2	4	B.2	6	C.2	2	D.2	6	E.2	2	F.2	5	G.2	7
A.3	3	B.3	3	C.3	4	D.3	1	E.3	0	F.3	5	G.3	1
A.4	4	B.4	1	C.4	3	D.4	5	E.4	1	F.4	6	G.4	4
A.5	4	B.5	4	C.5	2	D.5	0	E.5	3	F.5	1	G.5	3

Q	S
4. H.1	0
H.2	7
H.3	4
H.4	2
H.4	1

** For benchmark, not scoring, purposes

APPENDIX 2

PART I:
INITIAL EXPORT PLAN AND BUDGET

The initial plan and budget for exploring one or more target markets overseas should cover the fifteen steps specified in chapter 2. Below is an outline of a typical plan and budget, including the steps a company should consider. It is wise to set deadlines and a budget range (low and high) to establish the minimum and maximum a firm is willing to spend.

Item	Time	Budget	
		High	Low
Prepare at Home			
1. Learn the domestic trade infrastructure:			
– Export Assistance Center			
– Economic Development Center			
– World Trade Center			
– Trade Associations			
– Other			
2. Do market research domestically:			
– National Trade Data Bank			
– Internet			
– Other			
3. Learn the target country trade infrastructure:			
– Embassy			
– American Chamber of Commerce			
– World Trade Center			
– Trade groups			

Initial Export Plan and Budget (cont.)

Item	Time	Budget High	Low
4. Identify potential business partners from home: – Commercial News USA – Agent Distributor Service – Advertisements in international magazines – Catalog shows			
5. Identify attorneys in target markets: – International law firms – Embassy			
6. Learn trade finance and shipping options.			
7. Arrange appointments in target markets: – Export Assistance Center – World Trade Centers – Embassies			
Go Abroad			
8. Use tools to identify partners abroad: – Gold Key – Trade mission – Post-initiated promotion – Trade show – Other			
9. Travel to target market.			
10. Consult with the embassy, lawyer, and other trade infrastructure contacts.			

Initial Export Plan and Budget (cont.)

Item	Time	Budget	
		High	Low
11. Register product or service and company names.			
12. Hold preliminary meetings with potential business partners at their facilities.			
13. Conduct comparison shopping on 2Cs and 5Cs, perform gap analysis, and determine best timing for market entry.			
14. Determine best business arrangement and commit to any necessary product modifications.			
15. Develop a preliminary price for the product or service.			
16. Negotiate with business partner and finalize terms.			
17. Determine how best to market the product or service and negotiate with a marketing firm, if appropriate.			
18. Position the product or service.			
19. Set company objectives and draw up a market penetration budget.			
Total Exploratory Time and Budget (Per Target Market)			

PART 2:
COUNTRY
"COMMERCIAL GUIDE"
INFORMATION

The following are typical questions that *NTDB Commercial Guides* will likely answer:

1. How fast has the economy grown over the past five years and what is its projected growth this year?

2. What is total foreign investment? How has it grown over the past few years? Is the country experiencing capital growth or capital flight?

3. What are the government's policies on foreign investment: royalties on licensing agreements, repatriation of profits, etc.?

4. How stable is the currency relative to the U.S. dollar?

5. What is the level of inflation and what is the government's monetary policy?

6. What is the trade deficit or surplus? How has it improved or worsened in the past few years?

7. What is the population and per capita income of the country?

8. What is the demand for infrastructure services? How is the government addressing these needs?

9. What is happening in the country's capital markets?

10. What is the political situation? Does the country have a positive or negative relationship with the United States?

11. How strong are the country's intellectual property protection laws?

12. How does a company set up a business in the country? Can it buy local real estate, and does it need a local partner to do so?

13. What trade barriers are there to importing into the country or doing business in the country?

14. How strong are the local laws affecting trade? How important is it to have a local lawyer? How would a company identify a good one? Are agents treated as employees or contractors, eligible for severance benefits, etc.?

15. What is the country's standing with the World Trade Organization? To which international agreements is it a signatory?

16. Is management and skilled labor available in the country?

17. Is there corruption in the government?

18. Are the Export-Import Bank and the Overseas Private Investment Corporation active in the country? If so, what services do they provide?

19. What bilateral agreements does the country have with the United States? What do they cover?

20. Does the country have a tax treaty with the United States? If so, what are the conditions?

21. How strong are the courts? Does the country subscribe to international arbitration of trade disputes?

22. How effective is the national banking system?

23. What foreign exchange controls affect trade? How volatile is the currency?

24. Which U.S. banks have corresponding bank relationships in the country?

25. What trade and project financing is available locally?

26. What labeling and customs documentation are required? What is the policy on "sample" imports?

27. What are the best U.S. prospects for exporting to the country?

28. What product standards has the country set?

29. What are the requirements for selling to the government?

30. What steps is the government currently taking to improve foreign trade and investment?

31. What are some key cultural differences and traveling tips?

32. Where and what trade events (shows, exhibitions, etc.) are planned in the country for the coming year?

33. To what extent are companies privatized or government-run?

PART 3:
COMPARISON SHOPPING

The following questions are representative of those a company may use to explore the market (analyze the 2Cs and 5Ps). These questions should be asked of wholesalers, like the agents or distributors with which the exporter has made appointments, retailers, and customers.

Question	*Issue*
- Is there a product like mine already in the market?	Product
- What features does the product have?	Product
- How does the product get to the market (distribution)?	Place
- What is the retail market (type of retail store)?	Place
- Are there import restrictions for this product?	Place
- What are the most effective ways to advertise this product?	Promotion
- What restrictions are there on advertising?	Promotion
- How much would a customer be willing to pay for such a product?	Price
- What are the normal retail and wholesale markups on such a product?	Price
- What are the price differences between imports and local brands?	Price
- What are typical advertising marketing costs?	Price
- Can this product sell in this market?	Competition
- What are examples of comparable products?	Competition
- What are the most marketable features of such a product?	Competition
- How does this product compare to others like it (quality, price, etc.)?	Competition
- Does the product need to be changed to be successful in this market?	Competition
- Where would you go to buy a product like this?	Customer
- What do you like about this product?	Customer
- How often would you buy this product?	Customer
- How do you hear about products like this?	Customer

- What do you expect or want in a product like this?   Customer
- Would you be interested in representing this product?   Partner
- If yes, under what terms do you normally operate
  (type of agreement)?   Partner
- Can you provide after-sales service for this product?   Partner
- How much inventory space can you devote to this product?   Partner
- Do you handle complementary or competing products?   Partner
- What international shipping terms do you normally use
  (FOB, CIF, etc.)?   Partner
- Please describe the industry here and how it works.   Partner
- Do you have access to trade financing?   Partner
- How would you get this product through customs?   Partner
- Please describe the distribution and retail channel here.   Partner

PART 4

COMPARISION BETWEEN DOMESTIC AND INTERNATIONAL PRICING

A domestic and imported price of the same product may look like this:

Price Comparison

	Imported Product	Domestic Product
Factory price	$100.00	$100.00
Domestic freight (5.3%)	5.30	5.30
Insurance (2%)	2.00	none
International freight (12%)	12.00	none
CIF subtotal	$119.30	——
Import duties (25%)[a]	29.83	none
Merchant marine tax (3%)	3.58	none
Warehousing (1.5%)	1.79	none
Terminal handling fee (3.2%)	3.82	none
Custom brokerage fees (8%)	9.54	none
Financing charges (2%)	2.39	none
Landed cost subtotal	$170.25	$105.30
Value-added tax (5%)[b]	8.51	none[c]
Importer's commission and markup (35%)[d]	59.00	
Domestic wholesaler markup (12%)		12.64
Retail markup (50%)[e]	85.13	52.65
Total	$322.89	$207.44
Local tax (10%)	$355.18	$228.18

[a] Import duties to finance charges are based on the CIF subtotal.
[b] Value-added tax to retail markup is based on the Landed Cost subtotal.
[c] Sometimes domestic producers have to pay value-added taxes. Some countries do not have this requirement.
[d] Importer's commission (profit) and markup will vary from 15 to 300 percent, depending on the number of units projected to be sold, the size of the local market, and other factors. The length and breadth of the distribution channel, that is, the number of intermediaries involved in bringing the product to market (wholesalers and retailers) can also affect this expense.
[e] Retail markup will vary normally from 40 to 55 percent.

APPENDIX 3

TRADE FINANCING AND INTERNATIONAL SHIPPING

Coordinate Shipping and Trade Financing with Eyes Wide Open

Trade financing and international shipping are inexorably linked.

What happens if a company finds a distributor, sends him a shipment of 100 items, and never gets paid? Worse, what if this company has to try to collect the bad debt in the importer's country? It happens, but good preparation and using the right payment method can prevent this particular nightmare.

There are three things for a company to keep in mind in financing an export shipment:

The Currency of the Transaction

Exchange rates between currencies can move up or down unpredictably. From the time a company agrees to sell a product until the time it can deliver could take several months. In that time the value of the exporter's currency relative to the importer's could change and the exporter could make less or more money on the transaction than anticipated. This is why savvy exporters demand payment in U.S. dollars or another hard floating currency, such as yen or euros or British pounds; it increases the likelihood that the exporter will receive the full amount for the goods.

Companies that agree or are forced (in order to land the sale) to be paid in the importer's currency, run what is called "currency exchange risk" (see chapter 9). To reduce the risk and make their future cash flows predictable, these exporters can hedge. One way to do this is to buy an irrevocable forward contract in which the exporter and a commercial bank agree to deliver the importer's currency at a specified exchange rate at a future date, say, three or four months. This is the forward rate. Thus, the exporter knows exactly how much it will be paid at that point in the future.

Sound complicated? That's why it's best to insist on payment in a secure currency like U.S. dollars. The following sections will help the exporter gain a better understanding of trade financing and international shipping.

The Method of Payment

Cash in advance, credit cards, and confirmed letters of credit, if available, are the safest ways to go. Confirmed letters of credit are typically used only for larger orders.

The Documentation

It's important to make sure the financial documents conform to the shipping documents The letter of credit will have an expiration date. It will require specific shipping terms and documents. If the documentation does not follow those specifications, the exporter runs the risk of not getting paid.

Methods of Payment

The following are all ways of getting paid, depending on which party is bearing the risk:

Advance Payment

When the buyer or importer pays for goods in advance, the risk is on the buyer. This is the most common payment method because it is inexpensive and relatively easy to do. The importer or buyer makes an electronic transfer of funds. While the buyer bears most of the risk, the exporter should check with its bank to ensure that the credit to its account is made quickly and accurately. To do this, though, the buyer will need the exporter's routing and account numbers in advance. If the exporter is not comfortable giving the buyer its account information, a letter of credit should be used instead.

Open Account

This approach is also common even though the exporter bears the risk. The process works as follows:

1. The exporter ships the goods as soon as they are ready.

2. Once the goods arrive at the port of entry, the importer takes possession of them without bank documents.

3. The importer pays the exporter after the goods are sold.

Only after the exporter has a long-term arrangement with its importer, should the company consider this form of payment.

Documentary Collection

When commercial banks serve as the agents for both the importer and exporter, they share the risk. With the assistance of its bank, the exporter draws up a *draft* or bill of exchange telling the buyer to pay on a specific date. The exporter gives its bank the bill of lading, which tells that the goods have been shipped and serves as title to the goods, along with other required documentation. The importer's bank, serving as agent to the importer, rechecks the documents, debits the importer's account for the sale, and passes the documents to the importer.

The draft can be either a *sight* draft or a time (or *date*) draft. Under a time or date draft, the importer can pay at a specified date in the future. A sight draft requires the importer to pay immediately (upon sight of the draft). Because the banks are involved, the risk to the exporter is lessened, but since the banks themselves do not guarantee payment, there is still risk to the exporter.

Letter of Credit (L/C)

The several types of letters of credit (L/C), which are a subgroup of documentary collections, put the risk on the importer. A L/C names the type of shipment permitted, the time allowed for the shipment, the to and from points, the names of the banks involved, the names of the importer and exporter, the terms, conditions and documents required in shipment, and penalties for discrepancies. A revocable L/C may be amended or even cancelled by the issuing bank without notice to the exporter; an irrevocable L/C cannot be amended or cancelled without consent of all parties. Again, to protect the exporter and ensure the credibility of the importer, commercial banks (one for the importer and one for the exporter) serve as intermediaries between the parties to make the payment. Depending on whether the L/C is confirmed or not, either the importer's or the exporter's bank guarantees to pay the exporter if the company meets the terms of the L/C. L/Cs also use sight drafts and time drafts. An exporter may use a time draft if it wants to provide credit to a trusted importer who is experiencing temporary cash flow problems.

The L/C Process

To understand how a L/C works, the players should first be introduced:

The Issuing Bank

This is the importer's bank. It will have some relationship to the exporter's bank, either as a subsidiary, an affiliate, or a corresponding bank. (The last arrangement does not involve ownership ties between the two banks, only an understanding that they represent mutual clients.) This importer's bank will issue the L/C to the exporter's bank.

The Advising Bank

After reviewing the L/C, the exporter's bank will advise the exporter that the L/C is either valid or not; if it is, the shipment can move forward.

The Shipper

The freight company that is transporting the goods has to issue the exporter a *bill of lading* to show that the goods were sent as stipulated in the L/C and to serve as title to the goods for the importer.

The Confirming Bank

For an additional fee, the advising bank will serve as the *confirming* bank. In this capacity, when the exporter provides the shipping documents stipulated in the L/C, the bank will pay the exporter if the documents are in order and conform to the L/C. The confirming bank is then taking the risk because it now has to be compensated by the issuing bank. That is why the relationship between the two banks is so important.

Here is how the process works:

- The exporter and the importer agree on the pricing and shipping terms of the transaction. Usually the importer bears the cost of the L/C, normally 1 to 2 percent of the value of the transaction. The exporter sends the *pro forma invoice* to the importer.

- The importer accepts the invoice and conditions of sale and approaches her bank to apply for a L/C.

- The issuing bank checks to make sure the importer can pay for the shipment. If the importer is creditworthy and has the funds available, the bank will issue the L/C to the advising bank.

- The advising bank verifies that the L/C is valid, advises the exporter, and sends the documents to the company.

- The exporter arranges to ship the goods according to the instructions specified in the L/C. The company normally works through a freight forwarder, which secures the required export documents and delivers the goods to a shipper, which in turn provides the bill of lading. The freight forwarder then gives the exporter all the documentation.

- The exporter presents the documents to the advising or confirming bank. The bank checks to see that the documents are in order; if not, it will return them to the exporter for correction. Once it accepts the documents, the bank sends them and a draft to the issuing bank, demanding payment. If the L/C is confirmed, the confirming bank will pay the exporter and collect from the issuing bank.

- If the exporter's bank is the advising bank, the issuing bank makes payment electronically to the advising bank, which will advise the exporter and credit its account.

Problems with L/Cs

In working with L/Cs, an exporter should watch for the following potential problems:

Documents not in Order

If the paperwork is not in perfect shape and discrepancies are found, the company risks not getting paid and the documents being rejected. Discrepancies may be incorrect names and addresses; inconsistent weights, markings, or numbers; partial shipments if these are disallowed by the L/C; or incorrect insurance coverage, among other things. The exporter must pay a fee for each discrepancy and the transaction may be either delayed or nullified.

Expired L/C
An L/C is time–sensitive: the exporter must satisfy its terms by a certain date. If that is not done, the L/C expires, and the exporter may lose the transaction.

Unrealistic Shipment Dates
The importer wants the goods as soon as possible. If he specifies in the L/C an unrealistic shipping date that the exporter cannot meet, the exporter runs the risk of not getting paid. The two parties should agree on shipment timing before the L/C is issued. Revisions after the fact will cost time and money.

Limits on Shipping Costs
The importer will impose a limit on shipping costs unless the exporter agrees to pay all these expenses. If the costs exceed what the exporter and importer have agreed on, the exporter will have to cover any cost overages.

The Components of International Shipping
A simple way to remember the various parts of the shipping process is by spelling the word POET a different way: *P O W I T.*

- *Packing and marking:* How should the goods be packed and marked so that they do not get damaged or lost in shipment?

- *Other, including documentation:* What are the important documents in the shipping process, like the bill of lading and commercial invoice?

- *Warehousing of goods:* Where and for how long will the product be warehoused during shipment? How will that affect the condition of the goods when they arrive?

- *Insurance:* Who—exporter or importer—pays for insurance and how will that impact the cost of the shipment?

- *Transportation:* How will the product get from the exporter's factory to the importer? How will that affect the cost of the shipment?

tsrade Financing and International Shipping

The Process of Entering a Foreign Country

When the exporter's shipment arrives, the importer will normally file entry documents with the district or port director at the port of entry. The shipment has not legally entered the country until (a) it has arrived at the port of entry, (b) either the importer or exporter has paid any duties, and (c) customs has authorized delivery of the goods. It is the responsibility of the importer to arrange for examination and release of goods. She must understand and work with customs and use the right tariff nomenclature to get the goods released successfully.

Usually the carrier bringing the goods into the port of entry certifies the importer or her designee as the "owner" of the goods. The owner thus carries out the entry process.

Entering a shipment is a two-step process:

1. Filing the documents so that goods can be released by customs; and

2. Filing the documents to determine whether a duty applies to the shipment

Unless an extension is granted, these documents must be filed within a specific period of time, say five working days, of the shipment's arrival. The documents are: (a) entry manifest; (b) evidence of right to make entry; (c) commercial invoice; (d) packing lists, if any; and (e) other documents, such as consular invoices, needed to determine whether the merchandise is admissible. These last documents usually apply to agricultural products or others that need special country clearance.

Once the documents are entered, the goods are released. Entry summary documentation is then filed and any estimated duties are paid within a specified period, say ten working days of the release of the goods. Entry summary documentation consists of (a) the entry package that was returned to the importer along with the merchandise; (b) an entry summary; and (c) any other invoices that may be necessary to determine duties. The entry must also show that bond has been posted with customs to cover any potential duties, taxes, and penalties that accrue from importing the goods.

Goods that are not released in the specified timeframe may be placed in a customs-bonded warehouse for up to several years.

Perishable goods and explosives are normally not warehoused. If the importer fails to file an entry for the shipment in the time allotted, the customs director may put the goods in a warehouse at the importer's risk and expense.

The exporter may also give power of attorney to a customs broker and have the broker enter the goods into the country.

Customs may examine both goods and documents to determine the shipment's value, whether the goods are properly marked and invoiced, whether the amount stated in the invoices is proper, and whether the goods are legal. If a shipment contains more or fewer goods than the amount shown on the contents of each package, customs may assign additional duties. Goods that are damaged and lose value in shipment will not be taxed.

Packing and Marking

Proper packing, marking, and invoicing are very important. The exporter will speed customs clearance if it or its freight forwarder:

- *Packs Well:* Adequate packing is a must, but excessive or unnecessary packing should be avoided because it can increase shipping costs. The packing should be chosen for ease of handling and prevention of breakage, moisture damage, and pilferage en route.

- *Matches Invoices Properly:* Invoices should match the contents of each container.

- *Shows Exact Quantities:* The exact number in the containers must be listed on the corresponding invoices.

- *Puts Marks and Numbers on Each Package Shipped and on the Corresponding Invoices:* Markings might include "Hazardous" or "Not Hazardous" and cautionary markings, such as "Handle with Care" for fragile items and "This Side Up". Markings explain to handlers how best to treat the goods.

When packages or containers consist of one kind of good, their examination is much easier. Packing different products with different duty rates commingled together in the same container can cause problems and delay of customs clearance.

A critical part of inspections concerns how the goods are loaded. Putting cargo onto pallets for easy removal by forklifts speeds the inspection process, although other containerization may be more appropriate for certain cargo. Each shipment must be assessed to determine the best packing mode.

Shipping Documents

Key shipping documents are:

- *Pro Forma Invoice:* This document confirms to the importer the cost of the goods and all other costs related to the shipment. It describes the goods, terms of sale, payment method, length of time the quote on the goods is valid, weight and dimensions of the goods, mode of transportation, and banking information.

- *Commercial Invoice:* While very similar to a pro forma invoice, the CI also allows for decisions, such as the duty amount to be applied during the shipping process. It notes the port of entry, whether the merchandise is sold and to whom, a description of the goods, the quantities in weights and measures, the purchase price in the agreed currency, the kind of currency of payment, all charges in the shipment, the country of origin, and a list of all parts furnished for the production of the goods that are not included in the invoice price. The most common problems with commercial invoices are that the information on them is not truthful or accurate and that the document is not properly filled out.

- *Packing List:* This list shows the content of the shipment, weights, measures, type of package, and number of packages. The packing list should conform to the information in the commercial invoice.

- *Bill of Lading (Air Waybill):* The freight company or the shipper issues this document when the exporter signs a contract with the company. It serves both as a receipt and as title to the goods. The exporter presents this to the advising bank to confirm shipment of goods and the shipper transfers this document to the importer upon entry of the goods.

- *Certificate of Origin:* This document, which tells where the shipment or components of it originated, is used to determine import duties. The commercial invoice can also serve this purpose.

Shipping Terms

There are a number of specialized shipping terms, also called INCO terms for the International Chamber of Commerce that coined them. They indicate what costs in the shipping process are the responsibility of the importer or the exporter and affect the price quote an exporter makes. The most common terms are:

- *EXWorks:* Goods are available at the exporter's facilities. The importer makes all arrangements and bears all shipping and insurance expenses from that point to the destination.

- *FCA:* Free carrier to a named destination in the exporter's country. Used for overland shipments, this part of the journey is free to the importer. The exporter, usually working through a freight forwarder, delivers the goods to a carrier that the importer or buyer designates.

- *FAS:* Free along-side to a named port of exportation. The exporter bears all expenses to the exportation dock alongside the vessel and the importer pays to unload the shipments and all remaining costs.

- *FOB:* Free on board; restricted to waterborne shipments. The exporter agrees to pay all charges up to and including getting the goods on board the vessel. The buyer bears all costs from that point on, although the exporter has to clear the goods for export.

- *CFR:* Cost and freight to a named port of importation. While the exporter pays to ship the goods to the destination port, the importer bears the cost of insurance to protect against loss or damage of the goods during shipment.

- *CIF:* Cost, insurance, and freight to a named port of destination. Here the exporter buys at least minimum coverage insurance. This makes the shipper responsible for buying insurance and showing the certificate of insurance when entering the goods at the port of destination. The importer does not pay any costs of shipment until the goods arrive at the named port of importation.

- *DDP:* The exporter agrees to pay all costs to a named place in the country of importation, as designated by the importer. These costs include duties. If there are other costs, such as value-added taxes imposed at the point of entry, the parties need to determine in advance whether the importer or exporter will bear these expenses. If not, the terms should read: "DDP, VAT et al. Unpaid." If the exporter agrees to deliver to a point in the importer's country that is past customs but does not want to pay duties and other costs, the terms should read: "DDU": Delivered duties unpaid. The importer is then required to pay these expenses.

The Freight Forwarder
Are you reader thoroughly confused yet? Actually this entire process can be simplified if the exporter finds one or more good freight forwarders. Not all freight forwarders are competent, and a competent one is not necessarily expert in all destinations.

A reliable freight forwarder should provide the following services:

- Inform the exporter of routes and mode of transportation to the target markets.

- Determine freight and insurance costs, based on shipping terms, weight, size, method of shipment, and destination, and calculate the best and most affordable prices.

- Advise the exporter on special regulations that need to be met to enter the target markets and help the exporter obtain the necessary export licenses.

- Arrange for domestic shipping and any necessary warehousing of the goods.

- Arrange for packing, crating, and containerization and schedule space and overseas vessel transport.

- Draw up the shipper's export declaration, dock receipt, and bill of lading; ensure the commercial invoice is in order; and prepare and get necessary clearance for such documents as the consular invoice.

- Prepare or secure documents for the advising and issuing banks.

- Deliver the documents to the shipper and exporter and ensure proper loading of the shipment.

- Arrange for or provide insurance for the shipment.

- Follow up to see that the shipment arrives safely or, if damaged, draw up the necessary claim forms.

This significant series of tasks shows just how critical the shipping function is and why an exporter needs to be careful in selecting a freight forwarder.

APPENDIX 4

SAMPLE EXPORTER QUESTIONNAIRE FOR INTERVIEWING POTENTIAL AGENTS AND DISTRIBUTORS

Company Information

1. How large is your company?

2. How old is your company?

3. How many sales staff does your company employ?

4. How many products do you currently represent or distribute?

5. Please list them by name and the territory you cover for them:

Product	Territory
a. _____	_____
b. _____	_____
c. _____	_____
d. _____	_____

6. Does your company have the resources to do the following:
   ___ Product sales?
   ___ After-sales service?
   ___ Marketing and advertising?
   ___ Product assembly?
   ___ Inventory warehousing?
   ___ Distribution?
   ___ Customs?
   ___ Retail market?
   ___ Secure import licenses, if needed?
   ___ Get product liability insurance, if needed?

7. Can you provide or demonstrate:
    ___ Testimonials from other exporters?
    ___ Testimonials from industry contacts (retailers, etc.)?
    ___ Credit ratings from financial institutions?
    ___ Demonstrated use of tariff nomenclature?

8. Please list the major competitors in this market for my company's products:
    a._____
    b._____
    c._____

9. What are comparable prices for products like those of my company: _____

10. Why do my company's products appeal to you and why do you think they would sell in this market?
    a. _____
    b. _____
    c. _____

Business Arrangement
Prioritize by MOST (6) to LEAST (1) desirable.

1. Exclusive agency/distributorship   ____

2. Non-exclusive agency/distributorship   ____

3. Agency/distributorship plus local product assembly   ____

4. Contract manufacture of product   ____

5. Licensing agreement   ____

6. Joint venture with the following terms:
    — Ownership (by %) required or desired   ____

Terms of the Arrangement

1. Financing (check the methods of payment that are acceptable to you)
   ___ Letter of credit (L/C)
   ___ Confirmed L/C
   ___ Open account
   ___ Consignment
   ___ Documentary draft
   ___ Credit card
   ___ Advance payment
   ___ Other

2. How will you pay my company?
   ___ U.S. dollars
   ___ Local currency
   ___ Other (yen, euro, etc.)

3. Which shipping terms do you normally use?
   ___ ExWorks (from the exporter's factory)
   ___ Free Along Side
   ___ Free on Board
   ___ Cost and Freight
   ___ Cost, Insurance, Freight
   ___ Delivered Duties Paid
   ___ Delivered Duties Unpaid

4. What is your normal markup rate and what does it include? ___%
   ___ Marketing and advertising
   ___ Sales
   ___ Facilities and overhead
   ___ Other:

5. What is your normal commission rate?   ___%

6. How do you normally operate with an exporter?
    ___ Incentive pay
    ___ Performance goals
    ___ Reporting requirements
    ___ Length of contract:
    ___ Employee or contractor
    ___ Permission of both parties to change contract
    ___ Certain indemnities, i.e.
    ___ Set prices unilaterally or ___ with exporter's permission
    ___ Term of contract: ____ 6-month with extension
                          ____ one year
                          ____ two years
    ___ Product delivered assembled or ____ not assembled
    ___ Employee or contractual relationship with exporter

Appendix 5

Information Agents and Distributors Want to Know About Exporters

Company Information

1. How many people in your company? ____

2. What is annual sales or volume? ____

3. How old is your company? ____

4. Is the company committed to this new overseas market? ____

5. What percentage of your total sales is international? ____%

6. In which countries are you currently operating or selling?
   A. _____
   B. _____
   C. _____
   Others: _____

7. How many units of your product could you produce for this market? ____

8. Are you willing to modify your product to be successful in this market? ____

9. What is your current excess production capacity? ____%

10. What is the rate of turnover, especially in management positions, in your company? ____

11. Can your company afford to expand into
    this new market?   _____

12. What specifically will your company provide?
    ___ Marketing/advertising support
    ___ Staff training
    ___ Samples and promotional materials
    ___ Warranties _____ Replacement products_____
    ___ Product modifications, if needed

13. Describe your typical customer.

14. Please list your major competitors in this market, if known:
    a.
    b.
    c.

15. List up to five key features of your company and product that
    you would want a potential business partner to know, or that you
    would use to market your product:
    a.
    b.
    c.
    d.
    e.

Business Arrangement
Prioritize by MOST (6) to LEAST (1) desirable.

1. Exclusive agency/distributorship   _____

2. Nonexclusive agency/distributorship   _____

3. Agency/distributorship plus local product assembly   _____

4. Agency or sales representation   _____

5. Contract manufacture of product   _____

6. Licensing agreement   _____

7. Joint venture with the following terms:
   — Ownership (by %)   _____%

Terms of the Arrangement

1. Financing
   ___ Letter of Credit (L/C)
   ___ Confirmed L/C
   ___ Open Account or Consignment
   ___ Documentary Draft
   ___ Credit Card
   ___ Advance Payment
   ___ Other

2. Currency
   ___ U.S. dollars
   ___ Local currency
   ___ Other (e.g. yen, euro, etc.)

3. Shipping
   ___ Have you ever shipped to this country before?
   ___ What is the delivery time from your country to here?
   ___ What is your on-time delivery rate?
   ___ How do you normally ship?

4. Market Territory
   ___ Countrywide
   ___ Less than countrywide
   ___ More than countrywide

5. Incentives and Penalties
   ___ Incentive pay for meeting sales goals
   ___ Penalties for not meeting goals

6. Reporting
   ___ Extent of regular communications
   ___ Monthly written reports
   ___ Quarterly written reports
   ___ Exporter monitoring visits
   ___ Periodic oral reports

7. Delivery Schedules
___ Number of units _____ in 1 month
___ Number of units _____ in 2 months
___ Number of units _____ in 3 months
___ Number of units _____ in 4 months
___ Number of units _____ in 5 months
___ Number of units _____ in 6 months
___ Penalties for late shipments

8. Other Issues
___ Can importer change prices unilaterally? ____
___ With exporter permission? ____
___ Term of contract: 6 month_____ with extensions;
    1 year_____; 2 years_____
___ Product delivered whole_____or needs assembly_____
___ Can importer handle competing_____or
    complementary products?
___ Is importer considered employee_____ or
    contractor_____of exporting company?

9. Reasons exporter would want to terminate or renegotiate
   contract:
   a. _____
   b. _____
   c. _____
   d. _____

APPENDIX 6

WHAT EACH PARTY WANTS FROM INTERNATIONAL BUSINESS ARRANGEMENTS

Although each side may have different wants and objectives, international business arrangements should be win-win situations for all sides. The parties should keep this in mind when entering into negotiations since the purpose of a business arrangement is to accomplish something positive for all.

Agent or Distributor[1]

Agent/Distributor Wants	Exporter Wants
A unique product with modifications made and financed by the exporter	Share expense for product modifications with importer
Partial assembly of product and use of exporter's intellectual property (e.g. logos, trademarks, etc.)	Intellectual property protection[2]
Exporter to provide replacement products or warranties	Importer to provide after-sales service and warranties

---

[1] An agent represents the exporter overseas. Agent implies that the person or company operates relatively independently from the exporter and possibly can commit the exporter to certain things. A sales representative has less autonomy and cannot commit the exporter without permission. A distributor buys goods from the exporter and operates more independently than an agent or sales representative.

[2] An exporter must understand how well its technology will be protected before dealing with an agent or distributor overseas. Can the product be disassembled and the technology stolen? The proper intellectual property (patents, trademarks, etc.) needs to be filed, especially if the exporter fears the loss of proprietary technology.

275

Agent/Distributor Wants	Exporter Wants
Exporter to secure necessary export import licenses	Importer to secure necessary licenses
Exporter to produce and deliver on time, with penalties for late deliveries and incentives for meeting or exceeding sales goals	Importer to sell total inventory, with performance goals and penalties for nonperformance
Exporter to handle unpaid accounts	Importer to help collect unpaid accounts
Exporter to train importer staff[3]	Importer to provide marketing for product[4]
Exclusive contract with largest possible territory[5]	Nonexclusive contract with with limited territory for importer[5]
Long-term contract	Short-term contract with extensions based on meeting performance goals
To pay for goods in local designated currency	Importer to pay in exporter's currency
To deal on open account[6]	To deal on confirmed letters of credit[6]

[3] The exporter should welcome this. Agents or distributors who want training show they have a commitment to the exporter and its products. The more agents or distributors are trained, the more comfortable they will be in pushing the product. An untrained agent or distributor will get frustrated or lose interest in the product.

[4] Often an agent or distributor does not have the budget or ability to market the product well. An exporter should be prepared to have another local organization in the target market do the advertising campaign.

[5] An agent or distributor will want the longest possible leash in the largest possible territory, perhaps exclusive rights to an entire market, often covering several countries, like the entire Mercosur region in South America. The exporter should try to restrict the contract to a smaller area, at least until the value of the agent or distributor is proven. The exporter should tie territory growth to performance.

[6] Open account financing allows the agent to pay the exporter for the goods after they have been sold; a confirmed letter of credit allows the exporter to be paid when it ships the goods. In open account financing, the risk rests with the exporter; with letters of credit it rests with the importer (see 2).

Agent/Distributor Wants	Exporter Wants
To be treated as company employee with severance pay at termination[7]	Wants contractual, not employee, arrangement with no severance at termination[7]
Exporter to pay all shipping costs, including duties, and deliver goods to final destination	Importer to pay all shipping costs from exporter's factory to final destination, including duties
Information on exporter to determine ability to provide product reliably and that management will not change and renege on contract	Information on importers knowledge of market and ability to sell service and distribute from customs to market
To handle competing products[8]	Importer to handle complementary, not competing, products[8]
Maximize commissions and markup price	Minimize commissions to stay competitive[9]
Control over processing customer orders	Ability to monitor importer's order processing and collection
Flexibility to change prices	No ability to change pricing without exporter's permission
Exporter to provide promotional material	Importer to provide promotional material

[7] Contracts must be done in the importer's country. An exporter should investigate the local laws through a local attorney before trying to conduct business there.

[8] In many countries the market for products is small, so agents and distributors often handle similar, if not competing, products. An exporter should try to find an agent or distributor who handles complementary, not competing, products.

[9] In smaller markets, agents work on less volume and higher markups; in larger markets, they work on more volume and lower markups.

Agent/Distributor Wants	Exporter Wants
Exporter to buy product liability insurance	Importer to buy product liability insurance
Specific contact in exporting company	Specific contact in importing company
Written agreement of both parties to change contract	Written agreement of both parties to change contract
Penalties for breach of contract enforced through local courts only	Penalties for breach of contract with either strong local court action or international arbitration
Clear statement of exporter responsibilities	Clear statement of Importer responsibilities
Certain indemnities and force majeure	Certain indemnities and force majeure
Autonomy of operations	To control importer operations

Licensing

Licensee Wants	Licensor Wants
A saleable product with a license fee payable in installments over time	An upfront license fee
Technology transfer	Patent/design protection
A large territory in which to operate	Restricted territory for the importer
Long-term license to ensure market penetration	Short-term license in case licensee breaks the agreement in any way
Freedom to modify technology, if needed, to fit market[10]	Licensee not to change technology unless licensor approves in advance
Freedom to sell under private label, especially if licensor improves licensed technology and the licensee can then sell the older technology for less[11]	Licensee acknowledges licensor in all advertising and agrees to non-compete, nondisclosure clauses in license
Freedom to improve technology[12]	Licensee collaboration to improve technology[12]

---

[10] Some licensees have the wherewithal to modify the technology they license if they see a need for it in the target market. Licensors should be wary of this because an improved product could convert the licensee into a competitor.

[11] If the licensor improves the technology or the product, the licensee could take the older version of the product, put it under a private label, and sell the product as a less expensive competitive product. A licensor can prevent this by stating it clearly in the licensing agreement and issuing a new license for every new iteration of the technology or product.

[12] Often a licensee brings a fresh view to the product or technology or sees how it works in a different market. Licensees can thus be a good source of innovation and product modification, and can often make the modifications that will benefit the product and the licensor. There are advantages to collaboration.

Licensee Wants	Licensor Wants
Training provided by licensor for the manufacture, marketing, and distribution of the product; and provision of materials, etc., in a timely manner	Licensee not to alter licensor's registrations or intellectual property (patents, etc.); licensee will register in the target market as a registered user of the technology
Flexibility to change prices of product	Quality control of production marketing and distribution
Licensee can sublicense outside agreed territory	Licensor only can license outside agreed territory; licensee cannot sublicense under any circumstance without licensor permission
Royalties without per-unit monitoring	Royalties with per-unit monitoring and performance goals[13]
Trust of licensor in licensee's count of units sold	Semiannual inspection to determine accurate count of units sold and production and sales reports; unit production monitoring devices on manufacturing equipment
Licensee responsible for following local laws for producing and distributing product	Licensee responsible for following local laws for producing and distributing product
Licensor provides warranties	Licensee provides warranties

---

[13] It is imperative that the licensor have a way of tracking or monitoring the number of units sold. An unreliable licensee will often undercount units sold so that it will not have to pay royalties. Sometimes a licensor will require not just royalties and a license fee but will insist on equity shares in the licensee company.

Licensee Wants	Licensor Wants
Flexibility to sublicense or automatic license extension on any improvement licensor makes	New license for every technology on any new improvement licensor makes
Freedom to expand market based on performance	Penalties against licensee for nonperformance or noncompliance with license
Dispute resolution through local courts only	Dispute resolution through international arbitration if local courts are inadequate[14]
Indemnification of licensee against certain damages and costs[15]	Indemnification of licensor against certain damages and costs[15]

---

[14] Some countries' judicial systems are inferior; contracts are not well protected by the courts. If this is the case, a licensor's only recourse could be international arbitration or arbitration by a third party. If the country where the licensee operates does not honor international arbitration, the licensor may not have any recourse but the local court system.

[15] If the license is dissolved, the licensor can buy back the materials or tools used to make the licensed product.

Joint Venture

An international joint venture (JV), because it requires a heavy commitment of capital and technology, has several areas where both parties need to agree to establish a framework for the JV. These are summarized here to show you the complexity involved:

- *What Will Be the Fields of Activity?* What business operations will the joint venture cover: manufacturing, research and development, sourcing, marketing and distribution?

- *What Products Will Be Produced?* More important, which proprietary technology does each partner have to contribute?

- *What Will Be the Percentage Breakdown between the Parties (e.g. 50%/50%)?*

- *What Are the Preliminary Business Plans of Each Party?* To show good faith the parties should exchange preliminary business plans in which they describe how they view the pending business and joint venture. This is a way for each party to review the goals, objectives and estimates of the others. The preliminary plans should include, among other things, an analysis of strengths and weaknesses in view of the competition, a market analysis and demand estimates, an analysis of all business operations in the entire supply chain, capital structure and financing options, the projected cost of capital, and capital budgeting.

Once a framework and exchange of trust is in place, "the devil is in the details." How the joint venture will be set up and operated is key; the implementation scheme will be incorporated into the venturer's agreement, which must be approved by each party.

That document covers:

1. The name of the joint venture
2. The location and territory of the joint venture
3. How it will be organized
4. The pre-formation budget[16]

---

[16] The pre-formation budget includes all the costs leading up to the actual formation of the joint venture (e.g., document preparation and legal and registration fees).

5. Capital contributions of each party
6. Other contributions of each party
7. What happens in case of defaults and withdrawals of capital and technology[17]
8. Liabilities and indemnifications of each party
9. Management and officers of the joint venture, including from which parent companies (the parties) they will come
10. The board of directors, including how they are chosen
11. Hiring and firing practices for officers and employees
12. Method of decision-making and the execution of day-to-day business operations
13. How the joint venture will report to the parent companies
14. Internal controls of the joint venture
15. Financial disclosure of the joint venture[18]
16. Distribution of income (profit) and responsibilities for liabilities (loss) among all parties
17. Duties of each party
18. Non-competition and nondisclosure agreements[19]
19. Restrictions on transfer of shares of the joint venture to outside parties[20]
20. The term and termination date of the joint venture[21]
21. The terms of dissolution of the joint venture by the parties
22. Adherence to laws of the country where the joint venture will be located
23. Provisions for force majeure

---

[17] If either party fails to provide its agreed share of the capital or technology contributions, the percentage share of the joint venture will be adjusted to show the new percentage contributions of the other parties.

[18] The joint venture will provide to each parent company balance sheets and cash flow statements periodically and fully audited statements at the end of the fiscal year.

[19] The parties agree not to engage in any other business that would compete with that of the joint venture.

[20] Permission from all parties is normally required for any party to sell or transfer joint venture shares to third parties.

[21] The parties state the circumstances under which they can terminate the joint venture (e.g. , bankruptcy, accumulated losses, breach of agreement).

APPENDIX 7

SOURCES OF MARKET INFORMATION AND DATA

There are numerous sources of market information, many accessible by word search on the Internet. The following lists representative material and specific sources.

Factor	Source
Economic	
1. External debt	World Bank, World Development Indicators, International Monetary Fund
2. Sovereign credit ratings	Standard and Poor's, Sovereigns
3. Inflation/GDP/interest rates	National Trade Data Bank, Country Commercial Guides (CCGs) (www.STATUSA.com)
4. Monetary/fiscal policies	National Trade Data Bank, CCGs
5. Exports/imports	National Trade Data Bank, CCGs, country customs data, Port Import Export Reporting Service

Factor	Source
6. Currency rates	Wall Street Journal National Trade Data Bank
7. Tax collection/GDP	Grey House Publishing, Nations of the World, A Political, Economic and Business Handbook

Political

1. Political stability/ideology	National Trade Data Bank, CCGs
2. Restrictive government policies Tariffs, profit repatriation, etc.	National Trade Data Bank, CCGs, Heritage Foundation, *Economic Freedom Index* (IEF)
3. Property rights and law	Heritage Foundation, IEF
4. International arbitration	National Trade Data Bank, CCGs, Company's embassy abroad
5. Government/private GDP consumption	World Bank, *World Bank Atlas* (WBA)
6. Government entrenchment/ political freedom	Freedom House, *Survey of Freedom in the World*
7. Government intervention	World Bank, WBA Heritage Foundation, IEF
8. Red tape	Company's embassy abroad

Factor   Source

Market

1. Commercial infrastructure

   - Market size/growth/   S. Tamer Cavusgil, *Measuring*
     intensity   *the Potential of Emerging*
                                  Markets: An Indexing
                                  Approach, National Trade
                                  Data Bank, CCGs
                                  World Bank, WDI

   - GNP/GDP: per capita/   World Bank, WDI
     growth   National Trade Data Bank,
                                  CCGs

   - Electricity consumption/   Energy Information
     energy growth rate   Administration,
                                  International Energy –
                                  Annual

   - Telephones/television   International
     per capita   Telecommunication Union,
                                  ICT Indicators

   - Retail establishments per   Euromonitor, *European*
     capita   *Marketing Data and*
                                  Statistics

   - Middle class income   World Bank, WDI
     distribution

   - Distribution/communication   World Bank, WDI
     channels

   - Customs efficiency   National Trade Data Bank,
                                  Company's embassy abroad

   - Market/production factors   World Bank, WDI,
                                  National Trade Data Bank,
                                  CCGs

Factor	Source
2. Market receptivity	National Trade Data Bank, CCGs, World Bank, WDI

General

1. Country risk	Euromoney, *Country Risk Rankings*

APPENDIX 8
TRADITIONAL ORGANIZATIONAL FORMS[1]

In expanding abroad, companies typically follow one of the following broad strategic approaches, though they may evolve through all four of them:

International Strategy

Because of its success at home a firm decides to venture into foreign markets. This logical progression prompts the company to export and maybe invest offshore. In this case the company elects to keep product development activities at home and set up manufacturing and sales facilities in key overseas markets.

While major functions, such as finance and R&D, remain centralized, subsidiaries can customize marketing and the products themselves to a limited, cost-effective extent. Since manufacturing occurs in several markets under varying conditions, manufacturing changes can be costly and because of its expense customization is rare. A company uses this approach because it has a better product than local, or even other international, competition, so that changes are not that critical. Competitive advantage through product uniqueness or superiority enables the company to succeed.

Multidomestic Strategy

Here a company customizes marketing and product activities and gives subsidiaries a long leash. Because they are responsible for catering to the local or regional market, they are in charge of marketing and production and possibly other functions, operating as profit centers. The cost structure is high but the host government is

---

[1] Primary sources of these descriptions of traditional structures and strategies are Charles W.L. Hill, International Business, *Competing in the Global Marketplace*, 3rd ed. (Boston: Irwin McGraw Hill, 2000) and C.A. Barlett and S Ghoshal, *Managing Across Borders* (Boston: Harvard Business Press, 1989).

pleased and the company has a strong local image. However, many functions, including subsidiary cash flows, are often managed centrally so communications throughout the company are harder, as is transfer of core competencies and best practices. Competitive advantage largely relies on a subsidiary's ability to meet local market needs.

Global Strategy

Companies taking this approach want to achieve broad product coverage, a broad reputation, and greater market share by producing and selling a standardized, low-cost product and maximizing profit through volume sales. Production, marketing, and often R&D are positioned in key regional markets. While the company's supply chain is dispersed worldwide, this approach normally calls for a structure where subsidiaries report to a central product unit. Consequently, there is a greater need to coordinate and communicate well to ensure that the various stages of the supply chain function smoothly. The company works through both a formal organizational structure and informal networks to ensure strong coordination of activities. The low-cost nature of the product and the firm's ability to secure ample suppliers in a timely manner is what gives companies using this approach a competitive advantage.

Transnational Strategy

Here a company tries to combine global and multidomestic strategies, attempting to keep prices competitive while addressing the varying needs of local and regional markets. Unlike the more autonomous multidomestic strategy, the firm recognizes a greater need to share core competencies and best practices in order to stay competitive, but achieving both product customization and cost efficiencies is not easy. To do so, companies rationalize their manufacturing by using standard parts to the extent possible and concentrating production in a few well-placed regions.

To its network of manufacturing facilities, a company adds assembly plants where products can be altered to meet local needs. The same holds true of marketing and advertising as the company tries to standardize packaging at least region-wide. To ensure good communications and control over local changes, the company may organize on a matrix basis, where a subsidiary will answer to two bosses, say, a geographic manager and a product manager.

Within these broad approaches, companies will organize in different ways as follows:

Specialized

To stay simple and flexible, a firm will have subsidiaries focus on one or two activities only. An overseas division may be responsible for manufacturing just one product of the 10 or 12 the company makes. Or a subsidiary may simply market a product and report to the corporate president for that product, who is located in headquarters. The manufacture of the product is centralized to gain cost efficiencies but the subsidiary has some latitude in marketing locally.

A firm uses this approach when it wants to maximize its market share by keeping prices lower through centralized, low-cost production. The approach becomes problematic when demand reaches higher levels, requiring new production plants to service more markets, or when transportation costs from one facility worldwide become exorbitant and are no longer justified.

Geographic

Here a company organizes by divisions that are responsible for a geographic area, such as Asia or Latin America. While responsible for the manufacture and marketing of all or some products or services for that region or subregion, subsidiaries report to a geographic boss located in headquarters or in the region itself.

Functional

For simplicity, some companies organize along functional or process lines. The roles of the subsidiaries and responsible units are clear and focused, e.g., finance, marketing, manufacturing. or sales. Nevertheless, to work well, coordination is key. Confining functions, though, often creates coordination problems that require centralized supervision.

Customer

If companies have very distinct client groups, such as businesses within a single industry or other institutional consumers, they may organize along customer lines. While the products may be the same, how the customers buy the goods may vary significantly. Companies that manufacture industrial products or organizations that provide services to corporate clients often organize this way.

Project

Project teams allow for rapid deployment of people to meet unique market opportunities. Agile organizations trying to enter a market quickly or preempt a competitor's move typically use such teams.

Hybrid

This approach combines two or more organizational types at the same time. Companies employ this configuration when they are in transition, say during a merger or acquisition. For example, an acquired overseas company with two or three products might become a subsidiary reporting to a corporate division in charge of worldwide marketing. The subsidiary continues to manufacture the goods while a corporate product division markets them.

Matrix

Here two organizational forms interact. For example, Company A has both geographic and product divisions, with managers at the same level though not necessarily reporting to the same boss. The director of the subsidiary in Indonesia reports to both the Asian and product managers.

The matrix presumably helps coordinate interrelated functions and activities. However, to make it work managers have to agree to make sharp decisions and send clear direction to subsidiaries and other operating units. If not, compromises and delays set in and blurred lines of authority and responsibility prompt managers to pass blame or shirk their duties.

INDEX